JUNTOS

Fernando Rubio
The University of Utah

Timothy Cannon
The University of Utah

D1478129

CENGAGE

Australia • Brazil • Canada • Mexico • Singapore • United Kingdom • United States

Juntos
Fernando Rubio & Timothy Cannon

Product Director: Marta Lee-Perriard

Senior Product Team Manager:
  Heather Bradley Cole

Product Manager: Mark Overstreet

Senior Content Developer: Kim Beuttler

Product Assistant: Catherine Bradley

Marketing Manager: Sean Ketchem

Senior Content Project Manager: Aileen Mason

Manufacturing Planner: Fola Orekoya

IP Analyst: Michelle McKenna

IP Project Manager: Betsy Hathaway

Production Service: Lumina Datamatics, Inc.

Compositor: Lumina Datamatics, Inc.

Art Director: Brenda Carmichael

Cover Designer: Lisa Trager

Cover Image: pixelfit

For product information and technology assistance, contact us at
Cengage Customer & Sales Support, 1-800-354-9706.

For permission to use material from this text or product, submit all requests online at **www.cengage.com/permissions**. Further permissions questions can be emailed to **permissionrequest@cengage.com.**

Library of Congress Control Number: 2017948552

ISBN: 978-1-285-86896-7

Cengage
200 Pier 4 Boulevard
Boston, MA 02210
USA

Cengage is a leading provider of customized learning solutions with employees residing in nearly 40 different countries and sales in more than 125 countries around the world. Find your local representative at: **www.cengage.com.**

To learn more about Cengage platforms and services, visit **www.cengage.com.**

Purchase any of our products at your local college store or at our preferred online store **www.cengagebrain.com.**

Printed in the United States of America
Print Number: 02   Print Year: 2021

Welcome to *Juntos!*

Juntos is a complete introductory Spanish program that is unique in many ways. We built this program with the learning styles and needs of 21st century learners in mind. As you work with *Juntos*, we'd like to point out some features that set it apart from other language learning programs.

Chapter structure The structure of the chapters is very easy to follow and is built around a set of clear communicative goals. Every task and activity is designed to allow you to meet those goals. To meet them, you will need to learn many new vocabulary words and language structures, but *Juntos* breaks down the new information into small, manageable chunks that are always followed by comprehension checks and practice. In addition to written grammar explanations, short animated videos are available to help you grasp each new grammar topic.

Project-based assessment There is often little connection between what happens in the typical language class—with lots of group work, both in the classroom and online, and real-life communicative tasks—and the way language learning is usually tested using paper-and-pencil tests of grammar and vocabulary that students take individually.

People tend to learn a language more quickly when they need to use it in real-life situations. Accordingly, the best way to measure how much you have learned is for your instructor to have you use the language in the same real-life situations. That is why *Juntos* follows an unusual approach to testing: it assesses your learning by asking you to use the language in the same types of tasks that you complete as you work through each chapter. At the end of each even-numbered chapter, you will find a project-based assessment that covers materials from the previous two chapters, including vocabulary and grammar, and communicative functions. Each assessment includes a variety of activities that lead to a final task. The combination of your grades for these activities provides an excellent indication of how much you have learned and of your growing proficiency in Spanish.

What we ask of you *Juntos* is designed as a blended language learning program. That means that the program takes advantage of online learning and combines it with the benefits of classroom learning to "blend" them into a program that delivers the best of both environments. We did this because we know that is how people learn in the 21st century: we benefit from both face-to-face interactions with others as well as interaction with technology. And that's where *Juntos* needs your involvement. Your instructor will provide all the necessary support in the classroom, but *Juntos* will help you to become a successful language learner only if you also do your part by being a diligent online learner. Remember that you are responsible for completing all online assignments thoroughly and in a timely manner. Follow this advice and you will be well prepared to put what you learn online to use in the classroom. Do this consistently, and you'll be on your way to understanding and speaking Spanish before you know it.

Chapter Organization at a Glance

The Learning Path consists of five steps that characterize not only the stages of your progression through the materials, but also the ways in which you will interact with materials at each stage.

Ready?	→	Learn it!	→	Try it!

Ready? This step is your introduction to the topic at hand. The purpose of this step is to prepare you for learning either through learning objectives for the upcoming section or by reflecting on and drawing from your prior knowledge of the topic. In either case, activities are simple and low-stakes, geared towards preparing you to learn.

In *Juntos*, the **Ready?** step appears at the beginning of each chapter as well as at the beginning of grammar and skills sections wherever a strategy is presented.

Learn it! This step consists of presentational material paired with brief **Try it!** comprehension activities. Presentational material ranges from photos and illustrations with audio-enhanced labels to readings, videos, or written explanations with charts, model sentences, and sample dialogues. Presentations are broken down into manageable "chunks," each of which has a unique **Try it!** activity that allows you to put the new concepts to work right away. **Try it!** activities have two distinct advantages that support your learning: first, the activities appear on the same screen as the presentational materials, so you have the chance to refer to the presentation as you are working; second, these low-stakes activities give you immediate feedback, so that you can be sure you understand the concepts before moving on to more in-depth graded practice. All vocabulary and grammar **Learn it!** activities are paired with a **Try it!** activity that provides you with immediate feedback before you click submit.

| Practice it! | → | Use it! | → | Got it? |

Practice it! This step in the learning path consists of activities in which you have the opportunity to practice using the material in a variety of contexts. Activities include visual, audio, and written prompts. Formats include multiple choice, matching, fill-in-the-blank, true / false, and similar activity types. The **Practice it!** step appears in content sections such as grammar and vocabulary, where varied practice is necessary for thorough comprehension and retention of the material. All **Practice it!** activities in the grammar section contain embedded hints that identify and reinforce the key concepts addressed in the activity once you have submitted your answers. (The feedback appears regardless of whether you answer correctly or incorrectly.)

Use it! In this step, you have the opportunity to apply your new knowledge in a variety of contexts, often in a more personalized and open-ended way. Activity types include open-ended writing and speaking prompts. Most **Use it!** activities are instructor-graded, but some discourse-level activities can be computer-graded and are still considered an application of the content that was presented.

Got it? In this step, you are challenged to recall what you have learned. In a low-stakes environment, you are asked to revisit the learning goals first encountered in **Ready?** by viewing the opening video clip again and to assess your comfort level with these new tasks through a set of comprehension activities. In this chapter-end section, you are provided with references back to the relevant presentations associated with each skill, so that you can review whatever you need to before moving on to the next section.

Scope and Sequence

Preliminar: Greetings, the classroom, formal vs. informal address 1

Objectives: Greeting other people and introducing yourself

Vocabulary: The Spanish alphabet; numbers 0–100; classroom expressions; basic greetings and introductions

Grammar: Nouns and gender; definite and indefinite articles; article–noun agreement; subject pronouns; formal and informal address; use of **hay**

Pronunciation: The Spanish alphabet

	Objectives	Vocabulary	Grammar	Culture	Reading/Writing	Pronunciation
1 La familia y los amigos 15	Talking about yourself and your family; describing people's physical and emotional traits; asking basic questions; explaining and asking where someone is from	Family; physical characteristics; personality traits; colors, emotions; months; days of the week	Regular -**ar**, -**er**, and -**ir** verbs; noun–adjective agreement; **ser** and **estar** with adjectives; the verb **tener** to indicate possession and age; question words: **¿cuántos, cómo, quién, cuál, qué?**	Hispanic family life; Spanish around the world	Lectura: Cómo identificar el regalo ideal El blog de Bella: Introducción Writing a blog	Syllable-final **e** and **o**
2 ¿Qué te gusta hacer? 33	Talking about your pastimes; describing daily activities; talking about what you and others like; indicating possession; telling time	Pastimes; sports; additional -**ar** verbs; connecting words	Uses of **gustar**; possessive adjectives; telling time	Una ciudad biciamiga; Los deportes: El fútbol y el béisbol en el mundo hispano	Lectura: Librerías Gandhi El blog de Bella: Me gusta vivir en España	**a, i, u**

Proyecto 1: Looking for a new roommate (Capítulos 1 y 2)   57

	Objectives	Vocabulary	Grammar	Culture	Reading/Writing	Pronunciation
3 La comida 61	Expressing likes and dislikes regarding food; giving basic recipe instructions; talking about what you have to do and what you are going to do	In the kitchen; adjectives; food; at a restaurant	Irregular **yo** form verbs; informal commands; expressing obligation (**tener que**) and necessity (**hay que**); other expressions with **tener**; expressing future plans using **ir a**	La comida en el mundo hispano; Los chiles	Lectura: El origen de la comida hispana El blog de Bella: You say **patatas,** I say **papas . . .**	**b** and **v**
4 En la casa 83	Describing rooms in a house; talking about household chores and routines; making comparisons; indicating location; describing what someone is doing	The house; rooms and furniture; appliances; chores	Prepositions of location; the present progressive; comparatives and superlatives; stem-changing verbs	Las casas cueva; La casa Luis Barragán	Lectura: La arquitectura de España El blog de Bella: Mi piso nuevo	**p, t, k**

Proyecto 2: Una fiesta (Capítulos 3 y 4)   107

Scope and Sequence

	Objectives	Vocabulary	Grammar	Culture	Reading/Writing	Pronunciation
5 Por la ciudad 113	Asking for and giving directions; indicating location; talking about immediate future plans; giving formal commands	The city; city buildings and transportation; the university	Preterite of **ir, ser**, and **estar;** reflexive verbs; the personal **a;** formal commands	El transporte urbano; Las universidades en Latinoamérica	Lectura: "Picaflor II", Pablo Neruda El blog de Bella: ¡Me encanta Barcelona!	**b, d, g**
6 De viaje 137	Expressing travel preferences and discussing transportation; talking about past travel experiences by describing a sequence of events in the past; discussing the weather and seasons; talking about what you know and are familiar with	Lodging; travel; weather and seasons; adverbs	Verbs like **gustar;** preterite of regular **-ar, -er,** and **-ir** verbs; demonstrative adjectives; **saber** and **conocer**	La ruta del cacao; Lugares impresionantes en países hispanohablantes	Lectura: "12 signos de que eres adicto a los viajes", María Eugenia Mayobre El blog de Bella: Madrid con Lucía	**ll, y**

Proyecto 3: Feria de turismo (Capítulos 5 y 6)   165

	Objectives	Vocabulary	Grammar	Culture	Reading/Writing	Pronunciation
7 La tecnología 169	Narrating in the past; expressing basic opinions; discussing technology and social media	Technology; means of communication; social networking; blogs	Preterite of regular and irregular verbs; **hace** + time expressions; direct object pronouns; **por** and **para**	Las computadoras y las redes sociales en Latinoamérica; El periodismo digital	Lectura: "Mutaciones", José Emilio Pacheco El blog de Bella: Mi teléfono nuevo (simple past narration)	ll, y
8 Profesiones y carreras 191	Talking about majors, professions, and job qualifications; narrating in the past	Professions; majors; job qualifications	The imperfect; uses of the preterite and imperfect; stem-changing verbs in the preterite; indirect object pronouns; more verbs like **gustar**	Las profesiones; Las profesiones de personalidades hispanas	Lectura: "El carpintero", Eduardo Galeano El blog de Bella: La señorita del anillo	r, l

Proyecto 4: Metas profesionales (Capítulos 7 y 8)   209

Scope and Sequence

	Objectives	Vocabulary	Grammar	Culture	Reading/Writing	Pronunciation
9 Cultura popular 217	Talking about the visual arts and popular culture; discussing preferences	At the movies; television; music; art	Double object pronouns; uses of **se**; preterite and imperfect	Los Óscar; Las estaciones de radio universitarias	Lectura: La música de Latinoamérica El blog de Bella: Una película buena	Syllabification
10 La moda 239	Expressing opinions and subjective reactions; talking about hypothetical situations	Clothing; accessories; fabrics; fashion	Subjunctive mood to express indirect commands and opinions; the conditional; future tense	La ropa tradicional en Latinoamérica; Los blogueros de moda	Lectura: Los diseñadores hispanos más famosos El blog de Bella: Un paseo	Intonation and stress

Proyecto 5: Elaboración de película (Capítulos 9 y 10)   264

	Objectives	Vocabulary	Grammar	Culture	Reading/Writing	Pronunciation
11 La salud 269	Visiting the clinic, describing symptoms; talking about exercise routines; expressing emotions; discussing healthy living	The body; at the gym, the hospital, and the dentist's office	Subjunctive to express emotions, hopes, and wishes; irregular verbs in the subjunctive; past participles; present perfect	Estilos de vida; La medicina tradicional	Lectura: "Tía José Rivadeneira", Ángeles Mastretta El blog de Bella: Una visita a la clínica	Review I: Main challenges for English speakers
12 El mundo de hoy 295	Discussing and expressing subjective opinions and reactions to current events in the present and past	Environment; politics; media; immigration; energy	Relative clauses; subjunctive and indicative in relative clauses; review of present perfect and past participles; past perfect; present perfect subjunctive	Current events in the Spanish-speaking world; El ambiente	Lectura: "Una gigantesca ola de 19 metros de altura establece un nuevo récord mundial", National Geographic El blog de Bella: El mundo de hoy: *What I learned while living abroad*	Review II: Main challenges for English speakers

Proyecto 6: Artículo de opinión (Capítulos 11 y 12) 318

Spanish-English Glossary 323

Acknowledgments

We would like to acknowledge the helpful comments, suggestions, and ideas provided by our reviewers. Your contributions have enabled us to create a better program, and we are immensely grateful for your help.

In particular, we would like to thank the following instructors who took time to participate in online surveys, focus groups, and chapter reviews.

Maria Blackmon, *Ozarks Technical Community College*
Susana Blanco-Iglesias, *Macalester College*
Melanie Bloom, *University of Nebraska Omaha*
Evelyne Bornier, *Auburn University*
Alicia Bralove Ramirez, *Bronx Community College*
Julia Bussade, *University of Mississippi*
Maria Cabrera, *West Chester University of Pennsylvania*
Oscar Cabrera, *Community College of Philadelphia*
Lina Callahan, *Fullerton College*
Sara Casler, *Sierra College*
Aurora Castillo-Scott, *Georgia College*
Lisa Celona, *Tunxis Community College*
Rachel Clair, *University of Tampa*
Sofia Cook, *College of the Sequoias*
Mark Cox, *Presbyterian College*
Elizabeth Deifell, *University of Iowa*
Andrew DeMil, *University of Tampa*
David Detwiler, *MiraCosta College*
Dorian Dorado, *Louisiana State University*
Indira Dortolina, *ISCS UP*
Monica Duran, *University of Miami*

Edward Erazo, *Broward College*
Ronna Feit, *Nassau Community College, SUNY*
Amy George-Hirons, *Tulane University*
Amy Ginck, *Messiah College*
Inmaculada Gómez-Soler, *University of Memphis*
Jennifer Góngora, *Sam Houston State University*
Kate Grovergrys, *Madison Area Technical College*
Marie Guiribitey, *Florida International University*
Elizabeth Gunn, *Rutgers University—New Brunswick*
Loida Gutierrez, *South Mountain Community College*
Shannon Hahn, *Durham Technical Community College*
Judy Haisten, *College of Central Florida*
Michelle Harkins, *Burlington County College*
Dennis Harrod, *Syracuse University*
Mary Hartson, *Oakland University*
Dominique Hitchcock, *Norco College*
Katherine Honea, *Austin Peay State University*
Michael Hughes, *California State University, San Marcos*
Becky Jaimes, *Austin Community College*
Yun Sil Jeon, *Coastal Carolina University*
Carmen J. Jiménez, *The University of Tennessee at Chattanooga*
Keith Johnson, *California State University, Fresno*
Chris Kneifl, *University of Oklahoma*
Piet Koene, *Northwestern College*
Pedro Koo, *Missouri State University*
Bryan Koronkiewicz, *University of Alabama*
Marilyn Manley, *Rowan University*
Rob Martinsen, *Brigham Young University*

Cynthia Melendrez, *University of Northern Colorado*
Joseph Menig, *Valencia College*
Montserrat Mir, *Illinois State University*
Maria Monica Montalvo, *University of Central Florida*
Francisco Montaño, *Lehman College*
Markus Muller, *California State University, Long Beach*
Heather Nylen, *University of Hawai'i at Mānoa*
Sandy Oakley, *Palm Beach State University*
María de los Santos Onofre-Madrid, *Angelo State University*
Iliana Pagan-Teitelbaum, *West Chester University of Pennsylvania*
Lynn Pearson, *Bowling Green State University*
Gwendolyn Pearson, *University of Tampa*
Teresa Perez-Gamboa, *University of Georgia*
Pablo Pintado-Casas, *Kean University*
Anne Prucha, *University of Central Florida*
Jessica Rangel, *College of DuPage*
Judy Rodríguez, *California State University, Sacramento*
Paul Roggendorff, *Abilene Christian University*
Maria Rosales, *City College of San Francisco*
Gabriela Segal, *Arcadia University*
Nori Sogomonian-Mejía, *San Bernardino Valley College*
Sabrina Spannagel, *University of Washington*
Nancy Stucker, *Cabrillo College*
Samantha Swift, *Middle Tennessee State University*
Marta Tecedor, *Texas Tech University*
Veronica Tempone, *Indian River State College*
Joe Terantino, *Brown University*
Linda Tracy, *Santa Rosa Junior College*

Katica Urbanc, *Wagner College*
Kimberly Vitchkoski, *University of Massachusetts Lowell*
Lee Wilberschied, *Cleveland State University*
Helga Winkler, *Moorpark College*
Matt Wyszynski, *University of Akron*
U. Theresa Zmurkewycz, *Saint Joseph's University*

In addition to the reviewers and participants listed above, a great number of instructors took the time to provide early input via surveys regarding supplementary instructor resources, general approach, and other questions. We sincerely appreciate their invaluable time and advice.

We would especially like to thank the Graduate Teaching Assistants at the University of Utah for their help implementing our vision for blended learning in the Spanish language program and also the University of Utah's Teaching and Learning Technologies unit for their guidance and support. Special thanks to LeeAnn Stone, Heather Bradley Cole, and Beth Kramer for helping us turn our ideas into a real project and a very emphatic thank you to Kim Beuttler and Mark Overstreet for making sure that the project came to fruition. This would not have been possible without your unwavering support and patience.

Fernando Rubio
Tim Cannon

Preliminar

Objectives: In this chapter you will learn to

- greet people and introduce yourself
- say the Spanish alphabet and numbers 0–100
- use classroom expressions and identify objects in the classroom

Vocabulario

CP-1 El alfabeto   With a partner, take turns reading the Spanish letters below and writing
out the words they spell. One of you should read the odd-numbered items and the other
should read the even-numbered items. Then choose two more words each from page 10
and spell them in Spanish for your partner to write.

Modelo   Student A: *eme, e, ese, a*
         Student B: *mesa*

1. u, ene, o
2. a, de, i, o con acento, ese
3. ge, a, te, o
4. ene, o, ce, hache, e
5. eme, a, eñe, a, ene, a
6. a, erre, ge, e, ene, te, i, ene, a
7. pe, e, erre, ese, o, ene, a

8. eme, e con acento, equis, i, ce, o
9. jota, u, ele, i, a
10. hache, o, ele, a
11. ¿...?
12. ¿...?
13. ¿...?
14. ¿...?

CP-2 Las matemáticas   With a partner, take turns asking and answering these basic math
problems. Then create three to five of your own simple addition and subtraction problems
to ask each other. Follow the model.

Modelos $5 + 2 = ?$ Student A: *Cinco más dos son...*   Student B: *siete*
          $7 - 2 = ?$ Student A: *Siete menos dos son...*   Student B: *cinco*

1. $6 + 2 =$
2. $3 + 1 =$
3. $14 - 4 =$

4. $8 + 4 =$
5. $16 + 5 =$
6. $9 - 8 =$

7. $4 + 5 =$
8. $11 + 15 =$
9. ¿...?

Vocabulario

CP-3 El salón de clase With a partner, ask each other what is and is not in your classroom, then respond positively or negatively. Each of you should mention at least three objects.

Modelo   Student A: *¿Hay una mesa en el salón de clase?*
Student B: *Sí, hay una mesa en el salón de clase. / No, no hay una mesa en el salón de clase.*

CP-4 ¿Cuántos hay? With a partner, look around the classroom and say how many things there are and where they are found, based on the information provided below. Remember to use the correct plural forms and definite articles as needed.

Modelo   libro (2), mesa
*Hay **dos** libros en **la** mesa.*

1. persona (23), clase

2. profesor (2), clase

3. puerta (1), salón de clase

4. cuadernos (3), escritorio

5. sillas (30), salón de clase

6. borrador (1), pizarra

CP-5A ¿Qué hay en el salón de clase? **A** Work with a partner. Look at the illustration below while your partner looks at the illustration in CP-5B on the next page. Take turns asking each other what objects are in your rooms until you have identified five differences.

Modelo   Student A: *¿Hay un libro en el salón de clase?*
Student B: *Sí, hay un libro en el salón de clase. / No, no hay un libro en el salón de clase.*

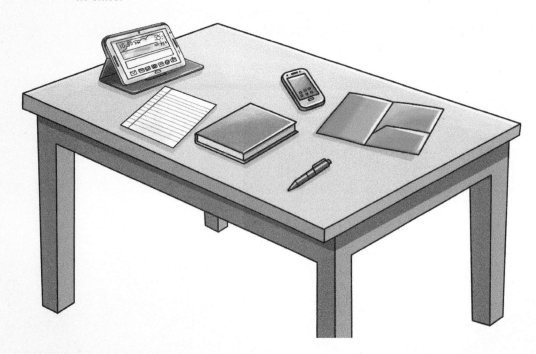

Gramática

CP-5B ¿Qué hay en el salón de clase? **B** Work with a partner. Look at the illustration below while your partner looks at the illustration in CP-5A on the previous page. Take turns asking each other what objects are in your rooms until you have identified five differences.

Modelo Student A: *¿Hay un libro en el salón de clase?*
Student B: *Sí, hay un libro en el salón de clase. / No, no hay un libro en el salón de clase.*

Gramática

CP-6   **¿Qué hay?**   In groups of three or four, find out how many of the items your group has.

Modelo   (libros)

> Student A: *¿Cuántos libros hay?*
> Student B: *Hay cuatro libros. / No hay libros.*

libros	lápices	apuntes	mujeres
mochilas	mapas	teléfonos celulares	(…)
cuadernos	marcadores	diccionarios	

CP-7   Los artículos

Step 1   With a partner, use the word bank to create four sentences. Write out your sentences and make sure to use articles that agree in gender and number with the nouns.

Modelo   *Hay unas ventanas en el salón de clase.*

hay	en	mesa	profesora	silla	salón de clase
ventana	clase	escritorio	estudiante	reloj	

Articles: el, la, los, las, un, una, unos, unas

Step 2   Work again with your partner to write three more sentences describing what is (or might be) in each of your backpacks. Use your imagination and be sure to include some false statements!

Modelos   *Hay dos lápices en mi mochila.*
              Hay unas mesas en mi mochila.

Step 3   Now travel around the classroom with your partner, take turns reading your sentences from **Step 2**, and ask other pairs to take turns guessing whether the sentences are true or false.

Modelos   Student A: *Hay dos lápices en mi mochila.*   Student B: *Es cierto.*
              Student A: *Hay unas mesas en mi mochila.*   Student B: *Es falso.*

Vocabulario

CP-8 ¡Mucho gusto!

Step 1 Ask three different people in the class the following questions and write their answers.

1. ¿Cómo te llamas?
2. ¿De dónde eres?

3. ¿Cuál es tu número de teléfono?
4. ¿Cuál es tu correo electrónico?

Responses: 1. Me llamo _____. 2. Soy de _____. 3. Mi número de teléfono es el _____.
4. Mi correo electrónico es _____.

Step 2 Now that you have basic information about some of your classmates, share that information with the class or another classmate using the model as your script.

Modelo   *Quiero presentar a mi amigo Juan. Juan (Él) es de California. Su número de teléfono es el… Su correo electrónico es…*

CP-9A Las oraciones *(sentences)* **A** Work with a partner to complete the following sentences. One of you will use the sentences below and the other will use the sentences in CP-9B on the next page. Without looking at each other's sentences, take turns spelling out the underlined words in your sentences and writing down the words that you are missing until you can complete all the sentences. After you have completed all of the sentences, read the sentences out loud with your partner.

1. Muy <u>bien</u>, ¿y tú?
2. Mucho _____. Me <u>llamo</u> Clara.
3. Bien, _____… ¿Cómo te _____?
4. ¿De <u>dónde</u> eres?
5. _____ de _____. Es un <u>placer</u>.

6. Me _____ Kris.
7. Hola, ¿<u>cómo</u> estás?
8. Soy de _____. ¿Y tú?
9. <u>Igualmente</u>. Hasta _____.

Vocabulario

CP-9B Las oraciones *(sentences)* **B** Work with a partner to complete the following sentences. One of you will use the sentences below and the other will use the sentences in CP-9A on the previous page. Without looking at each other's sentences, take turns spelling out the underlined words in your sentences and writing down the words that you are missing until you can complete all the sentences. Read the sentences out loud with your partner. Then put them in logical order to create a conversation.

1. Muy _____, ¿y tú?
2. Mucho <u>gusto</u>. Me _____ Clara.
3. Bien, <u>gracias</u>… ¿Cómo te <u>llamas</u>?
4. ¿De _____ eres?
5. Soy de <u>Uruguay</u>. Es un _____.

6. Me <u>llamo</u> Kris.
7. Hola, ¿_____ estás?
8. Soy de <u>Guatemala</u>. ¿Y tú?
9. _____. Hasta <u>luego</u>.

CP-10 Las preguntas personales Imagine that you're sitting next to a chatty stranger on a plane and he/she is asking you about yourself. You don't want to be rude, but you'd like some privacy. Make up new answers to the questions you answered in **CP-8.** Be creative and have fun with your cover story.

1. ¿Cómo te llamas?
2. ¿De dónde eres?

3. ¿Cuál es tu número de teléfono?
4. ¿Cuál es tu correo electrónico?

CP-11 Presentaciones With a partner, choose one of the images below and use as many expressions as you can to write a short paragraph of introduction. Take turns reading the paragraph out loud and correct any mistakes you notice. Then decide who will read your paragraph to the rest of the class.

Modelo *Buenos días. Me llamo Sofía.*
Soy de Albania…

©arek_malang/Shutterstock.com

michaeljung/Shutterstock.com

Charlotte Purdy/Shutterstock.com

Gramática

CP-12
Citas rápidas *(Speed dating)*
As a class, count off in threes in Spanish until everyone has a number. Write the word that corresponds to your number on a piece of paper:

> 1 = mañana   2 = tarde   3 = noche

When your instructor gives the signal, you will have two minutes to find a classmate with a matching number, greet each other correctly for your assigned time of day, and exchange two additional polite questions and answers. When you are finished, trade numbers with another classmate until you have completed all three greetings.

Otua Images/ Shutterstock.com

CP-13
Presentaciones
Using the expressions on page 11, work with a partner to create situations in which the following people greet and introduce themselves to each other. Make sure you choose the correct forms of address (formal or informal) according to the situation.

1. A doctor (**Dr. Rodríguez**) and a patient (**señora Mendoza**)
2. A professor (**la profesora Chacón**) and one of her students (**Antonio**)
3. Two university classmates (**Carlos and Patricia**) who are just meeting for the first time
4. **Señor Ávila** and his new ten-year-old neighbor (**Pedrito**)
5. Two high school students (**Álvaro and Ana**) who are introducing themselves to their teacher (**señor Aragón**) on the first day of class

Albertiniz/ Shutterstock.com

CP-14
Los saludos

Stuart Jenner/ Shutterstock.com

Step 1 Look at the four pictures of people meeting each other. In groups of three, create three or more conversations based on the pictures. Give the people names. Decide who will speak formally and who will not. Write down your conversation. Be creative.

Step 2 As a group, choose one of your conversations. Present it in front of the class. Your classmates will then try to guess which picture is being represented.

Ostvintsev Alexander/ Shutterstock.com

Síntesis: Vocabulario

A	*a*	Ana	**J**	*jota*	jamón
B	*be**	Barcelona	**K**	*ka*	kilo
C	*ce*	casa	**L**	*ele*	loco
D	*de*	dos	**M**	*eme*	Madrid
E	*e*	elefante	**N**	*ene*	nuevo
F	*efe*	Francia	**Ñ**	*eñe*	niño
G	*ge*	Guatemala	**O**	*o*	ocho
H	*hache*	hola	**P**	*pe*	Panamá
I	*i*	Italia	**Q**	*cu*	queso

R	*erre*	Roma
S	*ese*	sol
T	*te*	tomate
U	*u*	Uruguay
V	*uve, ve corta**	Valencia
W	*uve doble, doble u**	Washington
X	*equis*	xilófono
Y	*i griega, ye**	yo
Z	*zeta*	zapato

*The names of some letters vary around the Spanish-speaking world. Though each native speaker has his/her preferred term, all are acceptable. Here are a few examples of letters with multiple names:

> Latin America: **b** *be larga,* **v** *ve baja, ve corta,* or *ve chica,* **w** *doble u* or *doble ve*

> Spain: **b** *be,* **v** *uve,* **w** *uve doble*

The Real Academia Española changed the name of the letter **y** to *ye,* but many Spanish speakers still refer to this letter as **i griega,** which means *Greek i.*

Los números

0 cero	9 nueve	18 dieciocho	27 veintisiete	36 treinta y seis	51 cincuenta y uno
1 uno	10 diez	19 diecinueve	28 veintiocho	37 treinta y siete	60 sesenta
2 dos	11 once	20 veinte	29 veintinueve	38 treinta y ocho	70 setenta
3 tres	12 doce	21 veintiuno	30 treinta	39 treinta y nueve	80 ochenta
4 cuatro	13 trece	22 veintidós	31 treinta y uno	40 cuarenta	90 noventa
5 cinco	14 catorce	23 veintitrés	32 treinta y dos	41 cuarenta y uno	100 cien
6 seis	15 quince	24 veinticuatro	33 treinta y tres	42 cuarenta y dos	
7 siete	16 dieciséis	25 veinticinco	34 treinta y cuatro	43 cuarenta y tres	
8 ocho	17 diecisiete	26 veintiséis	35 treinta y cinco	50 cincuenta	

Síntesis: Vocabulario

Letras y sonidos

- The letter **h** has no sound in Spanish. **Hola, hermana, hay, La Habana,** etc.

- The letter **j** is pronounced like *h* in English. **Jota, joven, dijo, jugar, jamón,** etc.

- The letter **ñ** does not exist in the English alphabet. The sound is similar to the *nyuh* or *yuh* sound in words like *on̲i̲on* or *ca̲n̲yon.* **Niño, año, señor, mañana, baño,** etc.

- The letter *g* has two different pronunciations. When followed by a consonant or by the vowel **a, o,** or **u** it is pronounced much like English *g* as in *get.* When **g** is followed by **e** or **i,** it sounds like the Spanish **j** (see above). Note that if **g** is followed by **ue** or **ui,** it maintains a sound like the English *g.* **Agua, gato, gota, guitarra, guerra, guía, Gerardo, gente, general,** etc.

- The letter **r** also has two different pronunciations. At the beginning of a word and every time it is spelled **rr,** it is a "rolling" *r* sound. The same sound occurs when **r** follows **n, l,** or **s.** In all other cases, it is pronounced as a simple *r* sound (the tongue only taps the top of your mouth). **Roma, carro, Pedro, hora, libro, arroba,** etc.

El salón de clase   *The classroom*

el borrador   *eraser*
el escritorio   *desk*
el (la) estudiante   *student*
el mapa   *map*
el marcador   *marker*
la mesa   *table*
la muchacha / la chica   *girl, young woman*
el muchacho / el chico   *boy, young man*
la pared   *wall*
la persona   *person*
el piso / el suelo   *floor*

la pizarra   *blackboard*
el (la) profesor(a)   *teacher*
la puerta   *door*
el reloj   *clock*
el salón de clase   *classroom*
la silla   *chair*

¿Cómo se dice…?   **Se dice…**
   How do you say…?   *You say…*
¿Cómo se escribe…?   **Se escribe…**
   How do you spell…?   *You spell…*
¿Qué es…?   **Es…**
   What is…?   *It's…*

Presentaciones   *Introductions*

Para saludar   *To greet*
Hola.   *Hello.*
Buenos días.   *Good morning.*
Buenas tardes.   *Good afternoon.*
Buenas noches.   *Good night.*
¿Cómo estás (tú)? (informal)   *How are you?*
¿Cómo está (usted)? (formal)   *How are you?*
¿Cómo están (ustedes)? (plural)   *How are you?*
¿Qué tal?   *How are things going?*

Síntesis: Vocabulario

Para responder *To respond*

Bien, gracias. *Fine, thanks.*

(No) Muy bien. *(Not) Very well.*

Terrible. *Terrible.*

Fatal. *Awful.*

Regular. *Normal.*

¿Y tú? (informal) *And you?*

¿Y usted? (formal) *And you?*

Presentaciones *Introductions*

¿Cómo te llamas? (informal) *What's your name?*

¿Cómo se llama? (formal) *What's your name?*

¿De dónde eres? (informal) *Where are you from?*

¿De dónde es (usted)? (formal) *Where are you from?*

¿Cuál es tu número de teléfono?
(informal) *What's your phone number?*

¿Cuál es su número de teléfono?
(formal) *What's your phone number?*

¿Cuál es tu correo electrónico?
(informal) *What's your email address?*

¿Cuál es su correo electrónico? (formal)
What's your email address?

Me llamo… *My name is …*

Soy de… *I'm from …*

Mi número de teléfono es el… *My telephone number is …*

Mi correo electrónico es… *My email address is …*

Quiero presentarte a… *I would like to introduce you (informal) to …*

Quiero presentarle a… *I would like to introduce you (formal) to …*

Quiero presentarles a… *I would like to introduce you (plural) to …*

Mucho gusto en conocerte. (informal)
A pleasure to meet you.

Mucho gusto. *A pleasure.*

Encantado(a). *Delighted.*

Un placer. *A pleasure.*

Igualmente. *Likewise.*

Para despedirse *To say goodbye*

Adiós. *Goodbye.*

Hasta luego. *See you later.*

Hasta mañana. *See you tomorrow.*

Chau. *Bye.*

Tengo que irme. *I have to go.*

Nos vemos. *See you later.*

Emails

arroba @

guion *dash*

guion bajo *underscore*

punto *period / dot*

espacio *space*

Síntesis: Gramática

Hay

Hay is used to mean both *there is* and *there are*. Its form never changes. **No hay** means *there isn't* or *there aren't*.

Hay quince estudiantes en mi clase.	*There are fifteen students in my class.*
En mi mochila **hay** un cuaderno.	*In my backpack there is a notebook.*
No **hay** clase hoy.	*There is no class today.*

Nouns and Articles

The Gender of Nouns

A noun is a person, place, thing, or idea. In Spanish all nouns have gender, which means that they are either masculine or feminine. Although there are many exceptions, in general, nouns that refer to females and **most** nouns that end in **-a** are feminine and nouns that refer to males and **most** nouns that end in **-o** are masculine.

> **el** bolígraf**o** (masculine)
> **la** computador**a** (feminine)

Nouns ending in **-sión, -ción, -dad, -tud,** and **-umbre** are feminine. For example:

> **la conversación** (feminine)
> **la electricidad** (feminine)

Many nouns ending in **-ma, -pa,** and **-ta** are masculine. For example:

> **el programa** (masculine)

There are many exceptions to these rules, so it is always best to memorize the genders of new nouns that you are learning.

Definite and Indefinite Articles

In English, we use the definite article *the* to refer to specific nouns or to a noun that has been previously mentioned. In Spanish, definite articles are either singular or plural and either masculine or feminine. They agree in number and gender with the nouns to which they refer.

	Definite article		
Masculine	Singular	el	libro
	Plural	los	libros
Feminine	Singular	la	mochila
	Plural	las	mochilas

In English we use the indefinite articles *a, an,* and *some* to refer to non-specific nouns. Just like definite articles, indefinite articles in Spanish are either singular or plural and either masculine or feminine. They also agree with the nouns they modify.

Síntesis: Gramática

		Indefinite article	
Masculine	Singular	**un**	bolígraf**o**
	Plural	**unos**	bolígraf**os**
Feminine	Singular	**una**	ventan**a**
	Plural	**unas**	ventan**as**

Always use a masculine plural form for groups that include both masculine and feminine terms. **Unos estudiantes,** for example, means a group of male students or a group of male and female students.

Formal and informal address

The English pronoun *you* can be translated in Spanish as **tú, vosotros, vosotras, usted,** or **ustedes.** Which Spanish pronoun you use depends on how many people you are referring to and the level of formality of the situation.

tú   (singular, informal)
usted   (singular, formal)
vosotros / vosotras   (plural, informal, used in Spain)
ustedes   (plural, informal and formal)

Here are some other terms of address:

Señor (Sr.) *Mr.*
Señora (Sra.) *Mrs.*
Señorita (Srta.) *Miss*

La familia y los amigos

Objectives: In this chapter you will learn to

- talk about yourself and your family
- describe people's physical and emotional traits
- ask basic questions

- use verbs and expressions with **tener**
- indicate and ask where someone is from

Hero Images/Getty Images

Vocabulario

C1-1 La familia de Roberto   Work with a partner to determine the relationships between Roberto's family members. Read all of the sentences before you begin, as you may need information that appears in a later sentence to determine an answer. Don't forget to add the article before the noun where necessary.

1. Roberto y Tomás son los hijos de Alison. Roberto es _____ de Tomás.

2. Roberto y Tomás son los nietos de Patricia. Patricia es _____ de ellos.

3. El padre de Laura y la madre de Roberto son hermanos. Laura y Roberto son _____.

4. El padre de Laura se llama Nicolás. Nicolás es _____ de Roberto.

5. Nicolás está casado con *(is married to)* Liliana. Roberto es _____ de Liliana.

C1-2 Una familia famosa   With a partner, choose a celebrity, cartoon, political, or other family that is familiar to both of you. Then, working separately, write five true/false statements each about their relationships. Take turns reading your statements, identifying whether they are true or false, and correcting the false statements. Follow the model.

Modelo   Student A: *Marge Simpson es la hija de Homer Simpson. ¿Cierto o falso?*
Student B: *Falso. Marge Simpson es la esposa de Homer Simpson.*

Vocabulario

C1-3 Conversaciones Have a conversation with a partner using the following structure as a model. Before you begin the conversation, think about the verbs you will need to use and how you will conjugate them. Look only at your own lines. After you have gone through the conversation once, switch roles with your partner and have the conversation again.

Student A	Student B
1. Greet Student B.	2. Respond to Student A's greeting and ask how he/she is doing.
3. Respond to Student B's question saying that you are well. Ask Student B how his/her family is doing.	4. Respond to Student A by saying that your family is well. Tell Student A that you are a student (**estudiante**).
5. Ask Student B what he/she studies.	6. Tell Student A that you study biology (**biología**).
7. Tell Student B that you are studying biology, too (**también**). Then, ask Student B what his/her brother is studying.	8. Tell Student A that your brother studies literature (**literatura**).
9. Say goodbye to Student B.	10. Say goodbye to Student A.

C1-4

Relaciones familiares Work in groups of three. Using the family photo, take turns naming the people and then explain each person's relationship to the previous person. Add new identities to this fictional family until every person in the photo has a name and defined relationship. Follow the model.

Modelo Student A: *Él se llama Miguel.*
Student B: *Ella se llama Rosario. Es la esposa de Miguel.*
Student C: *Él se llama Ángel. Es el padre de Miguel.*

C1-5

Tu familia With a partner, describe three of your family members. Discuss one person at a time, using the script below as a model. To be more specific about your descriptions, say **un poco** *(a little)* or **muy** *(very)* before the adjective.

Modelo *Mi hermano se llama José. Tiene* (He has) *el pelo rubio y los ojos azules. Es (muy) alto y delgado.*

Mi _____ se llama _____. Tiene el pelo _____ y los ojos _____. Es _____ y _____.

Vocabulario

C1-6

Hablando de colores With a partner, talk about your favorite colors. Then use the adjectives on page 29 that you have learned to guess what kind of person your partner is, based on their favorite color. Continue your conversation by talking about other people's favorite colors. Follow the model.

Modelo Student A: *¿Cuál* (Which) *es tu color favorito?*
Student B: *Mi color favorito es el amarillo.*
Student A: *¿Eres una persona alegre* (happy)*?*
Student B: *Sí, soy una persona alegre.*

C1-7

¿Cómo es? With a classmate, look at the following pictures. Use as many physical descriptions as you can for each person. Remember to use **es** when you are describing inherent characteristics and **está** to talk about conditions or emotions.

Modelo

Es joven y gordo. Tiene el pelo rubio y liso.

1.  2.  3.  4.  5.

Vocabulario

C1-8 **¿Cómo son estos famosos?** With a partner, use adjectives and the verb **ser** to describe these famous people and characters.

1. Beyoncé
2. Emma Stone
3. Bugs Bunny

4. Harry Potter
5. Michael Jordan
6. Jennifer Lopez

C1-9 **¿Cómo soy yo?**

Step 1 Describe yourself to a classmate using as many adjectives as you can. Listen as your classmate describes himself/herself.

Step 2 Prepare a brief description in which you compare yourself with your classmate. Try to use more words than you used in **Step 1**. Some useful words are **pero** *(but)* and **también** *(also)*.

Modelo *Ann es alta y yo soy alto también, pero ella es rubia y yo soy moreno.*

C1-10 **¿Cómo es tu familia?** With a partner, look at a photo of your family or another family. Take turns describing people in the photo using adjectives you have learned in this chapter. Have your partner guess which family member you are talking about.

Gramática

C1-11A La familia Ricabo

Step 1 Look at the incomplete Ricabo family tree below. Your partner will be using activity C1-11B that includes all of the information that you are missing, but that activity is missing information that you have. As a first step, write a list of questions you will need to ask your partner to complete the family tree.

Modelo   *¿Cómo se llama el hijo de Alberto?*

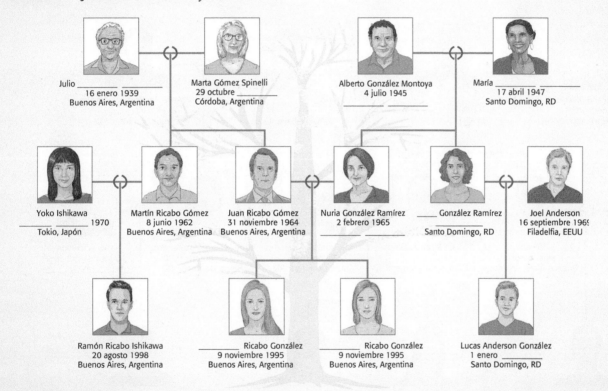

Julio _____
16 enero 1939
Buenos Aires, Argentina

Marta Gómez Spinelli
29 octubre _____
Córdoba, Argentina

Alberto González Montoya
4 julio 1945
_____ _____

María _____
17 abril 1947
Santo Domingo, RD

Yoko Ishikawa
_____ 1970
Tokio, Japón

Martín Ricabo Gómez
8 junio 1962
Buenos Aires, Argentina

Juan Ricabo Gómez
31 noviembre 1964
Buenos Aires, Argentina

Nuria González Ramírez
2 febrero 1965
_____ _____

_____ González Ramírez
_____
Santo Domingo, RD

Joel Anderson
16 septiembre 196?
Filadelfia, EEUU

Ramón Ricabo Ishikawa
20 agosto 1998
Buenos Aires, Argentina

_____ Ricabo González
9 noviembre 1995
Buenos Aires, Argentina

_____ Ricabo González
9 noviembre 1995
Buenos Aires, Argentina

Lucas Anderson González
1 enero _____
Santo Domingo, RD

Step 2 Using the questions you've written in Step 1, ask your partner for all the information you need to complete the family tree. Remember that you may need to spell out some of the names. Follow the models.

Modelos   *¿Cómo se llama el hijo / esposo / tío de...? ¿Cuántos años tiene...? ¿De dónde es...?*

Gramática

La familia Ricabo

Step 1 Look at the incomplete Ricabo family tree below. Your partner will be using activity C1-11A that includes all of the information that you are missing, but that activity is missing information that you have. As a first step, write a list of questions you will need to ask your partner to complete the family tree.

Modelo   *¿Cómo se llama el hijo de Alberto?*

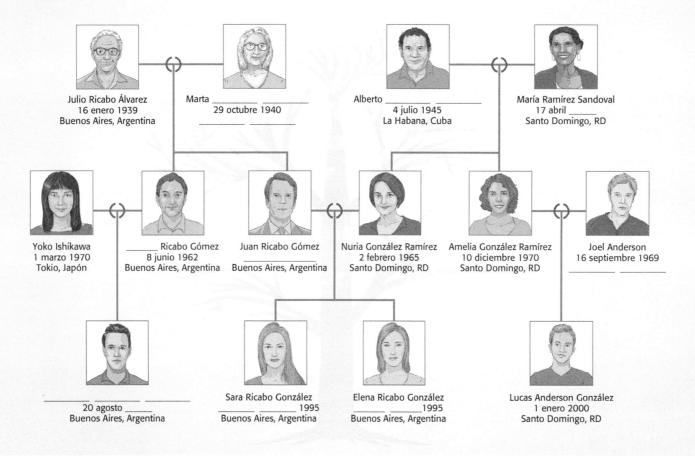

Julio Ricabo Álvarez
16 enero 1939
Buenos Aires, Argentina

Marta _____
29 octubre 1940
_____ _____

Alberto _____ _____
4 julio 1945
La Habana, Cuba

María Ramírez Sandoval
17 abril _____
Santo Domingo, RD

Yoko Ishikawa
1 marzo 1970
Tokio, Japón

_____ Ricabo Gómez
8 junio 1962
Buenos Aires, Argentina

Juan Ricabo Gómez
_____
Buenos Aires, Argentina

Nuria González Ramírez
2 febrero 1965
Santo Domingo, RD

Amelia González Ramírez
10 diciembre 1970
Santo Domingo, RD

Joel Anderson
16 septiembre 1969
_____ _____

_____ _____ _____
20 agosto _____
Buenos Aires, Argentina

Sara Ricabo González
_____ _____1995
Buenos Aires, Argentina

Elena Ricabo González
_____ _____1995
Buenos Aires, Argentina

Lucas Anderson González
1 enero 2000
Santo Domingo, RD

Gramática

Step 2 Using the questions you've written in Step 1, ask your partner for all the information you need to complete the family tree. Remember that you may need to spell out some of the names. Follow the models.

Modelos   *¿Cómo se llama el hijo / esposo / tío de…?*
           ¿Cuántos años tiene…?
           ¿De dónde es…?

C1-12

Preguntas sobre una foto   Work with a partner. Using the photo on page 18, take turns asking each other questions about one person in the photo and inventing answers. Follow the models.

Modelos   Student A: *¿Cómo se llama ella?*
           Student B: *Se llama Isabel.*
           Student A: *¿Cuántos años tiene Isabel?*
           Student B: *Tiene 22 años.*
           Student A: *¿De dónde es Isabel?*
           Student B: *Isabel es de Colombia.*

Vocabulario/Gramática

C1-13 **Encuesta** Walk around to interview your classmates and find out how many people have the things listed in the form below. Make sure to keep a tally. Add one more item of your own for the last box. Use the verb **tener** to ask questions. Be prepared to summarize the results and be ready to share your findings with the class.

Modelo Student A: *¿Tienes un perro?*
Student B: *No, no tengo perro.*

¿Tienes...?	Sí	No
un perro		
un gato		
hermanos		
hermanas		
una guitarra		
una bicicleta		
clase de biología		
una computadora portátil		
música en español		
¿…? (create your own)		

C1-14 **Resumen (Summary) de la encuesta** After conducting your survey, prepare a written summary of what you have learned.

Modelo *Cuatro personas tienen un perro. Seis personas tienen un gato. Tres personas no tienen una computadora portátil.*

Vocabulario/Gramática

C1-15 Preguntas personales

Step 1 With a partner, ask and answer the following interview questions. Write down the answers.

1. ¿Cómo te llamas? _____

2. ¿Cuántos años tienes? _____

3. ¿Cuándo es tu cumpleaños? _____

4. ¿Cuántos hermanos tienes? _____

5. ¿Cómo se llaman tus hermanos? _____

6. ¿Cuántos años tienen tus hermanos? _____

7. ¿Cómo se llaman tus padres? _____

8. ¿Cuándo es el cumpleaños de tu madre? _____

9. ¿Cuándo es el cumpleaños de tu padre? _____

Step 2 In groups of four, introduce your interviewee using the answers to the questions you just asked.

Modelo   *Él se llama Pedro. Tiene 21 años. El cumpleaños de Pedro es el 7 de noviembre.*
Tiene dos hermanos. Tiene un hermano y una hermana. El hermano se llama José
y la hermana se llama Rosa. José tiene 24 años y Rosa tiene 19 años. La madre de
Pedro se llama Verónica y el padre se llama Esteban. El cumpleaños de su madre es
el 25 de septiembre. El cumpleaños de su padre es el 21 de febrero.

Lectura

C1-16 Antes de leer What is the class's favorite holiday or celebration?

Step 1 Work with a partner. Choose your favorite holiday and list the reasons: you may like the family gathering, a special yearly tradition, or the historical meaning?

Step 2 Include information about the activities you do during this holiday, the people with whom you share it, and the food you prepare and eat.

Step 3 In class, share your list. Are there similarities in the responses from your classmates?

C1-17 Cuestionario: El regalo ideal Below is a survey that you will use in activity C1-18.

Cómo identificar el regalo ideal

Los favoritos	
Color:	Vacaciones:
Comida (*food*):	Libro:
Animal:	Artista:
Bebida (*drink*):	Vehículo:
Autor:	Tipo de música / bandas:
Flor:	Actividad / hobby:
Perfume:	

Lectura

¿Cuál?	Específicos
¿Té o café?	Signo del zodíaco:
¿Arte o ciencia?	Obsesión personal:
¿Día o noche?	Alergias:
¿Matemáticas o literatura?	Colecciones:

C1-18 Complete the questionnaire in C1-17 by answering with your own preferences.

Step 1 Exchange your answers with a partner. After reading your partner's answers, choose what you feel would be an ideal gift, write it down, and show your partner. Look up the Spanish word for your gift if you don't know it.

Step 2 Read the gift your partner chose for you and decide whether it's something you would really like. Exchange reactions.

Modelo ¿Qué tal una tableta iPad?
Es un regalo ideal. ¡Gracias! / No es un regalo ideal.

Step 3 Now compare your results with those of the entire class. Did the questionnaire work? Do you think that adding some questions or categories would help? Think of at least two additional categories that you would include and be prepared to share them.

Introducción

I am so excited! In a few short weeks I will be in Spain! I have decided that I need to keep this blog so that everyone can read about my experiences and I have a place to share my thoughts while I study Spanish in Spain. I have already taken **dos clases de español. Hablo un poco.** I'm a little nervous that I might have a hard time understanding people in Spain. However, I'm going to do my best to speak Spanish all the time and as I get better at Spanish I plan on writing my blog in **español.** :)

Entrada de Bella

¡Hola, buenos días! This morning I went to campus for the first time. The university is **muy grande y bonita.** :) I had to fill out some paperwork and it was all in Spanish. There were a few words I didn't know. For example, **apellidos** means *last names.* People here have two last names. The first one is your father's family name and the last one is your mother's. So, I had to fill out Johnson Roberts. Oh, which reminds me: when I told them my last name was *Johnson* they had a hard time understanding me. They asked me to spell it out letter by letter. They kind of pronounce the first part like a *y,* like **yo.** I also had to ask what **fecha de nacimiento** means. It is *birth date.* They told me that **cita** also means *date,* but the kind of date when you go out with someone. The last word I had to ask about was **dirección,** which means *address.* I guess it makes sense . . . **¿Cuál es tu dirección?** :) **Estoy muy contenta aquí en España. Estoy encantada de hablar español con las personas aquí.**

C1-19 Estudiar en el extranjero Have you ever thought about studying in a Spanish-speaking country? What are some of the challenges that you think you would encounter? If you could study in any Spanish speaking country, where would you study and why?

Síntesis: Vocabulario

La familia   *Family*

la madre (mamá)   *mother (mom)*

el padre (papá)   *father (dad)*

los padres   *parents*

el hijo / la hija   *son / daughter*

el abuelo / la abuela   *grandfather / grandmother*

el bisabuelo / la bisabuela   *great-grandfather / great-grandmother*

el hermano / la hermana   *brother / sister*

el nieto / la nieta   *grandson / granddaughter*

el sobrino / la sobrina   *nephew / niece*

el primo / la prima   *cousin*

el hermanastro / la hermanastra   *stepbrother / stepsister*

el esposo / la esposa   *husband / wife*

el cuñado / la cuñada   *brother-in-law / sister-in-law*

el suegro / la suegra   *father-in-law / mother-in-law*

el yerno / la nuera   *son-in-law / daughter-in-law*

los parientes   *relatives*

los gemelos   *twins*

el nombre   first *name; given name*

el apellido   *surname; last name*

Verbos útiles   *Useful verbs*

comer   *to eat*

escribir   *to write*

estudiar   *to study*

hablar   *to talk*

leer   *to read*

mirar   *to watch*

trabajar   *to work*

vivir   *to live*

usar   *to use*

Características físicas
Physical characteristics

grande   *big*

pequeño(a)   *small*

joven   *young*

viejo(a)   *old*

alto(a)   *tall*

bajo(a)   *short*

gordo(a)   *fat*

delgado(a)   *thin*

moreno(a)   *brunette*

rubio(a)   *blond(e)*

pelirrojo(a)   *redhead*

Los colores   *Colors*

amarillo   *yellow*

anaranjado   *orange*

azul   *blue*

blanco   *white*

café, marrón   *brown*

gris   *grey*

morado   *purple*

negro   *black*

rojo   *red*

verde   *green*

To conjugate Spanish verbs, start with the infinitive form. In Spanish, every infinitive consists of one word and ends in either -**ar, -er,** or -**ir.** To conjugate a regular verb in the present tense, start with the infinitive, drop the -**ar, -er,** or -**ir,** and add the appropriate ending to the stem of the verb.

estudiar *to study*

yo estudi**o**	nosotros(as) estudi**amos**
tú estudi**as**	vosotros(as) estudi**áis**
él / ella / usted estudi**a**	ellos / ellas / ustedes estudi**an**

comer *to eat*

yo com**o**	nosotros(as) com**emos**
tú com**es**	vosotros(as) com**éis**
él / ella / usted com**e**	ellos / ellas / ustedes com**en**

escribir *to write*

yo escrib**o**	nosotros(as) escrib**imos**
tú escrib**es**	vosotros(as) escrib**ís**
él / ella / usted escrib**e**	ellos / ellas / ustedes escrib**en**

Noun-adjective agreement

In Spanish, adjectives must agree with the nouns they modify in number (singular / plural) and gender (masculine / feminine). When an adjective describes a masculine noun, a group of masculine nouns, or a group that contains both masculine and feminine nouns, use the masculine form of the adjective. Masculine adjectives typically end in -**o.** For example:

> el chico alt**o**
> María y Rafael son chic**os** alt**os.**

To create the feminine form of an adjective, change the -**o** ending to -**a.** For example:

> la chica alt**a**
> las chic**as** alt**as**

Adjectives that end in -**e,** such as **café,** or in -**ista,** such as **optimista, don't** change in the feminine form. The same is true for most adjectives that end in a consonant, such as **popular.** However, if an adjective ends in -**dor,** like **hablador,** you have to add -**a** to make it feminine.

To make an adjective that ends in a vowel, such as **alto,** plural, add -**s.** If an adjective ends in a consonant, like **trabajador,** add -**es.** When a noun ends in -**z,** like **feliz,** change the **z** to **c** and add -**es: felices.**

Síntesis: Gramática

Ser and estar with adjectives

In Spanish there are two verbs that mean *to be*: **ser** and **estar.**

ser *to be*	
yo **soy**	nosotros(as) **somos**
tú **eres**	vosotros(as) **sois**
él / ella / usted **es**	ellos / ellas / ustedes **son**

estar *to be*	
yo **estoy**	nosotros(as) **estamos**
tú **estás**	vosotros(as) **estáis**
él / ella / usted **está**	ellos / ellas / ustedes **están**

Uses of the verb *ser*

- To describe characteristics of a person, place, or thing:

  Yo **soy** alto.
  I am tall.

- To identify a person's occupation or nationality or to identify someone by relationship:

  Carolina **es** española y **es** la hermana de Pedro.
  Carolina is Spanish and she is Pedro's sister.

- To tell time or give dates:

  Es el 7 de julio y **son** las cinco.
  It is July 7 and it is five o'clock.

- With the preposition **de** to tell where people are from and to express ownership or possession:

  La casa **es de** mi papá. Él **es de** Cuba.
  The house is my father's. He is from Cuba.

Uses of the verb *estar*

- To express a temporary condition or a state of being:

  Estoy cansado.
  I am tired.

- To describe where someone or something is located:

  Los estudiantes **están** en la cafetería.
  The students are in the cafeteria.

The verb *tener*

Tener means *to have,* but in some expressions it is better translated in English as *to be.*

tener *to have*	
yo **tengo**	nosotros(as) **tenemos**
tú **tienes**	vosotros(as) **tenéis**
él / ella / usted **tiene**	ellos / ellas / ustedes **tienen**

Síntesis: Gramática

The verb **tener** is used in Spanish to indicate possession:

> Yo **tengo** una mochila roja.
> *I have a red backpack.*

The phrase **tener… años** (which literally translates as *to have … years*) is used to talk about age:

> Mi prima **tiene** 22 **años.**
> *My cousin is 22 years old.*

Questions in Spanish

There are two basic types of questions: those that require a *yes/no* answer, and those that ask for specific information.

In Spanish, yes/no questions can be asked by changing the intonation of your voice, by adding a tag question like **¿no?** or **¿verdad?,** or by switching the order of a statement, so that the verb comes before the subject.

All questions in Spanish require a question mark at the beginning of the question as well as at the end.

To ask for information, use interrogative words like *Who? How? Where? Why? What?* and *When?* Here are some common interrogative words in Spanish:

¿Quién? *Who?*	**¿Quién** es tu amigo?
¿Quiénes? *Who?* (plural)	**¿Quiénes** son tus hermanos?
¿Cómo? *How?*	**¿Cómo** estás?
¿Dónde? *Where?*	**¿Dónde** estás?
¿Por qué? *Why?*	**¿Por qué** estás cansado?
¿Qué? *What?*	**¿Qué** haces?
¿Cuándo? *When?*	**¿Cuándo** tienes clase?
¿Cuál? *Which?*	**¿Cuál** es tu libro?
¿Cuánto? *How much?*	**¿Cuánto** cuesta el teléfono?
¿Cuántos(as)? *How many?*	**¿Cuántos** teléfonos quieres?

¿Qué te gusta hacer?

Objectives: In this chapter you will learn to

- talk about your pastimes and hobbies
- describe typical daily activities
- indicate possession
- tell time

RichVintage/Getty Images

C2-1

¿Qué hacen? Look at the photos of Bella and her friends. Choose four of the photos and write a sentence about each one. With a partner, take turns reading your sentences to each other and guessing which photos they describe.

Modelo   Student A: *Bella escribe una entrada de blog.*
              Student B: (pointing) *Es la foto correcta.*

1.    **3.**    **5.**

2.    **4.**   **6.**

C2-2 ¿Qué haces tú?

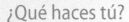

Step 1 With a partner, ask each other whether you do the following activities. Write down your partner's answers.

Modelo   Student A: *¿Cocinas?*
              Student B: *Sí, cocino. / No, no cocino.*

Vocabulario

1. tocar la guitarra
2. cantar
3. pintar

4. escuchar música
5. jugar al béisbol
6. jugar al tenis

7. comer tacos
8. esquiar
9. bailar

Step 2 Now work with another pair of classmates to find out how similar or different your interests are. Each person in your group of four will need to pair up with a new partner. With your new partner, ask each other the questions from **Step 1.** Make sure to write down the answers. Compare the new answers with your first partner's answers.

Modelo   Student A: *¿Cocinas?*
          Student B: *Sí, cocino. / No, no cocino.*

Step 3 As a group, now work together to complete your charts. Use check marks for positive answers.

Nombre	tocar la guitarra	cantar	pintar	escuchar música	jugar al béisbol	jugar al tenis	comer tacos	esquiar	bailar
Mark			✓	✓	✓		✓		

Step 4 Work together to write statements that describe your group's similarities and differences. Choose a representative to report to the class on your findings for each of the activities.

Modelos   *Mark y David cantan, pintan y escuchan música.*
           Laura y Tom juegan al béisbol, pero Mark y David no juegan al béisbol.
           Laura toca la guitarra.

C2-3A **¿Qué hace?** **A** With a partner, look at the images below or on the next page and ask what each person is doing. Ask each other questions until you have filled in all the missing information.

Modelo Student A: *¿Qué hace Marcela?*
Student B: *Marcela canta.*

Pablo

Claudia

Raúl

Ximena

Marcela

Ricardo

Lisa

Vocabulario

C2-3B

¿Qué hace? **B** With a partner, look at the images below or on the previous page and ask what each person is doing. Ask each other questions until you have filled in all the missing information.

Modelo   Student A: *¿Qué hace Marcela?*
                  Student B: *Marcela canta.*

Pedro

Andrea

José

María Olga

Marcela

Fernando

Pamela

Gramática

C2-4 ¿Te gusta?

Step 1 Look at the following list of eight things. For each item, check **Sí** if you like it and **No** if you don't. Add three topics of your choice. Then ask a classmate's preferences on all of these things and check the corresponding boxes. Remember to begin your questions with **¿Te gusta…?** or **¿Te gustan…?**

	Yo		Mi compañero(a)	
	Sí	No	Sí	No
los videojuegos	☐	☐	☐	☐
el hip hop	☐	☐	☐	☐
correr	☐	☐	☐	☐
las matemáticas	☐	☐	☐	☐
bailar	☐	☐	☐	☐
hablar español	☐	☐	☐	☐
levantar pesas	☐	☐	☐	☐
la guitarra	☐	☐	☐	☐
_____	☐	☐	☐	☐
_____	☐	☐	☐	☐
_____	☐	☐	☐	☐

Step 2 Form a group of three students and share the questions you added to the survey in **Step 1**, but don't answer them. As a group, choose the five best questions and make sure everyone in your group has a copy of all five. Once you all have the questions written down, each group member should find a new partner and ask these questions. Remember to make note of each answer.

Step 3 Now you have responses from numerous classmates for the provided questions as well as the new questions. Write up a summary of your findings and share the results with the class.

Modelo   *A tres personas les gusta nadar. A dos personas no les gusta nadar. A cinco estudiantes les gusta correr.*

Gramática

C2-5 Las rutinas

Step 1 With a partner, ask each other six questions about what you do and don't do during the week. Include the **palabras útiles** you have learned (**también, tampoco, y, o, pero**) to create a written summary of your answers.

Modelo   *Tom cocina pero yo no cocino. Yo estudio y Tom estudia también. No esquío. Tom no esquía tampoco.*

Step 2 Now imagine that you have decided to be roommates. Work together to figure out which tasks you each prefer to do; then assign responsibilities to find an apartment and move in. Use the phrases below to help guide your conversation. Be creative and make it interesting. Remember that your exchanges also need to make sense! Write your conversation in the space provided and then practice it with your partner.

Modelo   Student A: *¿Te gusta hablar por teléfono? Necesitamos llamar a agencias de apartamentos.*
Student B: *Sí, llamo a las agencias. ¿Y tú, qué haces?*

Phrase bank: leer descripciones de apartamentos, buscar apartamentos, comprar la comida, estar en el apartamento, llamar a los amigos, preparar la comida, regresar a la agencia, organizar una fiesta, sacar fotos, apagar las luces

_____

_____

_____

_____

_____

Gramática

C2-6 Caras y gestos *(Charades)* In groups of three or four, take turns pantomiming the following verbs and stating in Spanish what each member of the group is doing. Cross off the terms as you cover them. Then think of one or two more verbs apiece to act out and see who can identify them correctly first.

Modelo   *Ana habla por teléfono.*

buscar	desayunar	comprar	llamar	descansar	apagar	preparar	cocinar	llegar

C2-7 Conversaciones You and a friend have volunteered to pack school supplies and a couple of bonus items for needy children and you're getting organized. You will ask half of the questions and your partner will ask the other half.

Step 1 Have a conversation based on the cues below to determine whose table has each set of supplies.

Modelo   Student A: *Necesito las mochilas.*
              Student B: *Están en su mesa. / Hay mochilas en su mesa.*

1. You: need backpacks   Friend: her table
2. You: need pencils   Friend: their table
3. You: need notebooks   Friend: his table
4. You: need pens   Friend: my table
5. Friend: need paper   You: our tables
6. Friend: need books   You: your table
7. Friend: need markers   You: my table
8. Friend: need chocolate   You: their table

Step 2 Now that you have everything you need from the list, discuss and decide on one bonus item each that you'd like to add as a surprise (**una sorpresa**).

Gramática

C2-8 **Mis amigos** Now think about some of your friends. What are their favorite activities? Form small groups to complete the steps below.

Step 1 On your own, jot down a list of five activities that your friends like to do.

Step 2 Discuss with your group and compare what your friends like to what others' friends like.

Modelos *Mis amigos levantan pesas.*
Tus amigos estudian francés.
Nuestros amigos cocinan.

Step 3 Find at least two similarities or differences and write them in the space below.

_____

_____

_____

_____

_____

_____

_____

_____

_____

_____

Gramática

C2-9

¿Qué hora es? With a partner, look at the verbs and times below. Use this information to take turns asking each other what time it is and stating what you want to do at that time of day. Notice that the 24-hour clock format tells you whether it is morning, midday, or evening.

descansar	desayunar	cenar	estudiar	regresar a	hacer ejercicio
dormir	leer	ir a	mirar	llamar a	

Modelo 7:15

Student A: *¿Qué hora es?*

Student B: *Son las siete y cuarto de la mañana.*

Student A: *Quiero desayunar.*

1. 15:10	**3.** 16:55	**5.** 13:15	**7.** 18:50	**9.** 12:30
2. 6:30	**4.** 9:00	**6.** 8:00	**8.** 13:45	**10.** 14:15

C2-10A

¿A qué hora es? **A** It's new student orientation week. You have the opportunity to sample classes before registering and to attend welcome events. You and another student just received the schedule but some of the times are missing on both forms. Work with a partner. One will use the list of classes and events in this activity and the other will use the list in C2-10B on the next page. Take turns asking each other what time the classes and events that are missing on your list will take place. Once you've confirmed all the times, discuss what you each plan to attend.

Modelo clase de español / 10:30

Student A: *¿A qué hora es la clase de español?*

Student B: *La clase de español es a las diez y media.*

Student A: *¿Vas a la clase de español?*

Student B: *No, voy a la clase de francés.*

1. la clase de matemáticas / ____

2. la clase de biología / 8:30

3. la clase de historia / ____

4. la clase de francés / 10:15

5. la clase de arte / ____

6. el partido de fútbol americano / 14:00

Gramática

7. la clase de inglés / 14:20   **9.** la fiesta de estudiantes internacionales / _____

8. el partido (*game*) de baloncesto / 19:30   **10.** la fiesta del club de español / _____

C2-10B ¿A qué hora es? **B** It's new student orientation week. You have the opportunity to sample classes before registering and to attend welcome events. You and another student just received the schedule but some of the times are missing on both forms. Work with a partner. One will use the list of classes and events in this activity and the other will use the list in C2-10A on the previous page. Take turns asking each other what time the classes and events that are missing on your list will take place. Once you've confirmed all the times, discuss what you each plan to attend.

Modelo   clase de español / 10:30
         Student A: *¿A qué hora es la clase de español?*
         Student B: *La clase de español es a las diez y media.*
         Student A: *¿Vas a la clase de español?*
         Student B: *No, voy a la clase de francés.*

1. la clase de matemáticas / 8:00   **6.** el partido de fútbol americano / _____

2. la clase de biología / _____   **7.** la clase de inglés / _____

3. la clase de historia / 9:40   **8.** el partido (*game*) de baloncesto / _____

4. la clase de francés / _____   **9.** la fiesta de estudiantes internacionales / 20:00

5. la clase de arte / 10:15   **10.** la fiesta del club de español / 21:00

Gramática

C2-11A Programas y canales **A** You and a friend are trying to figure out what to watch on TV today. You have part of the TV schedule and he/she has the rest. Ask each other questions to get the information you don't have until the schedule is complete.

Modelos ¿Qué hay a las [time] en [channel]?
¿A qué hora es [program]?

Student A

CANAL 1

Programa	Hora
Noticias	5:00
El tiempo	
	6:00
	6:30

Teleglobal

Programa	Hora
Tenis: Wimbledon	5:00
	5:30
	6:00
	6:30

Tele2

Programa	Hora
	6:00
	6:30
Fútbol: Brasil–México	7:00
	8:30

CNN en español

Programa	Hora
Economía	7:00
Debate político	
Noticias internacionales	8:30

Gramática

Programas y canales **B** You and a friend are trying to figure out what to watch on TV today. You have part of the TV schedule and he/she has the rest. Ask each other questions to get the information you don't have until the schedule is complete.

Modelos *¿Qué hay a las* [time] *en* [channel]?

¿A qué hora es [program]?

Student B

CANAL 1

Programa	Hora
	5:00
El tiempo	5:30
Spiderman	6:00
	6:30

Tele2

Programa	Hora
Gran Hermano	6:00
	6:30
	7:00
	7:30

Teleglobal

Programa	Hora
Tenis: Wimbledon	
La semana	6:30

CNN en español

Programa	Hora
Economía	
Debate político	7:30
	8:00
	8:30

C2-12 Los programas de la televisión View the program guide for several TV channels in Spain that follows. Work with a partner to complete the next activities. Remember that the programs are color-coded according to the legend at the bottom of the guide.

Step 1 Using the guide, each of you should think of three questions to ask each other about the four categories of shows (Series, Noticias, Cine, Deportes) that are available. Remember to begin the questions with **¿A qué hora…?** and **¿En qué canal…?** Then, answer each other's questions according to the schedule.

Modelo Student A: *¿A qué hora hay un programa de música y en qué canal?*
Student B: *Hay un programa de música en TVE 2 a las 6 de la mañana.*

Step 2 You've both finished your class assignments and have some free time. Make a few viewing recommendations based on your partner's preferences.

Modelo Student A: *¿Qué programas te gustan?*
Student B: *Me gustan las comedias.*
Student A: *Te gustan las comedias… Miras Canal + a las 10:40, ¿verdad?*
Student B: *¿La Pantera Rosa 2 es comedia?*

Vocabulario

Guía de televisión

tve 1	tve 2	ANTENA 3	cuatro	5	laSexta	CANAL+
06:00 Noticias 24 horas •	**06:00** Es música	**06:00** Las noticias de la mañana •	**07:00** Matinal Cuatro: Emisión 16 •	**06:30** Informativos Telecinco matinal •	**07:00** LaSexta en concierto	**08:00** Nos gusta el cine: Emisión 2
06:30 Telediario matinal •	**07:00** Conciertos de Radio-3	**08:45** Espejo público •	**09:11** Alerta Cobra: Bajo sospecha •	**09:00** El programa de Ana Rosa	**08:10** Lo mejor de laSexta	**08:45** Cine: Asesinato justo •
09:00 Los desayunos de TVE •	**07:30** Para todos La 2	**12:30** La ruleta de la suerte	**10:07** Alerta Cobra: Sin vuelta atrás •	**12:45** Mujeres y hombres y viceversa	**08:30** La Tira	**10:25** Piezas: Especial Los Goyita
10:15 La mañana de La 1	**09:30** Aquí hay trabajo		**11:06** Alerta Cobra: Flashback •		**09:25** Futurama •	**10:40** Cine: La Pantera Rosa 2 •
	10:00 La aventura del saber		**12:02** Alerta Cobra: Bajo el fuego •		**09:50** Padre de familia •	**12:15** Serie: Archer: Episodio 4 •
	11:00 Los pingüinos papúa y sus enemigos		**13:00** Las mañanas de Cuatro: Emisión 16		**10:45** Crímenes imperfectos	**12:40** Saturday Night Live: Taylor Lautner / Bon Jovi •
	11:55 Elogio de la luz		**13:57** Noticias Cuatro •		**11:40** Crímenes imperfectos: ricos y famosos	**13:30** Serie: Crash: Da igual lo que hagas •
	12:30 Para todos La 2				**12:40** Las pruebas del crimen	
					13:05 Crímenes imperfectos	
14:00 Informativo territorial •	**14:30** A pedir de boca	**14:00** Los Simpson •	**14:50** Deportes Cuatro •	**14:30** De buena ley	**14:00** laSexta Noticias •	**14:30** Más deporte: Emisión 37 •
14:30 Corazón de verano	**15:00** Escala 1:1	**15:00** Antena 3 Noticias 1 •	**15:40** Tonterías las justas: Emisión 104	**15:00** Informativos Telecinco mediodía •	**14:55** laSexta Deportes •	**15:00** Serie: Weeds: Van Nuys •
15:00 Telediario 1 •	**15:30** Saber y ganar	**16:00** Cine •	**17:05** Fama revolution: Emisión 16	**15:45** Sálvame diario	**15:25** Sé lo que hicisteis…	**15:30** Cine: Lejos de la tierra quemada •
16:05 El tiempo •	**16:00** Grandes documentales	**17:45** 3D	**18:53** Dame una pista: El ansia, Colillas Nocturnas y Las Supermamás	**20:00** Pasapalabra	**17:10** Bones •	**17:15** Cine: Año uno •
16:15 Amar en tiempos revueltos: Episodio 16 •	**16:55** Biodiario	**19:15** El Diario	**19:56** Deportes Cuatro •	**20:55** Informativos Telecinco noche •	**18:05** Caso abierto •	**18:50** Telepatrulla, la tele dentro de la tele: Emisión 1
17:00 El clon: Episodio 9 •	**17:00** Documental	**21:00** Antena 3 Noticias 2 •	**20:30** Noticias Cuatro •		**19:00** Navy, investigación criminal •	**19:20** Documental naturaleza: Las fuerzas del planeta: Viento
17:30 Mar de amor: Episodio 81 •	**18:30** Creadores: Paloma Navarés, "Taller de sentidos"		**21:30** El hormiguero Next		**20:00** laSexta Noticias •	**20:15** El día después: Emisión 4 •
18:20 España directo •	**19:00** Universo matemático: Mujeres matemáticas		**21:38** El hormiguero 2.0: Emisión 19		**20:55** laSexta Deportes •	**21:30** Serie: True Blood (Sangre fresca): A mí también me duele •
20:00 Gente	**19:30** El hombre y la Tierra: Las aves esteparias (III)				**21:30** El intermedio	
21:00 Telediario 2 •	**20:00** La 2 Noticias •					
	20:30 Miradas 2					

Vocabulario

22:05 El tiempo •
22:15 Las chicas de oro: Sobre los años dorados: Entre damas anda el juego •
23:15 Cine •
01:25 Es Música
02:00 Noticias 24 horas •

21:00 La mitad invisible
21:25 Sorteo Bonoloto
21:30 Ciudad K
22:00 Río helado •
23:35 Festival de cine de San Sebastián •
23:55 Somos Cortos •
00:25 ZZZ
00:30 Centros en red
01:20 Festival de Jazz de San Javier 2010
02:30 La mitad invisible
03:00 Ciudad K
03:25 Somos Cortos •
03:55 El universo elegante (la teoría de cuerdas)
04:50 Documental
05:15 Es Música

00:00 Informe DEC
02:30 Astro Show

22:28 Callejeros viajeros: Tennessee
23:36 Tu vista favorita: Emisión 2
00:44 Callejeros viajeros: París
01:54 Gente extraordinaria: Niños de 80 años
02:42 Tonterías las justas
03:10 Cuatro Astros: Episodio 102
06:25 Shopping
06:43 Recuatro: Puro Cuatro
06:48 Recuatro: El zapping de Surferos: Emisión 76

22:00 C.S.I: Miami: Avión a la vista •
23:00 C.S.I. NY: Navegación por estima •
00:00 C.S.I.: Trenes y gafes •
00:45 C.S.I.: Abandonando Las Vegas •
01:30 C.S.I.: La dulce Jane •
02:15 Locos por ganar
04:00 Infocomerciales
05:00 Fusión sonora

22:15 Cine: Cine •
00:30 BFN
01:45 El intermedio
02:40 Astro TV
05:00 Teletienda

22:30 Serie: Hung (Superdotado) •
23:00 Cine estreno: Triage •
00:40 Fiebre Maldini: Emisión 4 •
01:50 Estrellas de Canal+: Megan Fox •
02:00 Serie: Archer: Episodio 4 •
02:25 Cómo debería haber acabado: Avatar
02:30 Fútbol americano: NFL: Chicago Bears–Green Bay Packers Monday night •
06:00 El Tamaño no importa: Emisión 1
06:30 Cine: Superhero movie •

● **Series** ● **Noticias** ● **Cine** ● **Deportes**

Vocabulario

C2-13A **¿A qué hora jugamos?** **A** Ernesto and Bella are trying to find a time that would work for both of them to schedule a tennis match. Working in pairs, one of you will be using Bella's schedule below and the other will use Ernesto's schedule on the next page in C2-13B. Ask each other questions about openings in the schedules for Bella and Ernesto to find a few times in the morning and a few times in the afternoon when they are both free.

Modelo   Student A: *¿Está libre Ernesto a las nueve de la mañana los lunes?*
               Student B: *No, tiene clase de matemáticas a las nueve.*

Ask each other similar questions until you are able to fill out the schedule and can come up with a time that would work for Ernesto and Bella.

Student A   El horario de Bella

	lunes	martes	miércoles	jueves	viernes	sábado	domingo
mañana	clase de biología (9:00–10:00)		clase de biología (9:00–10:00)		clase de biología (9:00–10:00)		bicicleta de montaña
	clase de español (10:00–11:00)	clase de español (10:00–11:00)	clase de español (10:00–11:00)	clase de español (10:00–11:00)			
tarde		gimnasio (2:00–3:00)		gimnasio (2:00–3:00)			
	baile (2:30–3:30)		baile (2:30–3:30)				

C2-13B ¿A qué hora jugamos? **B** Ernesto and Bella are trying to find a time that would work for both of them to schedule a tennis match. Working in pairs, one of you will be using Ernesto's schedule below and the other will use Bella's schedule on the previous page in C2-13A. Ask each other questions about openings in the schedules for Bella and Ernesto to find a few times in the morning and a few times in the afternoon when they are both free.

Modelo Student A: *¿Qué tiene Bella a las diez de la mañana los viernes?*
Student B: *Ella tiene clase de biología a las nueve.*

Student B   El horario de Ernesto

	lunes	martes	miércoles	jueves	viernes	sábado	domingo
mañana	clase de matemáticas (9:00–10:00)		clase de matemáticas (9:00–10:00)				acampar en el lago con amigos
	clase de francés (2:00–3:00)		clase de francés (2:00–3:00)		clase de francés (2:00–3:00)	nadar con mi hermano	
tarde			practicar tenis				
	clase de biología (4:00–5:00)		clase de biología (4:00–5:00)	practicar fútbol (5:00–6:00)	clase de biología (4:00–5:00)		

Lectura

C2-14 Antes de leer Below is a list of activities that people like to do in their spare time. Work with a partner to identify important benefits of participating in each.

practice a team sport	explore nature	solve puzzles
do yoga	read	play video games

Step 1 What do you feel is the single most important benefit of doing each of the activities in the list?

Step 2 Now, list other benefits for each activity that did not make your "most important" list in step 1.

Step 3 Which activities seem to have the most additional benefits? The least? Which ones are the most popular? Why do you think this is?

Anuncios de Librerías Gandhi

1.

2.

ordena Leer ideas. tus

gandhi.com.mx   *gandhi.*
                       libros·música·video·café

C2-15

Un anuncio original   Motivating people to think outside the box, to exercise more, to enjoy being outdoors, and to travel to other countries are some of the ways in which ads are used in marketing campaigns. The Librerías Gandhi ads you just read are examples. Can you think of other ads that you've seen on TV, in a magazine or newspaper, or online that promote a sport or pastime?

In groups of three or four, complete the following.

Step 1 Choose a sport or pastime that you have learned to talk about in Spanish.

Step 2 Brainstorm an ad that will use Spanish to promote the activity your group chose. What is the ad's main purpose? What elements do you want to highlight in your ads?

Step 3 Design your ad and write up to four sentences to complete the ad.

Step 4 As a class, present and discuss your ads. Are they effective? Do they entertain and/or educate? Why or why not?

El blog de Bella

Me gusta vivir en España

Hoy voy a escribir sobre las cosas que me gusta hacer en los Estados Unidos (EEUU) y las cosas que me gusta hacer aquí en España. En los EEUU, corro en el parque todos los días. Los lunes y miércoles voy al gimnasio. Los martes tengo clase de baile. Los fines de semana salgo *(I go out)* con mis amigos. Bailamos, cantamos, hablamos y nos divertimos *(we have fun)* mucho. Aquí en España hay muchas cosas que me gusta hacer. Cuando hace sol me gusta ir a la playa. Las playas aquí son muy bonitas. También me gusta hacer compras. Me gusta ir al centro comercial porque hay muchas tiendas buenas. Pero, mi lugar favorito para hacer compras es el mercado. Cada jueves y sábado hay un mercado grande. Puedes comprar muchas cosas. Me gusta mirar las cosas, ver la gente y practicar español. Los fines de semana me gusta salir con mis nuevos amigos españoles. Me gusta escuchar la música y bailar. España es muy divertida.

C2-16

Me gusta vivir en... In groups of three, think about why you like living in your hometown or another place you've lived. Or think of a place you'd like to live and why. Then list five things you like to do there and prepare two questions for each of your partners in Spanish. Use Bella's blog entry as a guide for your discussion. Be specific!

Modelo   Student A: *¿Qué haces los fines de semana?*
Student B: *Me gusta escuchar música en el club Knitting Factory. Hay música muy buena.*
Student C: *¿Te gusta ir a comer también?*

Síntesis: Vocabulario

Los deportes   *Sports*

el baloncesto   *basketball*

el béisbol   *baseball*

la bicicleta de montaña   *mountain biking*

el ciclismo   *cycling*

el fútbol   *soccer*

el fútbol americano   *football*

el golf   *golf*

el tenis   *tennis*

En el gimnasio   *At the gym*

bailar   *to dance*

correr   *to run*

caminar   *to walk*

esquiar   *to ski*

jugar   *to play (a sport)*

hacer gimnasia   *to do gymnastics*

hacer ejercicio   *to exercise*

levantar pesas   *to lift weights*

nadar   *to swim*

patinar sobre hielo   *to ice skate*

Más pasatiempos   *More pastimes*

cantar   *to sing*

escuchar música   *to listen to music*

mirar televisión   *to watch television*

navegar por Internet   *to surf the Internet*

pintar   *to paint*

conversar   *to talk*

hablar por teléfono   *to talk on the phone*

sacar / tomar fotos   *to take pictures*

salir con amigos   *to go out with friends*

tomar un refresco   *to have a soft drink*

Los instrumentos musicales
Musical instruments

tocar un instrumento   *to play an instrument*

la guitarra   *guitar*

el piano   *piano*

la trompeta   *trumpet*

el violín   *violin*

Más verbos   *More verbs*

apagar   *to turn off*

buscar   *to look for*

cenar   *to eat dinner*

cocinar   *to cook*

comprar   *to buy*

desayunar   *to eat breakfast*

descansar   *to rest*

llamar   *to call*

llegar (a)   *to arrive (at)*

necesitar   *to need*

preparar   *to prepare*

regresar (a)   *to return (to)*

usar   *to use*

Palabras útiles   *Useful words*

pero   *but*

y   *and*

o   *or*

también   *also; as well*

tampoco   *neither*

Síntesis: Gramática

El verbo *gustar*

To express that you like something, use the verb **gustar.** The sentence **Me gusta el fútbol** can be translated *I like football;* however, the verb **gustar** literally means *to be pleasing.*

To say that you like to do something (**nadar**) or to say that you like one thing (**fútbol**) use the form **gusta.** If what you like is plural (**los deportes**) use the form **gustan:**

Me gusta nadar.
I like swimming. / Swimming is pleasing to me.

Me gusta la música.
I like music. / Music is pleasing to me.

Me gustan los deportes.
I like sports. / Sports are pleasing to me.

The indirect object pronoun changes to indicate **to whom** something is pleasing. For example:

te gusta
you (informal) like / it is pleasing to you

le gusta
he, she, or you (formal) like / it is pleasing to him, her or you

nos gusta
we like / it is pleasing to us

os gusta
you (informal, plural) like / it is pleasing to you

les gusta
they, you (formal and informal, plural) like / it is pleasing to them or you

To clarify **le** and **les,** use the preposition **a** plus a noun, name of a person, or subject pronoun:

A Laura le gusta cantar.   *Laura likes to sing.*

You can also use the preposition **a** plus a noun, or pronoun, for emphasis:

A **nosotros** nos gusta nadar.

Use **a mí** to emphasize **me** and **a ti** to emphasize **te:**

A ti te gusta bailar pero a **mí** me gusta cantar.
You like to dance but I like to sing.

Los adjetivos posesivos

One way to indicate possession is by using possessive adjectives. Just like other adjectives in Spanish, all possessive adjectives agree in **number** with the nouns they modify. For example:

mi clase
mi**s** clase**s**

The possessive adjectives **nuestro** and **vuestro** agree in both number and gender with the nouns they describe. For example:

nuestr**a** amig**a**
nuestr**os** amig**os**

Síntesis: Gramática

A possessive adjective agrees with the gender and number of the thing that is possessed—**not** with the gender and number of the owner.

Possessive adjectives in Spanish are as follows:

Possessive adjectives			
mi, mis	*my*	**nuestro, nuestros, nuestra, nuestras**	*our*
tu, tus	*your*	**vuestro, vuestros, vuestra, vuestras**	*your*
su, sus	*his, her, its, your*	**su, sus**	*their*

La hora

To ask what time it is, use the expression **¿Qué hora es?** The verb **ser** is used to express time. Use **es la** with **una** and **son las** with all other hours.

To express time between the hour and the half hour, use **y** before the minutes. For example:

Son las cinco **y** diez.   *It is ten past five.*

To express time after the half hour, use **menos** plus the minutes until the next hour. For example:

Son las seis **menos** veinte.   *It is twenty till six.*

It is also common to express time as you see it on a digital clock:

Son las dos y cuarenta.   *It is twelve forty.*

Here are some common expressions for telling time:

3:15: Son las tres y **cuarto.**
It is a quarter past three.

11:45: Son las doce menos **cuarto.**
It's a quarter to twelve.

1:30: Es la una y **media.**
It is half past one.

9:00: Son las nueve **en punto.**
It's nine o'clock sharp.

To ask or tell at what time something is done, use the preposition **a** along with a time. For example:

—**¿A** qué hora corre Roberto?
At what time does Roberto run?
—Roberto corre todos los días **a** las ocho.
Roberto runs every day at eight o'clock.

Here are some phrases that are used to indicate whether a time is in the morning, the afternoon, or the evening:

de la mañana   *in the morning*
de la tarde   *in the afternoon*
de la noche   *in the evening*

Capítulos 1 y 2

For this project, imagine that you and your roommate are looking for a third roommate to share an apartment. You'll be given certain scenarios that people in shared living spaces often face, such as introducing yourself, describing yourself and others, talking about likes and dislikes, and comparing potential roommates. You'll use the grammar and vocabulary you've learned in Chapters 1 and 2 to do this.

Project components

Activity	Points
UP1-1 Presentaciones	20 points (individual)
UP1-2 Busco compañero(a) de apartamento	20 points (individual)
UP1-3 Responder	15 points (individual)
UP1-4 ¿Quién es mejor?	10 points (individual)
UP1-5 Conversación	15 points (individual / pair)
UP1-6 Correo electrónico	20 points (individual)

Proyecto 1: Looking for a new roommate

UP1-1 **Presentaciones** You have decided to start your roommate search online and need to set up an account on a social media site to begin your search. The site asks you to share some basic information about yourself. Write a description of 85–135 words that includes the following details.

- a basic self-introduction: name, age, hometown
- a physical description of yourself
- your likes and dislikes
- your favorite activities or hobbies
- your schedule: when you typically wake up, work, go to school, eat, study, sleep, etc.

Don't forget to proofread what you've written before posting!

UP1-2 **Busco compañero(a) de apartamento** The next step in your search is to state what type of roommate you are seeking. Write four sentences describing the ideal roommate. Then write five questions for a potential roommate.

> Modelo   *El/La compañero(a) ideal es un(a) estudiante trabajador(a) y divertido(a).*
> *Pregunta: ¿A qué hora tienes clase?*

UP1-3 **Responder** Now read two classmates' descriptions of their ideal roommate and answer their questions with relevant information about yourself.

UP1-4 **¿Quién es mejor?** Read the responses to your description. Write four sentences about each candidate that address what you will take into consideration in choosing your new roommate.

> Modelos   *Paula es estudiante y es trabajadora.*
> *A Juan le gusta el fútbol americano.*
> *María tiene clase a las 7:30 de la mañana.*

Proyecto 1: Looking for a new roommate

Now choose one of the candidates. Write a short message to this person (45–75 words) explaining why you liked his/her description and why he/she would be a good fit. Refer to the candidate's description and the sentences you wrote for UP1-3. Express your interest in becoming roommates by starting with:

Hola, quiero ser tu nuevo(a) compañero(a) de apartamento porque...

UP1-5

Conversación Now work with a partner as your existing roommate. You each must describe your choice from UP1-4 and explain why he/she would be a good roommate. Include physical descriptions, favorite pastimes and likes and dislikes. Ask your partner as many questions as needed to fill out the form below. Your goal is to gather all the information necessary to decide who would be the best roommate. Give three reasons for your final choice.

Name
Age
Occupation
Positive traits
Negative traits
Hobbies, pastimes
Other important info

UP1-6   Correo electrónico   You have now been living with your new roommate for a while. Your Spanish-speaking friend wants to hear how things are going. Write an email or record a voice message of 75–125 words describing your new roommate. Include the following:

- your new roommate's name, age, and hometown
- what he/she looks like
- what he/she does during the week and on weekends (Include a variety of verbs as well as likes and dislikes.)
- whether you are happy to have this new roommate
- three questions about your Spanish-speaking friend's roommates
- appropriate greetings and goodbyes

La comida

Objectives: In this chapter you will learn to

- express likes and dislikes regarding food
- give basic recipe instructions
- talk about what you have to do and what you are going to do

patty_c/Getty Images

Vocabulario

C3-1 ¿Qué se usa para…? With a partner, make a list of the thing(s) you need to do the following actions. Focus on the kitchen items you just learned, but feel free to use other vocabulary words.

1. limpiar la cubierta
2. cortar la comida
3. comer la sopa
4. recalentar la comida
5. guardar las comidas

C3-2 Conversaciones Have a conversation with a partner using the following structure as a model. Before you begin the conversation, think about the verbs you will need to use and how you will conjugate them. After you have gone through the conversation once, switch roles with your partner and have the conversation again.

Student A is helping Student B move into a new apartment.

Student A	Student B
1. Ask Student B where to put the microwave.	2. Reply to Student A saying a logical place to put a microwave.
3. Ask Student B what to do with the toaster. (¿Qué *[hacer]* con…?)	4. Tell Student A to place the toaster on the countertop. Ask Student A whether he/she knows where the forks and knives are.
5. Tell Student B that yes, you know. The forks and knives are in the kitchen.	6. Say thank you to Student A. Ask Student A what time he/she is going out to the restaurant tonight (**esta noche**).
7. Tell Student B that you are going out at 7 P.M.	8. Tell Student A to have a great time. (**¡Que lo pases bien!**)
9. Say goodbye to Student B.	10. Say goodbye to Student A.

Vocabulario

C3-3A

El juego de las cinco diferencias **A** With a partner, ask each other questions to identify five differences between the kitchens in the drawings on pages 63 and 64, but do not look at your partner's drawing. Describe your own drawing in as much detail as possible.

Modelo   Student A: *En mi cocina hay una mesa marrón y dos ventanas grandes.*
Student B: *¿Hay platos en tu cocina?*

C3-3B El juego de las cinco diferencias **B** With a partner, ask each other questions to identify five differences between the kitchens in the drawings on pages 63 and 64, but do not look at your partner's drawing. Describe your own drawing in as much detail as possible.

Modelo   Student A: *En mi cocina hay una mesa marrón y dos ventanas grandes.*
          Student B: *¿Hay platos en tu cocina?*

Gramática

C3-4

Encuesta Look at the pie charts below. In groups, write three or four statements about the results. Then, ask the people in your group the same survey questions and write three more statements based on their answers.

Step 1 Look at the pie chart below. In groups, write three or four statements about the results.

Modelo   *Muchas personas hacen la comida en la casa.*

Step 2 Ask the people in your group the same survey questions and write three more statements based on their answers.

Modelo   —*¿Haces ejercicio los fines de semana?*
          — *Nunca hago ejercicio los fines de semana.*

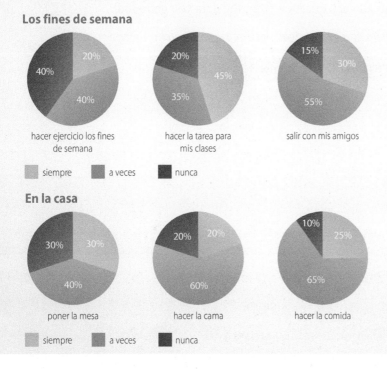

Los fines de semana

hacer ejercicio los fines de semana

hacer la tarea para mis clases

salir con mis amigos

siempre   a veces   nunca

En la casa

poner la mesa

hacer la cama

hacer la comida

siempre   a veces   nunca

Gramática

C3-5 **Entrevista** Interview three or more of your classmates to collect information about them.

Step 1 Write out these questions in Spanish and place them on the top row of the chart.

Pregunta 1: What do you do on the weekends?
Pregunta 2: Do you know someone famous?
Pregunta 3: How many miles (millas) do you drive per year?
Pregunta 4: How many days per week do you go out with friends?

Step 2 Write the name of each student you will interview in the left column and ask each interviewee the survey questions. Write out their answers in Spanish.

Step 3 Write two general statements about each question from the data you gathered.

Modelo *Los estudiantes no salen mucho con sus amigos porque tienen mucha tarea.*

	Pregunta 1	Pregunta 2	Pregunta 3	Pregunta 4
Student 1 _____				
Student 2 _____				
Student 3 _____				
Student 4 _____				
Student 5 _____				

Vocabulario

C3-6 **¿Qué ingredientes lleva?** Work with a partner to make lists of the different ingredients that are in each dish or meal.

1. ensalada de frutas

2. ensalada

3. una cena del Día de Acción de Gracias *(Thanksgiving)*

4. sushi

C3-7 **Las comidas preferidas**

Step 1 With a partner, ask each other your favorite foods, using the vocabulary list on pages 79–80. Note which category each food falls into. Take note of the category that has the most of your favorite foods.

Modelo —*¿Cuál es tu comida preferida?*
—*Mi comida preferida es el pollo? (categoría: las carnes)*

| las verduras | las frutas | las carnes | los pescados | las bebidas |

Step 2 Go around the class and ask at least four more people their favorite foods. What food categories do their favorite foods fall into?

Step 3 As a class, discuss what categories were the most popular.

C3-8A

Tenemos que hacer la compra **A** In some Spanish-speaking countries it is possible to call a market and place an order to be picked up or delivered later. With a partner, take turns playing the roles of a buyer and seller. Student A will be the **frutero** *(fruit vendor)* and the **pescadero** *(fishmonger)*. Student B will be the **carnicero** *(butcher)* and the **panadero** *(baker)*.

Each of you has a budget to spend and some specific things to buy. Use the information provided to find out what you need to buy and what questions you need to ask and use the drawing to provide the information that your partner needs.

Use the photos to answer your partner's questions. Be prepared to describe what you have in your store and how much it costs: e.g., **cuesta un euro y cincuenta céntimos el kilo / cuesta dos euros cada uno** *(each)*. Once your partner has all the information, it will be your turn to ask questions. This is the information that you need.

You have 30 euros and need to buy at least two types of bread / pastries and two types of meat. Try to use as much of your budget as possible.

Start by calling the butcher's. Use the following.

> **Buenos días. ¿Qué carne tiene?**
>
> **¿Cuánto cuesta…?**
>
> **Necesito / Quiero dos kilos / un kilo / medio kilo de…**

Then call the bakery and follow the same format you used at the butcher's.

manzanas, 5€/kilo

naranjas, 4,25€/kilo

cebollas, 3€/kilo

lechuga, 1€

limones, 3,50€/kilo

langosta, 13€/kilo

cangrejo, 7,50€/kilo

salmón, 9,50€/kilo

pulpo, 4€/kilo

Vocabulario

C3-8B

Tenemos que hacer la compra **B** In some Spanish-speaking countries it is possible to call a market and place an order to be picked up or delivered later. With a partner, take turns playing the roles of a buyer and seller. Student A will be the **frutero** (*fruit vendor*) and the **pescadero** (*fishmonger*). Student B will be the **carnicero** (*butcher*) and the **panadero** (*baker*).

Each of you has a budget to spend and some specific things to buy. Use the information provided to find out what you need to buy and what questions you need to ask and use the drawing to provide the information that your partner needs.

Use the photos to answer your partner's questions. Be prepared to describe what you have in your store and how much it costs: e.g., **cuesta un euro y cincuenta céntimos el kilo / cuesta dos euros cada uno** (*each*). Once your partner has all the information, it will be your turn to ask questions. This is the information that you need.

You have 30 euros and need to buy at least two types of fruit and two types of seafood. Try to use as much of your budget as possible.

Start by calling the fruit market. Use the following.

> **Buenos días. ¿Qué frutas tiene?**
>
> **¿Cuánto cuesta…?**
>
> **Necesito / Quiero dos kilos / un kilo / medio kilo de…**

Then call the fish market and follow the same format you used at the fruit market.

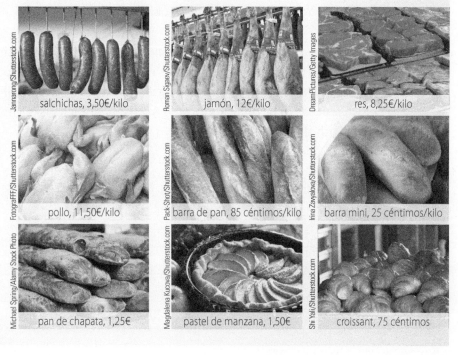

salchichas, 3,50€/kilo

jamón, 12€/kilo

res, 8,25€/kilo

pollo, 11,50€/kilo

barra de pan, 85 céntimos/kilo

barra mini, 25 céntimos/kilo

pan de chapata, 1,25€

pastel de manzana, 1,50€

croissant, 75 céntimos

Vocabulario

C3-9

¿Qué hago con la comida? With a partner, use the photos on pages 68 and 69 to take turns asking what to do with each of the food items. Use informal commands to tell your partner what to do. Try to use each of the verbs provided. Use the model as an example.

Modelo   Student A: *¿Qué hago con las uvas?*
          Student B: *Pon las uvas en el frigorífico.*

comer	lavar	poner	cortar	hervir	pelar

C3-10

¿Qué tengo que hacer? Use three small pieces of paper. Write your name on one of them and a Spanish verb on each of the other two and give them to your instructor. Then, using the name and two verbs you receive back from the pool, give two commands to a classmate. You may need to add an object to create a complete command.

C3-11

La fiesta You and two other classmates are in charge of getting everything ready for a surprise party for a friend. There are a lot of things that need to be done. Some things you will do individually and some will have to be done by two or all three of you. Make a list of what needs to be done and who is in charge of each task. Then be prepared to share the plans with the rest of the class.

Step 1 List all the things that need to be done here.

Modelo   *Hay que limpiar la cocina.*

_____

_____

_____

_____

_____

Vocabulario

Step 2 List who is in charge of every task here.

Modelo —¿Quién limpia la cocina?
—Yo limpio la cocina.

Yo _____.

Mi compañero de piso _____.

Mi compañero de piso y yo _____.

Mis compañeros de piso _____.

C3-12 **Las recetas** Working in small groups, come up with two dishes that you would like to prepare for the party. Then write a sentence for each ingredient that you need to buy (use the vocabulary list in this lesson or ask your instructor for additional items). Begin your sentences with the following expressions.

Tenemos que comprar…   *Hay que comprar…*   *Necesitamos…*

Do not share your ideas for dishes with the rest of the class. When everyone is ready, you will read your sentences out loud and the class will try to guess what your dishes are.

C3-13 **Preguntas personales**

Step 1 With a partner, ask and answer the following interview questions. Write the answers.

1. ¿Qué tienes que hacer los fines de semana?
2. ¿Cuánto tiempo tienes que estudiar para la clase de español?
3. Después de clase, ¿qué tienes que hacer?
4. Para tener una vida saludable *(healthy life)*, ¿qué hay que hacer?
5. Antes de *(before)* una fiesta, ¿qué tienes que preparar?
6. Para tener una casa limpia, ¿qué hay que limpiar?

Vocabulario

7. ¿Cuánta comida tienes que comprar para una fiesta?

8. ¿Qué hay que tener en una cocina?

Step 2 In groups of four, recount to the other members of your group what your interviewee said. After hearing each other's answers, note the similarities and differences between the responses.

C3-14 ¿Qué vas a hacer después de clase? Have a conversation with a partner using the following structure as a model. Before you begin the conversation, think about the verb phrases you will need to use. After you have gone through the conversation once, switch roles with your partner and have the conversation again.

Student A and Student B are talking about their plans for the day.

Student A	Student B
1. Greet Student B.	2. Respond to Student A's greeting and ask how he/she is.
3. Say that you are well. Ask Student B what he/she is going to do today.	4. Say that you have to go to class until **(hasta)** 5 P.M.
5. Ask what Student B is going to do after **(después de)** class.	6. Say that you do not know. Ask Student A what he/she is doing tonight.
7. Say that you are going to see a movie.	8. Ask what time Student A is going to see the movie.
9. Respond saying that the movie will start at 8 P.M.	10. Say that you are going to go to the movies too! Say goodbye to Student A.

Vocabulario

C3-15 Las preferencias With a partner, ask and answer the following questions about food and restaurants.

> ¿Qué te gusta comer para el desayuno?
>
> ¿Qué te gusta beber?
>
> ¿Qué no te gusta comer?
>
> ¿Cómo es tu sándwich ideal? ¿Qué ingredientes tiene?
>
> ¿Qué tienes que comer para tener una vida saludable?
>
> ¿Cuál es tu restaurante favorito?
>
> En un restaurante mexicano, ¿qué pides?
>
> En un restaurante chino, ¿qué pides?
>
> ¿Sabes cocinar? ¿Qué te gusta cocinar?

Now invent three of your own questions to ask your partner about food or restaurants and compare the answers with your own.

C3-16 Planes para el fin de semana

Step 1 Think about what plans you have for this weekend. Are you going to study for an exam? Are you going to see your friends? Are you going to a party? Are you going to work? Come up with at least four plans you have for this weekend and tell them to your partner. Your partner will tell you his/her plans.

Step 2 You and your partner will join another partner team. You will talk about your partner's plans for this weekend, and your partner will talk about yours. Your group should compare and contrast your different plans.

C3-17A ¿Qué hacen los Martínez Sierra? **A** Your drawing shows what some members of the Martínez Sierra family do on a typical day around 7:00 P.M., but you don't know what the others are doing. If you are student A, use the image below. If you are student B, use the image in C3-17B on the next page. Using your drawing, do the following:

Step 1 Ask each other questions to find out who does what until you know what everyone in the family typically does.

Useful vocabulary: **madre / padre / hija / hijo mayor (older) / hijo menor (younger)**

Step 2 Could someone in the family be doing something more important than what they are currently doing? Work with your partner to come up with one or two commands for different members of the family, telling them to do something else.

Modelos   *Pedro juega con videojuegos.*
            Pedro, ¡ayuda a tu padre a lavar los platos!

Vocabulario

C3-17B ¿Qué hacen los Martínez Sierra? **B** Your drawing shows what some members of the Martínez Sierra family do on a typical day around 7:00 P.M., but you don't know what the others are doing. If you are student B, use the image below. If you are student A, use the image in C3-17A on the previous page. Using your drawing, do the following:

Step 1 Ask each other questions to find out who does what until you know what everyone in the family typically does.

Useful vocabulary: **madre / padre / hija / hijo mayor (older) / hijo menor (younger)**

Step 2 Could someone in the family be doing something more important than what they are currently doing? Work with your partner to come up with one or two commands for different members of the family, telling them to do something else.

Modelos   *Pedro juega con videojuegos.*
            Pedro, ¡ayuda a tu padre a lavar los platos!

Lectura

C3-18 **Los orígenes de la comida** In this activity, you will explore favorite foods and their origins.

Step 1 Work with a partner to make a list of your favorite foods and key ingredients in them.

Step 2 Identify, to the best of your ability, which countries or regions the foods and ingredients come from. You may be able to identify multiple influences for certain dishes.

Step 3 As a class, share the foods and group them according to the regions or locations of origin. Does the class, as a whole, show a pattern in favorites?

C3-19 **Los ingredientes** Below is a list of ingredients found in a variety of cuisines.

oregano	cumin	tomatoes	corn	olive oil	garlic

Step 1 What foods or cuisines do you most identify with each ingredient?

Step 2 Now, try to make a list of foods in the U.S. or other cultures that also make use of those ingredients.

Step 3 Which ingredients seem to have the widest use? The most limited? Is there a factor that the most widely used ingredients seem to have in common?

Lectura

C3-20

Cognados Scan the text to find Spanish words that you did not know but can recognize because they are cognates of English words. Share your list with a classmate.

C3-21

Lectura: El origen de la comida hispana

Muchas de las comidas que ahora son típicas de España y Latinoamérica tienen su origen en otro lugar.

¿Puedes imaginar una tortilla española sin patatas? Pues, la patata tiene su origen en las montañas de Perú y solo aparece en la comida española después del viaje de Cristóbal Colón, o incluso más tarde. De manera similar, los tomates, esenciales para el gazpacho, y el chocolate, básico para muchos dulces populares de España, tienen su origen en Latinoamérica.

Pero la influencia de Europa también existe en Latinoamérica. Casi cada país caribeño tiene una forma de arroz con frijoles. En Cuba el nombre del plato se llama moros y cristianos, en Puerto Rico es arroz con habichuelas, y en Venezuela, pabellón criollo. El arroz es de origen asiático y fue introducido en la gastronomía latinoamericana por los españoles. También las frutas cítricas, como las naranjas y los limones, llegaron a Latinoamérica con los europeos.

Aunque estas comidas son esenciales en sus "nuevos" países, es importante recordar que tienen sus orígenes en otras partes del mundo.

Piénsalo Eating habits are different in different countries and cultures. For example, in many Spanish-speaking countries, the main meal of the day happens early in the afternoon as opposed to in the evenings as in the U.S. Would different eating times and habits be a perspective, a practice, or a product of a culture? What can be the causes and consequences of that difference, thinking again in terms of perspectives, practices, and products?

You say **patatas**, I say **papas...**

¡Me gusta la comida española! Hoy voy a escribir sobre una de mis comidas favoritas: la tortilla española. Las tortillas aquí en España son muy diferentes a las tortillas de México. Aquí están hechas *(made)* con papas, huevos y cebollas *(they are more like a big omelet with potatoes and other ingredients)*. Ayer, comimos en un restaurante que tiene muchas variedades de tortillas españolas.

Let me tell you about one funny thing that happened when I first learned how to make tortillas here in España. We were talking about **la comida** in my Spanish class and the teacher asked whether anyone knew the ingredients for tortillas and how to make them. One of my classmates raised her hand and shared with us "una lista de ingredientes." She used the word **patatas** for *potatoes*. When I was back home, I had learned the word as **papas**, not **patatas**. I raised my hand meaning to ask whether they meant the same. However, I said, **"¿Patata y papá significan lo mismo?"** This of course made my teacher smile. You see, **papá** is dad in Spanish and **papa** (without an accent) is potato. Our teacher said we could use either one. So, I decided to stick with **papas**. The embarrassment came later when I was talking about making mashed potatoes **(puré de papas)**. I said, **"Para un puré rico, tienes que hervir el Papa por veinte minutos,"** which is actually translated *"For a delicious puree, you have to boil the Pope for twenty minutes."* My roommate Marcela could not stop laughing! Now I always say **patata!**

El Papa = *the Pope*; **la papa** = *the potato*; **el papá** = *the dad!*

C3-22 Get together with the classmates whose blog recipes you reviewed online. Take turns talking about the recipes you posted, what makes them special, and what you liked about your classmates' recipes.

Síntesis: Vocabulario

En la cocina   *In the kitchen*

los armarios   *cabinets*

la batidora   *mixer*

la cacerola   *pan*

la cocina   *kitchen*

la cubierta, la encimera   *counter top*

la cuchara   *spoon*

el cuchillo   *knife*

la despensa   *pantry*

la escoba   *broom*

la esponja   *sponge*

la estufa   *stove*

el fregadero   *sink*

la heladera, el congelador   *freezer*

el horno   *oven*

el jabón de manos   *hand soap*

el jabón de platos   *dish soap*

el lavaplatos   *dishwasher*

la licuadora   *blender*

la mesa   *table*

el microondas   *microwave*

la olla   *pot*

el plato   *plate*

la servilleta   *napkin*

el plato hondo, el bol, el tazón   *bowl*

el refrigerador, el frigorífico, la nevera   *refrigerator*

la silla   *chair*

la taza   *cup*

el tenedor   *fork*

la tostadora   *toaster*

el vaso   *glass cup*

Los adjetivos   *Adjectives*

agrio(a)   *sour*

amargo(a)   *bitter*

caliente   *hot*

desordenado(a)   *messy*

dulce   *sweet*

frío(a)   *cold*

limpio(a)   *clean*

mojado(a)   *wet*

picante   *spicy*

seco(a)   *dry*

sucio(a)   *dirty*

Las frutas   *Fruit*

la banana, el plátano   *banana*

la cereza   *cherry*

la fresa, la frutilla   *strawberry*

el limón   *lemon*

el mango   *mango*

la manzana   *apple*

la naranja   *orange*

la pera   *pear*

la piña   *pineapple*

la uva   *grape*

Los vegetales / Las verduras   *Vegetables*

el ajo   *garlic*

la calabaza   *pumpkin*

la cebolla   *onion*

el chile, el pimiento   *pepper*

la lechuga   *lettuce*

la papa, la patata   *potato*

el pepino   *cucumber*

el tomate   *tomato*

la zanahoria   *carrot*

Las carnes   *Meats*

la carne   *beef*

el jamón   *ham*

el pavo   *turkey*

el pollo   *chicken*

la salchicha   *sausage*

Síntesis: Vocabulario

Los pescados y los mariscos
Fish and shellfish

la almeja   *clam*

el cangrejo   *crab*

la langosta   *lobster*

el pescado   *fish*

el pulpo   *octopus*

el salmón   *salmon*

Las bebidas   *Drinks*

la botella de vino   *bottle of wine*

el café   *coffee*

la cerveza   *beer*

el chocolate caliente   *hot chocolate*

el jugo, el zumo   *juice*

el jugo de manzana   *apple juice*

el jugo de naranja   *orange juice*

la leche   *milk*

el refresco   *soft drink*

el té   *tea*

Los condimentos   *Condiments*

el aceite   *oil*

el kétchup, la salsa de tomate   *ketchup*

la mantequilla   *butter*

la mayonesa   *mayonnaise*

la mostaza   *mustard*

la pimienta   *pepper*

la sal   *salt*

Los postres   *Desserts*

el helado   *ice cream*

la tarta, la torta, el pastel, el bizcocho   *cake*

el yogur   *yogurt*

Otras comidas   *Other foods*

el arroz   *rice*

los cereales   *cereal*

el hielo   *ice*

el huevo   *egg*

el pan   *bread*

el queso   *cheese*

Preparación de la comida
Food preparation

añadir   *to add*

beber, tomar   *to drink*

cocinar   *to cook*

comer   *to eat*

congelar   *to freeze*

cortar   *to cut*

hervir   *to boil*

lavar   *to wash*

limpiar   *to clean*

mezclar   *to mix*

pedir   *to order; to ask for*

pelar   *to peel*

servir   *to serve*

Síntesis: Gramática

Some common irregular verbs in the *yo* form

There are a number of verbs that have irregular **yo** forms that end in **-go.** They are often referred to as **-go** verbs. Notice that only their **yo** forms are irregular. Here are a few common **-go** verbs.

hacer *to do; to make*

yo **hago**	nosotros(as) hacemos
tú haces	vosotros(as) hacéis
él / ella / usted hace	ellos / ellas / ustedes hacen

poner *to put*

yo **pongo**	nosotros(as) ponemos
tú pones	vosotros(as) ponéis
él / ella / usted pone	ellos / ellas / ustedes ponen

salir *to go out; to leave*

yo **salgo**	nosotros(as) salimos
tú sales	vosotros(as) salís
él / ella / usted sale	ellos / ellas / ustedes salen

Another group of verbs, whose infinitives end in **-cer** or **-cir,** change from **c** to **zc** before **o** in the **yo** form.

conducir *to drive*

yo **conduzco**	nosotros(as) conducimos
tú conduces	vosotros(as) conducís
él / ella / usted conduce	ellos / ellas / ustedes conducen

conocer *to know; to be acquainted with*

yo **conozco**	nosotros(as) conocemos
tú conoces	vosotros(as) conocéis
él / ella / usted conoce	ellos / ellas / ustedes conocen

Here are some other verbs that have irregular *yo* forms.

dar *to give*

yo **doy**	nosotros(as) damos
tú das	vosotros(as) dais
él / ella / usted da	ellos / ellas / ustedes dan

saber *to know*

yo **sé**	nosotros(as) sabemos
tú sabes	vosotros(as) sabéis
él / ella / usted sabe	ellos / ellas / ustedes saben

traer *to bring*

yo **traigo**	nosotros(as) traemos
tú traes	vosotros(as) traéis
él / ella / usted trae	ellos / ellas / ustedes traen

Síntesis: Gramática

Affirmative informal commands

Affirmative informal commands are used when talking to a friend or family member or in any situation that would require he use of **tú.** To form affirmative informal commands of regular **-ar, -er,** and **-ir** verbs, use the *él / ella* present tense form of the verb. For example:

> **hablar: ¡Habla** español!
> **comer: ¡Come** la ensalada!
> **escribir: ¡Escribe** tu nombre!

Some common verbs have irregular affirmative **tú** command forms. Here are some examples.

> **poner: ¡Pon** los libros en tu escritorio!
> **tener: ¡Ten** cuidado!
> **hacer: ¡Haz** la tarea!
> **ser: ¡Sé** honesto!

Expressing obligation and necessity

If you want to say in Spanish that someone has to do something, you use the expression **tener que,** followed by a verb in the infinitive. For example:

> Carlos **tiene que estudiar** en la biblioteca y yo **tengo que ir** al gimnasio.
> *Carlos has to study in the library and I have to go to the gym.*

If you want to express obligation in a more general sense, use the expression **hay que** followed by an infinitive. Notice that, because there is no specific subject, the verb form is always **hay.**

> **Hay que** conservar energía.
> *One has to conserve energy.*

> **Hay que** encontrar una cura para el cáncer.
> *It is necessary (We must) find a cure for cancer.*

Expressing future plans: *ir a*

To express future plans in Spanish, use the verb **ir** followed by the preposition **a** and a verb in the infinitive.

> En el verano **voy a viajar** a Perú.
> *In the summer, I am going to travel to Peru.*

> Mañana mis padres **van a conocer** a mi amiga Carolina.
> *Tomorrow my parents are going to meet my friend Carolina.*

4

En la casa

Objectives: In this chapter you will learn to

- describe the different parts of a house
- indicate where something is located
- talk about chores and parts of your daily routine
- talk about what you or other people are doing
- compare two or more people or things
- identify different architectural styles of the Spanish-speaking world

JPagetRFPhotos/Shutterstock.com

Vocabulario

C4-1 ¿Dónde está?

Step 1 With a partner, take turns using the word bank and prepositions of location to create sentences and rough drawings to match. Each partner must form three sentences and create three sketches. Use the space at the bottom of the page for your sketches.

| el escritorio | la lámpara | la mesa | la puerta | el sofá |
| la frazada | el libro | la mesita de noche | la silla | la ventana |

Modelo   Student A: *La frazada está debajo de la almohada.*
Student B draws a picture of a blanket under a pillow.

Step 2 Now switch partners, and take turns asking your new partner to describe your sketches.

Gramática

Un cuarto **A** Work with a partner. One of you will use the picture of the room in this activity and the other will use a different picture in C4-2B. Take turns asking each other where things are in your rooms until you have identified the locations of all of the objects listed below.

el bolígrafo	los cuadernos	el espejo	la guitarra	los libros	la silla
el calendario	el cuadro	la foto	la lámpara	la mesa	el teléfono celular
la computadora	el escritorio	el gato	los lápices	la mochila	

Modelo Student A: *¿Dónde está la guitarra?*
Student B: *La guitarra está debajo de la cama.*

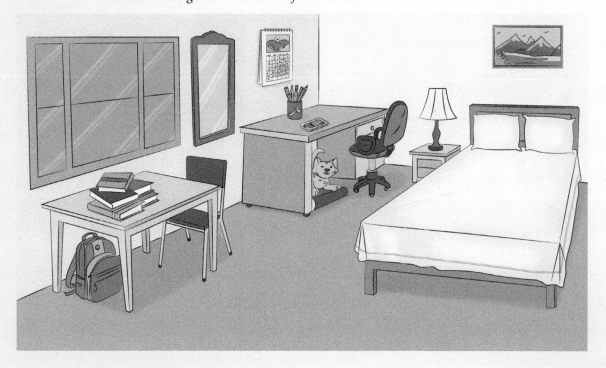

C4-2B **Un cuarto** **B** Work with a partner. One of you will use the picture of the room in this activity and the other will use a different picture in C4-2A. Take turns asking each other where things are in your rooms until you have identified the locations of all of the objects listed below.

el bolígrafo	los cuadernos	el espejo	la guitarra	los libros	la silla
el calendario	el cuadro	la foto	la lámpara	la mesa	el teléfono celular
la computadora	el escritorio	el gato	los lápices	la mochila	

Modelo   Student A: *¿Dónde está la guitarra?*
Student B: *La guitarra está debajo de la cama.*

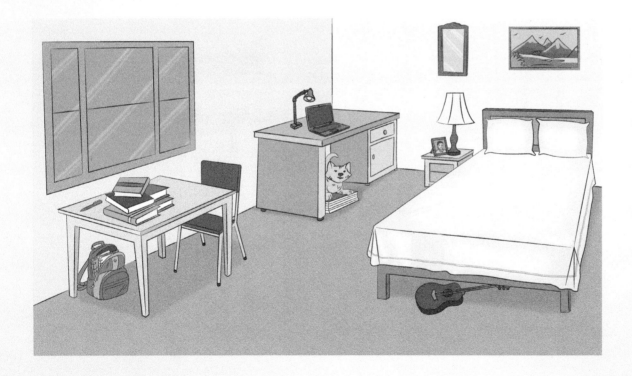

Gramática

C4-3 Mi cuarto

Step 1 Come to class with a picture of a room from a magazine or printed from the internet. Describe the room to a partner without revealing your drawing. Your partner will try to draw the room based on your description. Switch roles and draw the room your partner describes.

Modelo *Hay un escritorio y una silla a la derecha de la puerta.*

Step 2 After you both have drawn each other's rooms, see how well you did. Are all the objects in the room in the correct locations? Compare your original room with your partner's original room and state five similarities or differences.

Modelo *Yo tengo una silla, pero tú tienes dos sillas.*

C4-4 ¿Cómo organizar la sala? Imagine that you have just moved into a new apartment with some college roommates. In groups of three or four, decide how you're going to arrange the living room. Whose furniture will go where? What will you put on the walls? What needs to stay in your own rooms?

Step 1 Make a list of what you each have to contribute to the room and share your lists with each other.

Modelo *mi sofá blanco, el televisor HD, la silla de rayas*

Step 2 Agree with your new roommates on where everything will go and write a declarative statement to capture each decision. Even though it will be more time-consuming, be sure to use only Spanish as you are discussing your decisions. One person should draw the layout of the room to confirm that you are all talking about the same thing.

Modelos *La silla de rayas va al lado del sofá blanco.*
El televisor HD va en mi cuarto porque el televisor 3D va en la sala.

Step 3 Choose one student to represent your group and report out to the class.

C4-5 **¿Qué están haciendo?** With a partner, look at the picture together. Take turns creating and responding to true / false statements with the present progressive until you have stated what every person, cat, and dog is doing here. Correct the false statements.

Modelos   Student A: *La niña está corriendo.*
Student B: *¡Cierto!*
Student B: *El perro pequeño está durmiendo.*
Student A: *¡Falso! Está nadando.*

Gramática

C4-6

Conversaciones Have a conversation with a partner using the following structure as a model. Before you begin the conversation, think about the verbs you will need and their present participle forms. After you have gone through the conversation once, switch roles with your partner and have the conversation again.

Student A's parents are coming to visit. Student B is helping to clean up the apartment they share.

Student A	Student B
1. Express an emotion about your parents' upcoming visit. (**Estoy contento(a) / nervioso(a) porque…**)	2. Acknowledge Student A's comment with an appropriate expression.
3. Tell Student B two household chores that you need to do to get ready. (**Tenemos que…**)	4. Use the present tense to tell Student A what you each will do. Ask where something is if you need to. (**¿Dónde está la aspiradora?**)
5. It's fifteen minutes later. Use the present progressive to ask what Student B is doing right now.	6. Tell Student A what you are doing and then ask what Student A is doing.
7. Reply to Student B. Then identify two more chores to accomplish and ask which one Student B prefers. (**¿Quieres… o…?**)	8. Reply to Student A and ask whether that's OK. (**¿Está bien?**)
9. Confirm that Student B's preference is fine with you, but also say that you're tired and you are now taking a rest.	10. You've decided that you need a break, too. Tell Student A what you're doing right now instead of the rest of the chores. (Use a different verb from Student A.)

Gramática

C4-7A ¿Qué está haciendo la familia Gómez? **A** Work with a partner. You will use the image in this activity of the Gomez family working in their yard. Your partner will use the image in C4-7B of the family working inside. They are exhausted! Take turns asking about each family member until you know what everyone in the family is doing in the house and outside.

Modelo Student B: *¿Qué está haciendo Pedro?*
Student A: *Pedro está cortando el césped.*

C4-7B **¿Qué está haciendo la familia Gómez?** **B** Work with a partner. You will use the image in this activity of the Gomez family working inside. Your partner will use the image in C4-7A of the family working in their yard. They are exhausted! Take turns asking about each family member until you know what everyone in the family is doing in the house and outside.

Modelo   Student B: *¿Qué está haciendo Pedro?*
Student A: *Pedro está cortando el césped.*

Gramática

C4-8 Encuesta

Step 1 Work in groups of three or four to identify what chores each of you do. Using the chart below, interview each other and place check marks next to each chore you and your partners normally complete.

Modelo   Student A: *¿Lavas la ropa?*
                 Student B: *Sí, lavo la ropa pero no plancho la ropa.*
                 Student C: *Yo lavo la ropa también, pero no me gusta lavar ropa.*

Nombre	lavar la ropa	lavar los platos	pasar la aspiradora	barrer	planchar	sacudir los muebles	arreglar el cuarto	limpiar el baño

Step 2 Analyze your chart. Who does what? Write a statement for each chore that reflects your group's routines. Who does the most work around the house? Who does the least?

Modelo   *Laura y Tom lavan los platos.*
                 *Mark y David lavan la ropa y planchan sus camisas pero no planchan
                 los pantalones.*

 Step 3 Choose the most interesting finding from your survey and share it with the class.

Vocabulario/Gramática

C4-9 Comparando casas

Step 1 With a partner, look at the real estate ads below and compare the different properties for sale and rent. Note that **Q** is the symbol for **quetzal**, the currency in Guatemala. Make five observations about the properties and write them down. Be sure to vary your comparisons.

Modelo   *El apartamento número 1 es el más barato. Es bueno para una persona.*

Guatemala, zona 1. Alquilo apartamento pequeño independiente en zona 11, Las Charcas, incluye agua y cable. Detalles: Habitaciones: 1. Baños: 1. Precio: Q8.000,00. Teléfono: 54370624
Guatemala, zona 14. Alquilo precioso apartamento amueblado en nivel alto, con 165 m², 2 habitaciones, 2.5 baños, 2 salas, 2 parqueos y habitación de servicio. Totalmente amueblado y equipado, ideal para ejecutivos y/o extranjeros (*foreigners*), 1 línea telefónica. Detalles: Área de cons.: 165 m². Habitaciones: 2. Baños: 2. Precio: Q10,900. Teléfono: (502) 5016-8689 Oscar
Guatemala, MIXCO, SAN CRISTÓBAL. VENDO CASAS DE DOS NIVELES DE TRES DORMITORIOS, SALA, COMEDOR, COCINA, TRES BAÑOS, LAVANDERÍA, INDEPENDIENTES, AGUA PROPIA, SUPER PRECIO Q425,000 ENGANCHE (*down payment*) Q55,000 CUOTA BANCARIA (*bank fee*) Q3,330 TEL 43970067 Precio: Q425,000.00

Step 2 You and your partner need to find a fully furnished short-term rental apartment together. Interview each other to pinpoint your key requirements and note them in writing.

Modelo   Student A: *¿Necesitamos una sala con sofá y televisor?*
    Student B: *Sí, y una cocina. ¿Qué necesitamos en la cocina?*

Step 3 Now imagine that you are a Guatemalan realtor who specializes in temporary housing for international students. With your partner, write an ad that fits your requirements. Use the ads you compared for **Step 1** as your model. As the finishing touch, add a comparative or superlative statement that is guaranteed to appeal to prospective tenants.

Gramática

C4-10 Los verbos nuevos

Step 1 With a partner, take turns choosing verbs from the bank to complete the questions below logically.

cerrar	decir	empezar	hervir	perder	repetir
costar	dormir	freír	pedir	preferir	servir

1. ¿_____ la mesa roja o la mesa azul?

2. ¿Siempre _____ Juan enchiladas verdes en el restaurante?

3. ¿Cuánto _____ los tacos?

4. ¿Cuántas horas _____ Sara cada noche?

5. ¿Tu padre siempre _____ a cocinar a las siete de la mañana?

6. ¿Cuántas veces _____ el entrenador los ejercicios con pesas?

Step 2 Use two new verbs from the bank in step 1 to create two original questions.

Step 3 Ask each other your questions and answer them.

C4-11 Conversaciones Have a conversation with a partner using the following structure as a model. Before you begin, think about the stem-changing verbs you will need and their forms. After you have gone through the conversation once, switch roles with your partner and have the conversation again.

Student A and Student B are at a department store. Your apartment is mostly set up, but you still need some appliances and other items that none of your roommates have brought from home.

Student A	Student B
1. You need to visit more than one department. Ask where Student B prefers to begin.	2. Say that you should start with small appliances. Ask whether Student A remembers what you need to buy.
3. Remind Student B of the two appliances you need. (Decide on what you would like to purchase ahead of time.)	4. Look at the items and compare two models.
5. Say which choice you think you can purchase and ask whether Student B wants to choose the second item.	6. Look at the new items and say which is the best one.
7. Agree with Student B's choice. **(Está bien. Me gusta…)** Say that you also need a couple of heavy blankets for the living room sofa.	8. Agree with Student A. Point out that roommates and friends often sleep in the living room, in front of the TV.
9. Check the prices of what you've selected and tell Student B how much everything costs. Then state the total cost.	10. Uh-oh, you spent too long deliberating over your choices and have run out of time. Say that the store is closing and decide when you are coming back to finish your errand.

C4-12

Citas rápidas   It's time to get to know your classmates a little better.

Step 1 Individually, prepare 6 questions that you might ask your classmates to get to know them better.

Step 2 Look at the six questions you prepared for class today. Find a partner and take turns asking and answering your questions. As soon as you're finished, find another partner and repeat the process until you've spoken to two or three classmates. Take notes on their responses.

Student 1: _____

Student 2: _____

Student 3: _____

Step 3 Write a summary of your findings and present it to the class or post it for comments.

C4-13

La ruleta de la fortuna *(Wheel of Fortune®)* Congratulations! You're the winning contestant on Wheel of Fortune®, and it's time to choose your prizes.

una alfombra azul	un escritorio grande	una licuadora	una silla pequeña
unos altoparlantes gigantes	un horno eléctrico	un horno de microondas	un sofá amarillo
una aspiradora	una lámpara de oro (gold)	una pintura elegante	un televisor
una batidora	un lavaplatos	un refrigerador blanco	una tostadora

Step 1 With a partner, use the word bank to identify the prizes to choose from and make some comparisons. Create five statements each.

Modelo   *Hay una aspiradora. Es más útil que la silla pequeña.*

Step 2 Choose three prizes and write out sentences to explain why you are choosing them.

Step 3 Play the roles of Vanna White (the hostess that presents the prizes) and the winning contestant. Use the sentences from step 1 and 2 to make further statements about 3 prizes you are picking. Vanna can ask why you want or need them? How might you use them? Switch roles so that everyone is able to pick three prizes.

Lectura

Antes de leer

Step 1 With a partner, make a list of four buildings that you would consider important landmarks in your city or in a city near you.

Step 2 Now think about the roles of the buildings. What are they used for? Are their architectural styles historic, traditional, contemporary? Do the styles of the buildings match the character of the neighborhoods where they are located? Jot down some notes in Spanish to describe each one.

Step 3 Share your list with the class and discuss. Did many classmates describe the same buildings? Which landmark is most significant, in your opinion?

Fernando Rubio

La arquitectura de España

El estilo de la arquitectura española varía según la época *(according to the time period)* histórica. Hay mucha arquitectura clásica en España. Dos sitios famosos son el acueducto de Segovia y el teatro romano de Mérida. El acueducto romano de Segovia tiene casi *(almost)* dos mil años. El teatro es Patrimonio de la Humanidad de la UNESCO *(UNESCO World Heritage site)*.

En el norte, la Catedral de Santiago de Compostela es uno de los mejores ejemplos de iglesia románica de España. También hay muchas iglesias góticas con vidrieras *(stained glass)* preciosas como la Catedral de Burgos y la Catedral de León.

Los moros llegaron a España en 711 y la influencia árabe es muy evidente en la arquitectura ibérica. Dos ejemplos importantes son la mezquita de Córdoba y la Alhambra de Granada.

Fernando Rubio

Barcelona es conocida por la arquitectura de Antoni Gaudí (1852–1926). Gaudí diseñó muchos edificios interesantes. La construcción de la Sagrada Familia comenzó en 1882 pero no va a estar finalizada hasta el año 2026. Otro edificio diseñado por Gaudí es la Casa Batlló.

El museo Guggenheim en Bilbao es un ejemplo impresionante de arquitectura contemporánea. Fue construido en el año 1997 por Frank Gehry. Está hecho de planchas de titanio *(titanium plates)*, piedra caliza *(limestone)* y mucho vidrio *(glass)*. El museo tiene muchas instalaciones de arte permanentes y otras que cambian.

Lectura

 La arquitectura en… Using the text as a model and your list of buildings from **C4-14,** create a short summary of buildings titled **La arquitectura en…**

Step 1 Work with your partner to review the list you created together in C4-14. Add or replace buildings on the list so that you have a group of buildings that are representative of the city.

Step 2 Organize your list and write a sentence or two about each building, including the architectural style, location, and the reason for its significance.

Modelo   *El Empire State es un rascacielos en Nueva York, diseñado por William Lamb.*

Step 3 Present your summary to the class.

Mi apartamento nuevo

¡Hola, amigos! Esta semana estoy buscando un apartamento nuevo. Quiero vivir en un apartamento con mis amigos Carlos y Luis. Me gusta mi apartamento ahora, pero quiero tener más espacio. Quiero un dormitorio grande. No tengo ganas de compartir un baño con dos chicos. Entonces quiero tener por lo menos dos baños en el apartamento. Ya sabes que a mí me gusta cocinar, así que una cocina buena es importante. Algunos apartamentos tienen cocinas pequeñas y algunos tienen cocinas grandes. Hemos encontrado *(we have found)* dos apartamentos buenos. Could you please help me decide which one is the best? Por favor tell me which one you think is el mejor and tell me why it is better than the other two. Gracias por la ayuda.

Lo importante In groups of three, discuss what's most important to Bella and compare it with what's most important to you in your own living space, especially one that you have to share, and why. List three priorities and compare notes. Decide whether your group could get along as roommates.

Modelo　Student A: *A mí me gusta tener una sala grande.*
　　　　Student B: *Yo no puedo vivir sin un cuarto para mí sola.*
　　　　Student C: *Necesito tener un espacio tranquilo.*

Síntesis: Vocabulario

La casa   *The house*

el ático   *attic*

el baño   *bathroom*

la chimenea   *fireplace*

el clóset, el armario   *closet*

la cocina   *kitchen*

el comedor   *dining room*

la escalera   *stairs*

el garaje   *garage*

la habitación, el dormitorio   *bedroom*

el salón, la sala   *living room*

el sótano   *basement*

Afuera de la casa   *Outside the house*

el césped   *lawn*

el jardín   *garden; yard*

las flores   *flowers*

el patio   *patio*

la planta   *plant*

la piscina   *pool*

el porche   *porch*

En la casa   *Inside the house*

la alfombra   *rug*

la almohada   *pillow*

la cama   *bed*

las cortinas   *curtains*

el cuadro   *picture*

el cuarto   *room*

el escritorio   *desk*

la lámpara   *lamp*

la manta, la frazada   *blanket*

la mesa   *table*

la mesita de noche   *night stand*

la pintura   *painting*

la puerta   *door*

las sábanas   *sheets*

la silla   *chair*

el sofá   *sofa*

el techo   *ceiling*

el tocador, la cómoda   *dresser*

la ventana   *window*

El cuarto de baño   *The bathroom*

la bañera, la bañadera, la tina   *bathtub*

la ducha   *shower*

el espejo   *mirror*

el inodoro   *toilet*

la toalla   *towel*

Los quehaceres   *Chores*

arreglar   *to tidy up*

barrer   *to sweep*

cortar el césped   *to cut the lawn*

darle de comer a   *to feed (the pets)*

lavar el coche   *to wash the car*

lavar la ropa   *to wash clothing*

lavar los platos   *to wash the dishes*

limpiar   *to clean*

pasar la aspiradora   *to vacuum*

pasear (al perro)   *to walk (the dog)*

pintar   *to paint*

planchar   *to iron*

regar las plantas   *to water the plants*

sacudir   *to dust*

secar la ropa   *to dry clothing*

Más sobre la casa   *More about the house*

el apartamento   *apartment*

la residencia estudiantil   *student residence, dorms*

Síntesis: Vocabulario

Los electrodomésticos *Appliances*

el (aparato del) aire acondicionado
  air conditioner

los altoparlantes *speakers*

la aspiradora *vacuum cleaner*

el calefactor *heater*

el hornillo *stove*

el horno *oven*

el horno de microondas *microwave oven*

la lavadora *washer*

el refrigerador *refrigerator*

el reproductor de DVD *DVD player*

la secadora *dryer*

el televisor *television*

Prepositions of location

a la derecha (de) *to the right (of)*

a la izquierda (de) *to the left (of)*

al lado (de) *next to; beside*

alrededor (de) *around*

cerca (de) *close to; near; nearby*

debajo (de) *under; below*

delante (de) *in front of*

detrás (de) *behind*

en *in; at; on*

encima / arriba (de) *on; over; on top of*

enfrente (de) *facing*

en medio (de) *in the middle of*

entre *between*

lejos (de) *far from*

Comparatives and superlatives

más… que *more … than*

menos… que *less … than*

… más que *… more than*

… menos que *… less than*

… tanto como *… as much as*

tan… como *as … as*

tanto(a)… como *as much … as*

tantos(as)… como *as many … as*

Síntesis: Gramática

Prepositions of location

In Spanish to indicate where something is located, use **estar** or other verbs along with a preposition of location. Here is a list of other common prepositions of location.

a la derecha (de)   *to the right (of)*

a la izquierda (de)   *to the left (of)*

al lado (de)   *next to; beside*

alrededor (de)   *around*

cerca (de)   *close to; near; nearby*

debajo (de)   *under; below*

delante (de)   *in front of*

detrás (de)   *behind*

en   *in; at; on*

encima / arriba (de)   *on; over; on top of*

enfrente (de)   *facing*

en medio (de)   *in the middle of*

entre   *between*

lejos (de)   *far from*

The present progressive

The present progressive is used in Spanish to refer to actions that are in progress at the time of speaking. To form the present progressive in English, use the present tense of the verb *to be* plus a present participle, which is the *-ing* form of a verb. In Spanish, the present progressive tense combines a present tense form of **estar** with a present participle. The present participles of **-ar** verbs are formed by adding the ending **-ando** to the stem. To form present participles of **-er** and **-ir** verbs, add the ending **-iendo** to the stem of the verb.

hablar ⟶ habl**ando**

comer ⟶ com**iendo**

escribir ⟶ escrib**iendo**

> Carlos está estudiando en casa y sus hermanas están estudiando en la biblioteca.
> *Carlos is studying at home and his sisters are studying in the library.*

> La profesora está escribiendo y los niños están haciendo la tarea.
> *The professor is writing and the children are doing the homework.*

Some **-er** and **-ir** verbs, like **leer** and **traer,** have stems that end in stressed vowels. In order to maintain the expected sound, the present participles of these verbs end in **-yendo** instead of **-iendo.** For example:

leer ⟶ le**yendo**

traer ⟶ tra**yendo**

Although the verb **ir** is not commonly used in the present progressive, it does follows the same pattern:

ir ⟶ **yendo**

Síntesis: Gramática

Comparatives and superlatives

In English, to compare things that are equal, we use words and phrases such as *as, as many as,* and *as much as.* To compare things that are not equal, we use the phrases *more than* and *less than.* Words and phrases such as *the most, the least, the best,* and *the worst* are called superlatives.

Comparisons of inequality

In Spanish, to make comparisons of inequality with adjectives, adverbs, or nouns, use the following formula.

más / menos + (adjective / adverb / noun) + **que**

For example:

> Carlos es **más** alto **que** María.
> *Carlos is taller than María.*

To compare actions that are not equal, use this formula.

(verb) + **más que / menos que**

For example:

> Antonio estudia **más que** tú.
> *Antonio studies more than you.*

To say that there is *more* or *less than* a certain number or quantity, use **de** instead of **que.** For example:

> En mi universidad hay **más de** 2.000 estudiantes internacionales.
> *In my university there are more than 2,000 international students.*

Comparisons of equality

To compare things that are equal using adjectives and adverbs in Spanish, use the following formula.

tan + (adjective / adverb) + **como**

For example:

> Mi apartamento no es **tan** grande **como** tu casa.
> *My apartment is not as big as your house.*

To compare nouns of equal quantity, use **tanto** *(as much),* **tanta** *(as much),* **tantos** *(as many),* or **tantas** *(as many),* followed by a noun plus **como.**

tanto / tanta / tantos / tantas + (noun) + **como**

For example:

> Yo tengo **tantas clases como** mi hermana y por eso tengo **tanto trabajo como** ella.
> *I have as many classes as my sister and that's why I have as much work as her.*

Notice that **tanto** agrees in number and gender with the noun to which it refers.

Síntesis: Gramática

To compare actions that are equal, use a verb plus **tanto como** (*as much as*).

(verb) + **tanto como**

For example:

> Alejandro baila **tanto como** Laura.
> *Alejandro dances as much as Laura.*

Superlatives

To form superlatives in Spanish, start with a definite article and noun; then add **más** or **menos** followed by an adjective.

el / la / los / las + (noun) + **más** / **menos** + adjective

For example:

> **El cuadro más caro** de la colección es un Picasso.
> *The most expensive painting in the collection is a Picasso.*

Irregular comparatives and superlatives

Some of the most common adjectives in Spanish have irregular comparative and superlative forms.

Adjective		Comparative		Superlative	
bueno	*good*	**mejor**	*better*	el / la **mejor**	*the best*
malo	*bad*	**peor**	*worse*	el / la **peor**	*the worst*
joven	*young*	**menor**	*younger*	el / la **menor**	*the youngest*
viejo	*old*	**mayor**	*older*	el / la **mayor**	*the oldest*

> **La mejor fruta** está en el Caribe.
> *The best fruit is in the Caribbean.*

When talking about a person's age, use **menor** and **mayor,** but when you want to express that an object is older or newer, use **más viejo(a)** or **más nuevo(a).** For example:

> Mi coche es **más viejo que** tu coche.
> *My car is older than your car.*

Stem-changing verbs

In Spanish, there are three types of stem-changing verbs in the present tense: **o → ue, e → ie,** and **e → i.** The stem of the verb is the part of the infinitive that remains after dropping the **-ar, -er,** or **-ir** ending. The endings of stem-changing verbs are the same as regular verbs in the present tense; however, the stems change in all forms except **nosotros / nosotras** and **vosotros / vosotras.**

Verbs like **contar** are **o → ue** stem-changing verbs.

contar (o → ue) *to count*	
yo **cuento**	nosotros(as) **contamos**
tú **cuentas**	vosotros(as) **contáis**
él / ella / usted **cuenta**	ellos / ellas / ustedes **cuentan**

Síntesis: Gramática

Instead of changing from **o → ue,** the stem **o** of the verb **jugar** changes from **u → ue.**

jugar (u → ue) *to play*	
yo **juego**	nosotros(as) **jugamos**
tú **juegas**	vosotros(as) **jugáis**
él / ella / usted **juega**	ellos / ellas / ustedes **juegan**

Verbs like **querer** are **e → ie** stem-changing verbs.

querer (e → ie) *to wish, to want*	
yo **quiero**	nosotros(as) **queremos**
tú **quieres**	vosotros(as) **queréis**
él / ella / usted **quiere**	ellos / ellas / ustedes **quieren**

Verbs like **pedir** are **e → i** stem-changing verbs.

pedir (e → i) *to ask for; order*	
yo **pido**	nosotros(as) **pedimos**
tú **pides**	vosotros(as) **pedís**
él / ella / usted **pide**	ellos / ellas / ustedes **piden**

Here are some other common stem-changing verbs in the present tense.

o → ue	e → ie	e → i
contar *to tell*	cerrar *to close*	repetir *to repeat*
dormir *to sleep*	comenzar *to start; begin*	servir *to serve*
encontrar *to find; encounter*	empezar *to start; begin*	
morder *to bite*	entender *to understand*	
morir *to die*	hervir *to boil*	
mover *to move*	pensar de *to think of; to have an opinion*	
poder *to be able to*	pensar en *to think about; to consider*	
probar *to test; to prove; to taste*	perder *to lose*	
recordar *to remember*	preferir *to prefer*	
volver *to return*	sentir *to feel*	

Capítulos 3 y 4

Imagine that you will be studying abroad next semester and living with a host family in Mexico. The tasks that follow will require you to introduce yourself, talk about your likes and dislikes, learn more about Mexican culture, and provide information about your own culture. Use the grammar and vocabulary from Chapters 3 and 4 to complete this project online and in class. Refer to the chart below to see the topics covered and the number of points that correspond to each task.

Project components

Activity		Points
UP2-1 Presentación		15 points (individual)
UP2-2 Receta	Step 1	5 points (individual)
	Step 2	5 points (individual)
	Steps 3 and 4	10 points (individual)
UP2-3 Descripción		15 points (individual)
UP2-4 Solos en casa	Step 1	5 points (individual)
	Step 2	5 points (pair)
	Step 3	10 points (pair)
UP2-5 Llamada		15 points (individual)
UP2-6 Reflexión		15 points (individual)

UP2-1 Presentación As part of your application to study abroad, you need to compose an email introducing yourself to your host family. Describe yourself physically, and tell them about your personality as well as your hobbies and interests. Make sure to include information about your food preferences. State what you think you are going to do in Mexico. End your email by telling your host family that you are looking forward to meeting them.

UP2-2 Receta Now imagine that you have been placed with a Mexican family for the semester and you're living with them now. Your host family is great. Your host brother really likes to cook and even has his own cooking website with recipes and instructional videos. You have been in Mexico for a few weeks and one day during class, you get a voicemail from him asking you for a favor. Listen to the message to find out what it is.

Your host family has asked you to contribute a recipe from your home country for a family gathering at their house. They also want you to make a video describing how to prepare the recipe for their cooking website.

Step 1 You are not sure which recipe from your home country you want to make for the party. Research three recipe ideas and choose the one you like the best.

Step 2 Once you decide on a recipe, you need to record a video clip to upload to your host family's website. Use your host family's video about guacamole as a model. Start your recording by explaining what food you are going to prepare. Then list the ingredients and state approximately how long it takes to prepare the dish. Finally, you should provide a complete, detailed explanation of how to make it. Your instructor will decide how you will share your video with the class.

Step 3 Your host family loved your video submission, but they would still like one more recipe to include on their website. They have sent you two videos that describe recipes you did not choose. Watch the videos; then decide which one you recommend and tell why.

Step 4 Send an email to your family or friends back home, telling them what your host family has asked you to do and explaining which recipe you decided to prepare and why. To explain your choice, you should compare the three recipes. Write six reasons, comparing characteristics such as the following.

>¿Cuántos ingredientes tiene?
>
>¿Cuánto tiempo necesita?
>
>¿Tu receta es más cara o más barata que las otras?
>
>¿Cuál es la receta más fácil o más difícil de preparar? ¿Por qué?
>
>¿Cuál te gusta más?

UP2-3

Descripción You are posting about the family gathering on your video blog. Your friends and family back home will be watching it, so you want to describe the house where the party will take place, comparing it to your own home. And you want to impress them, so you are going to do it in Spanish. It is a large house and your host mom has told you that there will be quite a few chores to do to prepare for the party and to clean up after the party, such as: cook, do the dishes, vacuum, tidy up every room, sweep the floor, water the plants. As you describe the house, explain what chores you all will have to do and where.

>Modelos *Vamos a limpiar.*
>*Tenemos que limpiar.*
>*Hay que limpiar la cocina.*

UP2-4 Solos en casa

Step 1 Preparación *This step should be completed online.*

Write out what you and your friend will do to take care of the house while your host family is away. Organize the chores in three categories: things you like to do, things you don't care about, and things you don't like to do. Bring your list of chores to class.

Step 2 Conversación

You and your partner will receive a drawing of the house where you are staying and some information about the chores that need to be done in some of the rooms, but not in others. Ask each other questions to identify all the chores that your host family wants you to do. Follow the model to form and answer questions.

Modelo   Student 1: *¿Qué tenemos que hacer en el salón?*
          Student 2: *Tenemos que regar las plantas.*

Step 3 Los quehaceres

After exchanging the information and figuring out what needs to be done, share with your partner the list that you prepared in **Step 1.** Based on your lists, decide who is going to do what. You will have five minutes to complete this dialogue. You may need to compromise on some of the chores that neither of you likes to do.

Modelo   *A mí no me gustan los perros. ¿Quieres tú pasear al perro?*

Proyecto 2: Una fiesta

UP2-5 **Llamada** The day of the party is here and all of the guests have arrived. In the middle of the party you get a phone call from a friend who is also an exchange student in Mexico. You describe to him/her what is going on and show everything using your cell phone camera.

UP2-6 **Reflexión** The party is over now. This was your first party in Mexico and you are going to post a reflection about the experience on your blog. Write a couple of paragraphs (175 words or more) explaining what you like and don't like about aspects of Mexican culture that you learned about, such as family, food, or housing. Be sure to compare these cultural aspects to aspects of your own culture back home.

> **Modelo** *Voy a describir cómo es mi casa, mi familia y cómo son las fiestas que celebran…*

Por la ciudad

Objectives: In this chapter you will learn to

- ask for and give directions; indicate location; talk about immediate future plans and give formal commands
- talk about the city, city transportation, and the university
- use verbs in the preterite, reflexive verbs, and the personal **a**

C5-1 Transporte

Step 1 With a partner, read the following situations and write sentences to describe the best mode of transportation to get from one place to another.

Modelo   Estamos en la universidad y queremos ir a casa.
Vamos a tomar un autobús o el tren. / Vamos a caminar porque yo vivo cerca.

1. Estamos en Nueva York y tenemos que ir a Los Ángeles.

2. Estamos en la clase de español y queremos ir a tu casa.

3. Tenemos que viajar setenta millas, de una ciudad a otra.

4. Estamos en una ciudad grande y tenemos que viajar veintisiete cuadras.

5. Estás en tu casa y quieres ir a la casa de tu novio(a), que está cerca de tu casa.

6. Estamos en tu casa y queremos ir a la casa de tus padres o abuelos que están en otro barrio.

Step 2 Find a new partner and read your transportation sentences from step 1 in random order. Your partner should guess which of the situations in step 1 (1–6) would be applicable for each of your sentences. Then switch roles.

C5-2 Dos ciudades

Step 1 Your group will be assigned one of two cities. Read the description of the city to yourself. Then work with a partner to answer the questions that follow.

Fernandina   El pueblo Fernandina está situado en una costa hermosa. Es un pueblo tranquilo y un destino muy popular entre los turistas que quieren escaparse de las ciudades grandes. Las personas de Fernandina son muy amables y les encantan los turistas. Hay muchas actividades para hacer durante el verano *(summer)*. Hay muchas playas bonitas. La playa más popular es Santa Lucía. En la plaza central hay tiendas y conciertos. Es una ciudad pequeña y perfecta.

Vocabulario

Algunos datos sobre la ciudad:

- Tiene tres escuelas primarias y una escuela secundaria *(high school)*.

- Hay una línea de autobús que funciona de mayo a septiembre.

- Los fines de semana del verano hay un mercado en la plaza central.

- No hay hospital en el pueblo. Hay uno en la ciudad de al lado.

- El restaurante El Café de Clara es muy popular. Se cierra *(closes)* de diciembre a marzo.

Preguntas sobre Fernandina

1. ¿Es una ciudad grande?

2. ¿Está cerca del océano?

3. ¿Es popular entre los turistas?

4. ¿Cómo se llama la playa más popular?

5. ¿Cuándo está abierto *(open)* El Café de Clara?

6. ¿Qué hay en la plaza central?

7. ¿Cuántas escuelas hay en la ciudad?

San Timón   La ciudad San Timón está situada en las montañas. Es fácil viajar a San Timón. Hay un aeropuerto internacional y una estación de tren. Muchas personas vienen a la ciudad para estudiar o para trabajar. Por la noche hay vida nocturna y por el día hay actividades para las familias. Hay muchos hermosos lugares naturales en las montañas cerca de la ciudad, por ejemplo, el lago *(lake)* del Quijote. Es una ciudad diversa y bonita.

Vocabulario

Algunos datos sobre la ciudad:

- Tiene una universidad grande y muchos estudiantes.

- En el invierno *(winter)* se puede esquiar en las montañas.

- Hay un hospital grande que es un centro de investigación del cáncer.

- Hay muchos restaurantes con una gran variedad de comida: mexicana, china, japonesa, peruana, brasileña, americana, tailandesa y más.

- Tiene muchas opciones de transporte público: un metro, autobuses, trenes, taxis y un aeropuerto internacional.

Preguntas sobre San Timón

1. ¿Es un pueblo pequeño?
2. ¿Está cerca de las montañas?
3. ¿Es popular entre los estudiantes?
4. ¿Cómo se llama el lago en las montañas?
5. ¿Qué medios de transporte hay en la ciudad?
6. ¿Qué investigan en el hospital?
7. ¿Qué tipo de comida hay en la ciudad?

Vocabulario

Step 2 Now that you have information about the city, find a partner who knows about the other city. Ask each other questions about the buildings, transportation, and activities in each other's cities and write the answers. Answer to the best of your knowledge based on what you know about the city.

Step 3 Based on the answers, compare the two cities. What do they have in common and what is different about them? Identify four to six differences between the cities and note them in writing.

Step 4 Think of the city where you currently live. What does it have in common with Fernandina and San Timón?

C5-3 En nuestra ciudad

Step 1 With a partner, answer the following questions about the city where you live or the nearest city.

1. ¿Es grande o pequeña?
2. ¿Qué actividades son populares?
3. ¿Qué opciones hay para la educación?
4. ¿Qué medios de transporte hay?
5. ¿Es un destino popular para turistas? ¿Por qué?
6. ¿?

Step 2 Based on the answers from **Step 1**, create a description of your city to share with the class. Your description should be at least four sentences long.

Gramática

C5-4   En el pasado

Step 1 With a partner, ask and answer the following questions about your past. Use the preterite forms of **ir**, **ser**, and **estar** in your answers. After you have answered, add the question **¿y tú?** to find out the same information about your partner. Make sure to write down the answers you get.

Modelo ¿Adónde fuiste ayer?
Ayer, yo fui a la casa de mi madre, ¿y tú?

1. ¿Adónde fuiste en las últimas vacaciones?
2. ¿Adónde fuiste para tu cumpleaños?
3. ¿Cuál fue tu clase favorita el semestre pasado?
4. ¿De qué te disfrazaste *(What did you dress up as)* para Halloween el año pasado?
5. ¿Dónde estuviste en 2019?
6. ¿Adónde fuiste la semana pasada?
7. ¿Dónde estabas cuando estudiaste *(you studied)* la semana pasada?

Step 2 Pick two of the questions your partner answered in step 1 and prepare to share with the class. One question you will answer truthfully and another you will make up a false answer. The class will then guess which of your partner's answers is true (**cierto**) and which is false (**falso**).

Modelo Student A: *La clase favorita de Caitlin el semestre pasado fue estadísticas.*
Class: *Cierto.*
Caitlin: *Falso. Mi clase favorita fue biología.*

Gramática

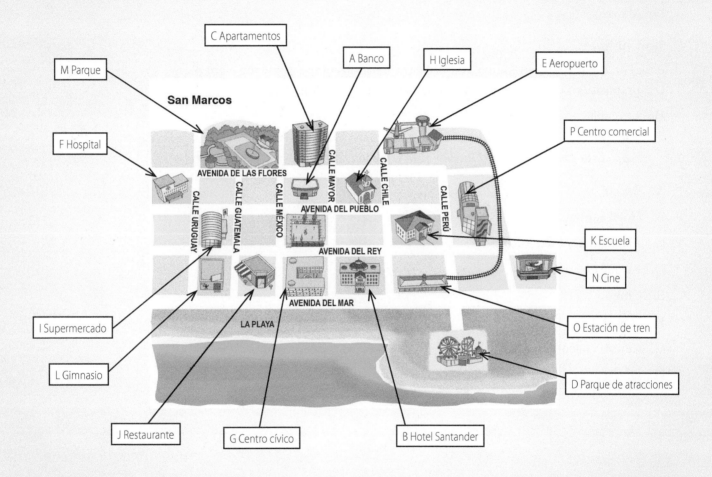

C Apartamentos

A Banco

H Iglesia

E Aeropuerto

M Parque

San Marcos

P Centro comercial

F Hospital

AVENIDA DE LAS FLORES

CALLE MAYOR

CALLE CHILE

CALLE PERÚ

K Escuela

AVENIDA DEL PUEBLO

CALLE URUGUAY

CALLE GUATEMALA

CALLE MÉXICO

AVENIDA DEL REY

N Cine

I Supermercado

AVENIDA DEL MAR

O Estación de tren

L Gimnasio

LA PLAYA

D Parque de atracciones

J Restaurante

G Centro cívico

B Hotel Santander

Step 1 Your instructor will assign you to be either Student A or Student B. Find a classmate who is assigned to the same group as you and answer the questions about the city of San Marcos.

Student A

Based on the map of San Marcos, describe the locations of the following eight places. Use prepositions of location and street names to complete this step.

Modelo Plaza Mayor

La Plaza Mayor está en el centro de la ciudad y está más o menos cerca de la playa. Está en la avenida del Pueblo. Está entre la calle Mayor y la calle México.

A. Banco

B. Hotel Santander

C. Apartamentos del Pueblo

D. Parque de atracciones

E. Cine

F. Hospital

G. Centro cívico

H. Iglesia

Student B

Based on the map of San Marcos, describe the locations of the following eight places. Use prepositions of location and street names to complete this step.

Modelo Plaza Mayor

La Plaza Mayor está en el centro de la ciudad y está más o menos cerca de la playa. Está en la avenida del Pueblo. Está entre la calle Mayor y la calle México.

I. Supermercado

J. Restaurante de Félix

K. Escuela

L. Gimnasio

M. Parque de la Libertad

N. Aeropuerto

O. Estación de tren

P. Centro comercial

Step 2 Imagine you are standing in the Plaza Mayor in San Marcos and a couple asks you how to get to a specific location in the city. Use the word bank and **ustedes** commands to tell them how to get to the eight locations from your list.

caminar *to walk*	seguir *to follow / continue*	tomar *to take*	doblar *to turn*	cruzar *to cross*
pasar *to pass*	cuadra *block*	esquina *corner*	hasta *until / to*	

Modelo la playa

Para llegar a la playa, crucen la Plaza Mayor y caminen por la calle México hasta la avenida del Mar. La playa está enfrente.

Gramática

Step 3 Find a new partner. If you are Student A find a Student B and vice versa.

You need to tell your new partner where you are starting from and where you would like to go. Your partner may not know where the starting location is on the map, so you will need to indicate its location on the map. As you learn where things are in your city, make note of the location names.

Modelo   del Parque de la Libertad a la playa

        Student A: *Queremos ir del Parque de la Libertad a la playa.*

        Student B: *¿Dónde está el Parque de la Libertad?*

        Student A: *Está en la avenida de las Flores y la calle México.*

        Student B: *Caminen por la calle México. Pasen por la Plaza Mayor. Crucen la avenida del Mar. La playa está enfrente.*

Student A

1. del banco al supermercado
2. del hotel Santander al aeropuerto
3. del centro comercial al Restaurante de Félix
4. del centro cívico al Parque de la Libertad

Student B

1. del gimnasio a la iglesia
2. de la escuela al parque de atracciones
3. de la estación de tren al hospital
4. del cine a los Apartamentos del Pueblo

Gramática

C5-6 Preferencias With a partner, ask and answer the following questions. Include where each place is located and how to get there from campus.

Modelo ¿Dónde hay buenos tacos aquí? ¿Cómo puedo llegar allí?
El restaurante El Tío Bueno tiene tacos buenos. Está en el centro, al lado de la policía. Camine por la calle central. Doble a la izquierda y el restaurante está enfrente del banco.

1. ¿Cuál es uno de tus restaurantes favoritos? ¿Dónde está? ¿Cómo puedo llegar allí?

2. ¿Dónde puedo comprar un coche aquí? ¿Dónde está? ¿Cómo puedo llegar allí?

3. ¿Adónde vas para tomar café y estudiar? ¿Dónde está? ¿Qué medio de transporte usas para llegar allí?

4. ¿Dónde está un hospital? ¿Qué hay cerca del hospital? ¿Qué medio de transporte va al hospital?

5. ¿Hay discotecas y bares aquí? ¿Cuál es el mejor? ¿Dónde está?

6. ¿Hay gimnasio aquí? ¿Dónde está el gimnasio más cerca? ¿Cómo puedo llegar allí?

C5-7 Sugerencias escolares

Step 1 Your instructor has asked you to create a list of at least five things students should do to succeed in school and to learn Spanish. Work with a partner to create your list. Your sentences should use both affirmative and negative **ustedes** commands. Be prepared to share your ideas with the class. Several verbs are listed here to help you, but you may use other verbs.

| estudiar | leer | dormir | asistir (a) | descansar | mirar | hablar | escribir | usar |

Modelo *Lean la tarea todos los días. No hablen durante la clase.*

Step 2 Form a group with another pair. Look at the commands you have all created and decide which ones will help you succeed in school, and in Spanish class in particular. Try for a list of at least ten unique commands that offer solid advice to students.

Gramática

C5-8 La rutina With a partner, use reflexive verbs from the verb bank to ask and answer at least six questions about your routines. If possible, include reasons for your answers.

acostarse	ducharse	cepillarse los dientes
relajarse	vestirse	lavarse el pelo

Modelo   relajarse
  Student A: *¿Dónde te relajas?*
  Student B: *Me relajo en casa porque puedo dormir o ver televisión.*

Write up a summary of your classmate's answers.

C5-9   Entrevista

Step 1 You have several new classmates in your Spanish class and you're looking forward to getting to know them. In groups of three or four, work together to create six questions using verbs from the verb bank. When appropriate, add adverbs like **generalmente** and **normalmente**. Each person in your group should make a written copy of all the questions.

cepillarse	comer	despertarse (ie)	relajarse	trabajar	divertirse
estudiar	acostarse (ue)	levantarse	reírse	preocuparse	

Question words: qué, cuándo, dónde, a qué hora, cómo, con quién, por qué

Modelos   *¿Generalmente a qué hora te acuestas por la noche?*
  ¿A qué hora trabajas?

Step 2 Now that you have your questions ready, find a partner and take turns asking and answering questions. Write down the answers, as you will need them in the following step.

Modelo   Student A: *¿Generalmente cuándo te acuestas por la noche?*
  Student B: *Generalmente me acuesto a las 11:30.*

Gramática

Step 3 Return to your original groups. Verbally share and compare the results for each question.

Modelo   Student A: *Generalmente Juan se acuesta a las 11:30.*
              Student B: *Generalmente Jacob se acuesta a las 11:00.*

Step 4 Based on the results you just shared, compare yourselves to the interviewees.

Modelos   *Juan y Jacob se acuestan tarde, pero yo me acuesto a las 9:00.*
           Ellos estudian en la biblioteca, pero yo estudio en casa.
           María se relaja con sus amigos y yo me relajo con mi familia.
           Nos divertimos los fines de semana.

C5-10

¿Adónde puedo ir? You're an incoming transfer student and a staffer from the new student center is helping you to get oriented. With a partner, take turns creating statements and formal commands to address each situation or need.

Modelo   comer pizza
          Student A: *Quiero comer pizza.*
          Student B: *Vaya a la pizzería en el centro.*

1. ver una película
2. estar enfermo(a) *(sick)*
3. comprar leche, huevos y yogur

4. tomar un café
5. tener tiempo libre
6. hacer ejercicio

C5-11

El nuevo semestre You need help finding certain places on campus at your school. With a partner, take turns asking and answering where the following locations are and questions about your daily routine.

Modelo   la librería
          Student A: *¿Sabes dónde está la librería?*
          Student B: *Sí, la librería está al lado de la biblioteca.*

1. el centro estudiantil
2. la cafetería
3. la biblioteca
4. el edificio administrativo
5. el gimnasio
6. el estadio
7. ¿Dónde te gusta estudiar?
8. ¿Qué medio de transporte usas para llegar a clase?

Gramática

C5-12 Sugerencias para estar en forma

Step 1 One of your classmates has a number of bad habits and the demands of student life are starting to take a toll. You need to provide suggestions to help your classmate get in shape, reduce stress, and feel better in general. With a partner, make a list of things that your classmate should do and not do. For your list, use the infinitive forms of at least five different verbs.

Modelo   *dormir ocho horas*

Step 2 Now use both your list and the word bank below to identify six pieces of advice that you and your partner consider essential for college students. Write a sentence using an **ustedes** command form to express each piece of advice. Each of you should make a copy of all the sentences.

comer	caminar	hacer yoga	estudiar	descansar
bailar	hacer ejercicio	beber	dormir	mirar la televisión

Modelos   correr
Corran tres veces por semana.
no comer
No coman helado todos los días.

Step 3 In groups of three or four, take turns sharing the advice you came up with. React to each suggestion by agreeing or stating why you don't think it's a good idea. What do you recommend instead?

Modelo   Student A: *Corran tres veces por semana.*
Student B: *Estoy de acuerdo.*
Student C: *No es una buena idea. Tres veces por semana es mucho.*

Gramática

C5-13 Consejos para turistas

 Step 1 Some acquaintances from Latin America are coming to visit and have asked you for recommendations on what to do and see. They don't have much time and you want to help them make the most of it. In groups of three or four, think of six to eight local attractions they should not miss or had better avoid. Include a range of suggestions for landmarks, restaurants, shopping, sports, arts, or outdoor activities. Begin each suggestion with an **ustedes** command. Write down all of your sentences to share in the next step.

Modelo   *Visiten el museo de arte en el centro de la ciudad. Hay una exhibición de Dalí muy buena.*

Step 2 Form new groups of three or four and read your suggestions to each other. Write down any new suggestions that sound good. (When it's your turn to read, be sure to allow time for your classmates to make notes.) As a group, decide on the ten best recommendations.

Step 3 Now share your top ten suggestions with the class. After each group has presented their lists, choose the ten best ideas and rank them from one to ten for a final set.

PICAFLOR II

(Sephanoides II)

Pablo Neruda

El colibrí[1] de siete luces,
el picaflor[2] de siete flores,
busca un dedal[3] donde vivir:
son desgraciados[4] sus amores
sin una casa donde ir
lejos del mundo y de las flores.

Es ilegal su amor, señor,
vuelva otro día y a otra hora:
debe casarse el picaflor
para vivir con picaflora:
yo no le alquilo este dedal
para este tráfico ilegal.

El picaflor se fue por fin
con sus amores al jardín
y allí llegó un gato feroz
a devorarlos a los dos:
el picaflor de siete flores,
la picaflora de colores:
se los comió el gato infernal
pero su muerte fue legal.

————
[1]*hummingbird*
[2]*hummingbird; womanizer*
[3]*thimble*
[4]*unfortunate*

C5-14 Tu poema picaflor

Step 1 Work with a partner. Create a new character for the poem "Picaflor"; you may choose another animal or a person. Write three sentences that describe your character using figurative language (remember that your language must create a vivid image in the mind of the reader).

Step 2 Based on the appearance of this new character, write a different ending for the poem, changing the fate of the hummingbirds in the garden. Keeping in mind the subject of the poem, see whether you can work in a final twist or surprise ending.

Step 3 Present your new ending to the class. Discuss how you decided to use your figurative language and the different ideas you came up with for the story.

¡Me encanta Barcelona!

Tengo el fin de semana libre. Entonces fui a Barcelona. Estoy escribiendo esta entrada en un café aquí en Barcelona. Me encanta Barcelona, tienes que visitarla. Ayer fui a visitar la Sagrada Familia (la iglesia famosa del arquitecto Gaudí). Es un edificio muy interesante. Me gustan los detalles del edificio. Después de la visita a la iglesia, yo fui a otro edificio de Gaudí, La Pedrera. Allí puedes ver un apartamento genial diseñado por Gaudí. También puedes subir al techo *(roof)*, donde se ve toda la ciudad y es un buen lugar para sacar fotos.

Hoy por la tarde voy al mercado de San Luis para comprar comida. Después, voy a la playa. Hace mucho sol hoy y estoy animada para estar ahí algunas horas. Pero tengo bloqueador que voy a usar para protegerme del sol. No sé si voy a bañarme. Creo que solo voy a tomar el sol.

La Pedrera

Sagrada Familia

Esta noche voy a pasear con unos amigos en La Rambla y luego vamos a comer en el Barrio Gótico y entrar en algunas discotecas para bailar. La Rambla es una calle grande peatonal, *just for foot traffic,* que es el corazón de la ciudad. Es muy divertido mirar las personas allí… *there are a lot of street performers as well.* El Barrio Gótico es la parte antigua de Barcelona. Los edificios son antiguos y hay una catedral gótica muy hermosa. Es un buen lugar para caminar. La verdad: hay que caminar mucho en esta ciudad. Todavía no conozco bien los medios de transporte aquí. Yo sé que hay taxis, buses, trenes y metro, pero… *I have walked everywhere! :) It's nice to sit here in the café resting my feet and watching the world go by while making plans for the rest of my time here.*

Barcelona… el próximo día: Hola amigos, ayer fue fantástico. Aquí pueden ver algunas fotos de mi día en la playa, la Rambla y el Barrio Gótico.

C5-15

¡Me encanta…! In pairs or small groups, think of a city you've visited and loved (or one that you've always wanted to visit). Make a list of your three favorite spots or activities in that city and prepare questions in Spanish to learn about your classmates' visits. Use Bella's blog entry as a guide for your discussion.

Modelo   Student A: *¿Cuál es tu ciudad favorita y por qué?*
Student B: *Me encanta New Orleans porque me gusta la comida y la celebración de Mardi Gras en la ciudad, ¿y tú?*

Síntesis: Vocabulario

La ciudad   *The city*

el banco   *bank*

el café   *café*

la carnicería   *butcher shop*

el centro comercial   *shopping center*

el cine   *cinema*

la cuadra   *block*

la discoteca   *club*

la esquina   *corner*

el gimnasio   *gym*

el hospital   *hospital*

la manzana   *block (Spain)*

el mercado   *(farmer's) market*

el museo   *museum*

la oficina de correos   *post office*

la panadería   *bakery*

el parque   *park*

la piscina   *pool*

la plaza   *plaza*

el restaurante   *restaurant*

el supermercado   *supermarket*

el teatro   *theater*

la tienda (de música, ropa, videos, etc.)   *store*

Vocabulario adicional
Additional vocabulary

el barrio   *neighborhood*

el centro   *city center (downtown)*

la ciudad   *city*

la comunidad   *community*

el pueblo   *village, town*

El transporte   *Transportation*

el aeropuerto   *airport*

el autobús   *bus*

el avión   *airplane*

la bicicleta   *bicycle*

el coche, el carro, el auto   *car*

la estación de autobuses   *bus station*

la estación de metro   *subway station*

la estación de trenes   *train station*

el estacionamiento   *parking lot*

la parada de autobús   *bus stop*

el tren   *train*

a pie   *by foot*

Cómo llegar   *Getting there*

bajarse (del tren, etc.)   *to get off (the train, etc.)*

caminar, andar   *to walk*

conducir, manejar   *to drive*

correr   *to run*

cruzar   *to cross*

doblar   *to turn*

hasta   *until, to*

montar a caballo   *to ride a horse*

montar en bicicleta   *to ride a bike*

seguir   *to follow; to continue*

subirse (al tren, etc.)   *to get on (the train, etc)*

tomar   *to take*

Reflexive verbs

acordarse   *to remember*

acostarse   *to go to sleep*

bañarse   *to take a bath*

casarse   *to get married*

cepillarse el pelo   *to brush one's hair*

despertarse   *to wake up*

divertirse   *to have fun*

Síntesis: Vocabulario

dormirse *to fall asleep*

enamorarse *to fall in love*

irse *to leave*

levantarse *to get up*

olvidarse *to forget*

peinarse *to comb one's hair*

ponerse (ropa) *to put on (clothes)*

preocuparse *to worry*

quedarse *to stay*

quitarse *to take off (clothes)*

reírse *to laugh*

relajarse *to relax*

sentarse *to sit down*

vestirse *to get dressed*

La universidad *The university*

la biblioteca *library*

la cafetería *cafeteria*

el campus (la ciudad universitaria) *campus*

el centro estudiantil *student center*

el edificio administrativo *administration building*

el estadio *stadium*

el gimnasio *gym*

la librería *bookstore*

la oficina *office*

la residencia estudiantil *dormitory*

Síntesis: Gramática

The preterite of ir, ser, and estar

The verbs **ser, ir,** and **estar** are irregular in the preterite, which means that they don't follow the same pattern of conjugation as regular -**ar,** -**er,** and -**ir** verbs. Notice that the preterite conjugations of **ser** and **ir** are identical.

ser *to be*

yo **fui**	nosotros(as) **fuimos**
tú **fuiste**	vosotros(as) **fuisteis**
él / ella / usted **fue**	ellos / ellas / ustedes **fueron**

ir *to go*

yo **fui**	nosotros(as) **fuimos**
tú **fuiste**	vosotros(as) **fuisteis**
él / ella / usted **fue**	ellos / ellas / ustedes **fueron**

estar *to be*

yo **estuve**	nosotros(as) **estuvimos**
tú **estuviste**	vosotros(as) **estuvisteis**
él / ella / usted **estuvo**	ellos / ellas / ustedes **estuvieron**

Antoni Gaudí **fue** el famoso arquitecto de la iglesia de la Sagrada Familia en Barcelona.
Antoni Gaudí was the famous architect of the Sagrada Familia church in Barcelona.

Juan **fue** a Barcelona en 2016 y **estuvo** allí por tres semanas.
Juan went to Barcelona in 2016 and was there for three weeks.

Reflexive verbs

Reflexive verbs express actions that people do **to** or **for** themselves. In other words, reflexive verbs indicate that the subject of the verb also **receives** the action of the verb. For example:

Roberto **se despierta** tarde en las vacaciones.
Roberto wakes up late on vacation.

Roberto is the subject of the sentence, but he is also receiving the action; he is waking himself up. Therefore, the verb is being used reflexively.

Reflexive pronouns

In Spanish, a reflexive verb is **always** accompanied by a reflexive pronoun. The reflexive pronouns are:

Singular		Plural	
me	*myself*	**nos**	*ourselves*
te	*yourself (informal)*	**os**	*yourselves (informal)*
se	*itself, himself, herself, yourself (formal)*	**se**	*themselves, yourselves (formal)*

The reflexive pronoun can always be placed before the conjugated verb. If the verb is in the infinitive or present progressive, you have the option of placing it before the conjugated verb or attaching it to the end of the infinitive or present participle:

Marianita **quiere ponerse** los zapatos.
Marianita **se quiere poner** los zapatos.
Marianita wants to put on her shoes.

Síntesis: Gramática

Marianita **se está poniendo** los zapatos.
Marianita **está poniéndose** los zapatos.
Marianita is putting on her shoes.

Notice how **poniéndose** has an accent mark. An accent mark is required when attaching the reflexive pronoun, in order to maintain the original stress of the present participle.

Grammar summary: The personal a

In Spanish, when the direct object is a specific person, the preposition **a** must come before it. This is called the *personal* **a.** For example:

Invito **a mi amigo.**
I invite my friend.

Whenever the Spanish preposition **a** is followed by the definite article **el,** you have to combine the two words to form the contraction **al.** For example:

Escucho **al** amigo de Miguel tocar la guitarra.
I listen to Miguel's friend play the guitar.

¡OJO! You do **not** use the personal **a** with the verb **tener,** even if the direct object refers to a person. For example:

Tengo **una abuela** venezolana.
I have a Venezuelan grandmother.

Usted / ustedes commands

Formal commands are used whenever you are giving commands to people you would usually address using **usted** or **ustedes.**

To form regular **usted** and **ustedes** commands of -ar verbs, start with the present tense **yo** form of the verb, drop the **-o** ending, and add **-er** endings: **-e** for **usted** commands and **-en** for **ustedes** commands. For example:

llamar → yo llamo → llame / llamen

To form regular **usted** and **ustedes** commands of **-er** and **-ir** verbs, start with the present tense **yo** form of the verb, drop the **-o** ending, and add **-ar** endings: **-a** for **usted** commands and **-an** for **ustedes** commands. For example:

poner → yo pongo → ponga / pongan

escribir → yo escribo → escriba / escriban

Negative informal commands are used whenever you are giving commands to people you would usually address using **tú.** They are formed much like formal commands. Start with the present tense **yo** form of the verb, drop the **-o** ending, and add **-es** for **-ar** verbs and **-as** for **-er** and **-ir** verbs. For example:

hablar → yo hablo → no hables

leer → yo leo → no leas

decir → yo digo → no digas

Síntesis: Gramática

Formal commands and negative informal commands of verbs that have infinitives ending in **-car, -gar,** and **-zar** have spelling changes.

For verbs ending in **-car,** change the **c** to **qu** and add the appropriate ending.

tocar ⟶ yo to**c**o ⟶ to**qu**e / to**qu**en / no to**qu**es

For verbs ending in **-gar,** change the **g** to **gu** and add the appropriate ending.

jugar ⟶ yo jue**g**o ⟶ jue**gu**e / jue**gu**en / no jue**gu**es

For verbs ending in **-zar,** change the **z** to **c** and add the appropriate ending.

empezar ⟶ yo empie**z**o ⟶ empie**c**e / empie**c**en / no empie**c**es

Common irregular verbs like **dar, estar, ser,** and **ir** also have irregular **usted / ustedes** commands and irregular negative **tú** commands.

dar ⟶ dé / den / no des

estar ⟶ esté / estén / no estés

ir ⟶ vaya / vayan / no vayas

ser ⟶ sea / sean / no seas

De viaje

Objectives: In this chapter you will learn to

- Express travel preferences and talk about transportation
- Talk about travel experiences by describing a past sequence of events
- Discuss the weather and seasons

- Use adverbs and demonstrative adjectives
- Talk about what you know and are familiar with
- Use regular verbs in the preterite and verbs like **gustar**

Vocabulario/Gramática

C6-1 Un hotel excelente

Step 1 You and your partner are talking about past hotel experiences. Working together, come up with five questions to ask each other about your most memorable hotel experiences. Below is a list of words and expressions you can use to form questions about the hotels.

nombre	precio	cuántas noches	camas
lugar	compañeros de viaje	comida	habitación

Modelos *¿Cómo se llama el hotel?* *¿Dónde está?* *¿Cuánto costó?*

Step 2 Now ask each other the questions and note the answers. Identify common points and differences between your experiences. Be prepared to share with the rest of the class.

C6-2 Los hoteles Imagine that you are part of a tourism committee that has been assigned to research preferences for a new hotel being built in your community. As part of the committee, you will conduct surveys, analyze the information, and then present the results.

Step 1 What do you look for in a hotel? In groups of three, develop and write down the questions you'll need to ask to get the information for the survey below. You will ask questions on the importance of the following areas: El precio, la piscina, tener restaurante, el transporte al aeropuerto, la calidad de la cama, la calidad del baño, aire acondicionado, las personas que trabajan en el hotel, la ubicación del hotel.

Modelo *¿Es importante tener aire acondicionado?*

Step 2 Now, using the interview questions from step 1 and the 4 final questions from the survey, interview two or three other classmates each, for a total of six to nine unique responses (in other words, each of you must interview different students). For each interview, one of you should be the potential traveler and answer the questions asked by your partner, who is conducting the survey on behalf of the tourism committee. Write down the answers for use in the next step.

Vocabulario/Gramática

Modelo el aire acondicionado
Student A: *¿Es importante tener aire acondicionado?*
Student B: *Para mí el aire acondicionado es más o menos importante. Un tres.*

Encuesta de hoteles

¿Qué cosas buscas en un hotel? Indica tus preferencias usando una escala de uno a cinco. Cinco indica que es muy importante para ti y uno no es importante.

	no es importante 1	2	3	4	es muy importante 5
el precio	☐	☐	☐	☐	☐
la piscina	☐	☐	☐	☐	☐
tener un restaurante	☐	☐	☐	☐	☐
el transporte al aeropuerto	☐	☐	☐	☐	☐
la calidad de la cama	☐	☐	☐	☐	☐
la calidad del baño	☐	☐	☐	☐	☐
el aire acondicionado	☐	☐	☐	☐	☐
las personas que trabajan en el hotel	☐	☐	☐	☐	☐
la ubicación (*location*) del hotel	☐	☐	☐	☐	☐

1. ¿De esta lista qué cosa te importa más? ¿Por qué?
2. ¿Normalmente con quién viajas?
3. ¿Cuántas veces por año duermes en un hotel?
4. ¿Generalmente cuánto dinero pagas por noche en un hotel?

Vocabulario/Gramática

Step 3 With your original group, discuss the results of the survey. Identify the most important features of a hotel and which amenities are less important. For your presentation you will need to be able to answer the following questions.

1. ¿Cuáles son las tres cosas más importantes según *(according to)* la encuesta? ¿Por qué son importantes?

2. ¿Cuál es la cosa menos importante? ¿En su opinión por qué es menos importante?

3. ¿Cuál sería el precio aceptable por una noche en un hotel? ¿Cuál sería el precio más alto aceptable?

Step 4 Now each committee will share their ideas and observations based on the survey results and the committee's discussion.

Step 5 Based on all the information from the presentations, your committee needs to determine the two most important features of a hotel, the best nightly rate, and a name for the new hotel.

Modelo *Nos parece muy importante tener piscina.*
Nos parece que _____ dólares es un precio aceptable.
Nos parece que el nombre del hotel debe ser _____.

Gramática

Encuesta: Me/le/les/nos gusta

Step 1 Using the chart below, make a list of things and activities in the first column, and then use a verb to describe your feelings about each one in the second column.

Step 2 Find two classmates and ask them questions to find out how they feel about the same things. Write down your classmates' names and responses in columns 3 and 4.

Cosa(s) y actividades	A mí	A _____	A _____
Modelo *comida mexicana*	**Modelo** *A mí me gusta(n)…*	**Modelo** *A Joel le gusta(n)…*	**Modelo** *A Jessica le molesta(n)…*
la música clásica			
viajar			

Gramática

Step 3 Based on the information you collected from the in-class survey, write sentences summarizing the results and share them with the class.

Modelos *A mí me aburre la música clásica, pero a John le gusta...*

A mí me gusta viajar, pero a John y a Amy les molesta...

A Paul y a mí nos interesan los...

C6-4 ¿Qué prefiere la clase?

Step 1 In groups of three, discuss things that bother you, are important to you, and interest you. In addition to the following topics, you can think of your own topics: **el viaje, la escuela, el tiempo, la comida, la música, los pasatiempos y las personas famosas.**

Modelo *A mí me interesan los coches. Me molesta el aeropuerto. Me importa mi familia.*

Step 2 With a new partner, write two true statements and one false statement about each of you.

Modelo *A mí me interesan los coches. A mí me molesta el aeropuerto. A mí me importa mi familia.*

In groups of three, discuss things that bother you, are important to you, and interest you. In addition to the following topics, you can think of your own topics: **el viaje, la escuela, el tiempo, la comida, la música, los pasatiempos y las personas famosas.**

Step 3 Now interview two different classmates and exchange the statements you created in step 2. Have each person guess your false statement, and you guess theirs. Write down their true information.

Modelo *A nosotros nos importa estudiar. Nos molestan los aviones. Nos interesa el fútbol.*

Step 4 Write comparison statements about yourself and the two classmates you interviewed and report to the class on your false statement. Was anyone able to guess it?

Modelo *A nosotros nos importa la clase de español. Nos molestan los aviones. Nos interesa el fútbol americano.*

Vocabulario

En el aeropuerto

Step 1 Imagine that you and a classmate are waiting for a flight and need a wifi connection. Your classmate's mobile device needs to be charged, so you have only one device with Internet capabilities. To connect, you must complete a short survey, with a chance to win a free flight to anywhere in the United States after completing the survey. Work together to answer the questions.

¿Cuál fue el destino de tu último viaje? _____

¿Cuál es tu línea aérea favorita? _____

¿Prefieres un boleto electrónico o físico? _____

¿Prefieres un asiento de ventanilla o de pasillo? _____

¿Qué servicios son más importantes para ti? (Elige dos.)

restaurantes	○	centro de información	○
espacios tranquilos	○	conexión de Internet	○
tiendas	○		

¿Normalmente qué haces cuando estás esperando un vuelo?

_____

_____

Step 2 You have successfully connected to the Internet. As promised, at the end of the survey you have the chance to win a free flight to anywhere in the United States. However, there is one additional step. You need to describe your experience at the airport and provide details about what the airport is like. The best descriptions will be used to create promotional videos on social media. Work with your partner to write up a description of at least six sentences.

Step 3 Now that you have an idea of what you will say and show about the airport and your experience there, you need to share your ideas with the whole class.

Vocabulario

C6-6 Agencia de viajes

Step 1 Planning a trip can be a fun but sometimes stressful experience. Many people seek the help of a travel agency. With a partner, imagine you are a team of travel agents with two clients who want to visit Latin America. What information do they need to know? What questions can you ask to discover this information? Work together to write questions to get specific information about your clients' expectations and situation.

Step 2 With a new partner, take turns playing the roles of travel agent and client. Take careful notes of what your client says in order to take his/her expectations back to your original partner.

Step 3 With your original partner, compare the expectations of the two people you worked with. Would they travel well together? Why or why not?

C6-7 Equipaje perdido

Step 1 With a partner, look at the two photos and answer the following questions for each image. Come up with answers together based on what you see.

1. ¿De quién es?
2. ¿Adónde fue?
3. ¿Qué hizo?

Step 2 With your partner, make a list of what you needed to pack for your respective vacations to your favorite destinations.

Step 3 Now go around the class and read your packing list. Have your classmates guess your destination.

Gramática

C6-8

Un viaje favorito Imagine you are working as an intern for a travel agency. Your supervisor has given you and the other interns the job of creating a survey. She wants to get a good idea of where students have traveled, what they like to do on trips, and anything else you think would be useful information. She wants the survey to focus on the interviewee's most recent or favorite trip.

Step 1 To start the creative process, get into groups of three (other interns) and talk about your own favorite trips. Discuss the following key points: **dónde, cuándo, con quién, qué actividades, qué comida.**

Work together to write statements describing the key information.

Step 2 In the same group, create six questions about past vacations. Use the preterite tense in your questions. Use the **tú** form and make the questions meaningful. Everyone needs to have a written copy of the questions for the next step.

Step 3 Now it is time to ask the questions. Find a new partner and ask your questions and answer his/her questions. Write down the responses. Once you finish with one person, find a new partner. Gather as much information as you can in the time allowed.

Step 4 Return to your original group. Discuss and compare the results question by question. Make note of the information you think will be the most useful and important to your supervisor.

Step 5 There is a meeting coming up and you all have been asked to share your ideas from the interviews. Prepare three statements about students and their past travel. You will then be asked to share these statements in the meeting.

Gramática

C6-9 De viaje

Step 1 With a classmate, ask and answer the following questions that are part of a survey. Make sure you write down your partner's name and answers.

1. ¿Dónde te gusta pasar tus vacaciones? ¿Por qué te gusta ese destino?

2. ¿Prefieres destinos donde hace calor o frío? ¿Por qué? ¿Cuando viajas en avión te importa tener un asiento de ventanilla?

3. ¿Compras tus billetes en una agencia de viajes o por Internet?

4. Normalmente, ¿viajas con mucho equipaje?

5. ¿Te gusta usar guías turísticas o prefieres improvisar *(improvise)* tus viajes?

Step 2 Working individually, write a paragraph including some of the things you learned about your classmate. Include information about yourself as well. Your paragraph should be between six and twelve sentences.

Vocabulario/Gramática

C6-10 El tiempo

Step 1 Compare what your partner likes and dislikes doing in a variety of weather conditions with your own likes and dislikes. Some weather conditions you can talk about are: **sol, frío, nieve, lluvia, viento, calor, buen tiempo, mal tiempo, fresco, nublado.**

Modelo   Student A: *¿Qué te gusta hacer cuando hace calor?*
          Student B: *Cuando hace calor me gusta jugar en la piscina.*
          Student A: *A mí no me gusta la piscina. Me gusta jugar en el parque cuando hace calor.*

Step 2 You and your classmate(s) are planning a fun weekend to one of three cities. Which activities are you most likely to do in each location based on the weather?

	Día	Máx. / Mín.	Descripción	Precipitación	Viento
Nueva York	viernes	62° / 50°	mayormente nublado	70%	poco
	sábado	64° / 57°	parcialmente nublado	10% solo por la mañana	por la mañana
	domingo	67° / 56°	mayormente soleado	0%	nada

	Día	Máx. / Mín.	Descripción	Precipitación	Viento
Los Ángeles	viernes	87° / 56°	soleado	0%	nada
	sábado	84° / 55°	soleado	0%	nada
	domingo	82° / 68°	parcialmente nublado	5% solo por la mañana	por la mañana

	Día	Máx. / Mín.	Descripción	Precipitación	Viento
Chicago	viernes	52° / 36°	parcialmente nublado	0%	nada
	sábado	44° / 32°	mayormente nublado / viento	15%	mucho
	domingo	41° / 29°	parcialmente nublado / viento	10%	mucho

Step 3 Make a more detailed itinerary for one city. You will arrive early on Friday afternoon and stay until Sunday evening. Say what you are going to do each day.

Step 4 It is the day before your trip and the weather forecast has changed. You need a Plan B. Look at the new weather conditions and come up with a new plan for the weekend.

Nueva York

Día	Máx. / Mín.	Descripción	Precipitación	Viento
viernes	65° / 52°	parcialmente nublado	0%	por la mañana
sábado	69° / 59°	soleado	0%	nada
domingo	70° / 56°	mayormente soleado	0%	nada

Los Ángeles

Día	Máx. / Mín.	Descripción	Precipitación	Viento
viernes	88° / 54°	soleado	10% por la noche	poco por la noche
sábado	79° / 53°	mayormente nublado	25%	poco
domingo	80° / 54°	parcialmente soleado	0%	nada

Chicago

Día	Máx. / Mín.	Descripción	Precipitación	Viento
viernes	63° / 38°	mayormente nublado / viento	0%	nada
sábado	37° / 31°	mayormente nublado / viento	75%	mucho
domingo	33° / 18°	parcialmente nublado / viento	80%	mucho

Gramática

C6-11

Conversaciones Have a conversation with a partner using the following structure as a model. Before you begin the conversation, think about the demonstrative adjectives you will need to indicate what you are talking about. After you have gone through the conversation once, switch roles with your partner and have the conversation again.

Modelo Student A: *¿Cuánto cuestan **estas** manzanas?*
Student B: *Son 25 pesos el kilo.*

Student A	Student B
1. Greet Student B, a stall keeper at an outdoor market.	2. Respond to Student A's greeting and ask what he or she wants to buy.
3. Respond to Student B's question by asking how much those oranges are.	4. Respond to Student A by saying that those oranges are fifty pesos each **(cada una)**.
5. Ask Student B how much those grapes over there are.	6. Tell Student A that those grapes over there are thirty pesos per kilo.
7. Tell Student B that you also want to know how much these carrots are.	8. Tell Student A that the carrots are forty-five pesos per kilo.
9. Tell Student B that you will buy those pears there.	10. Tell Student A how much they are.

Gramática

C6-12 ¿De quién es?

Step 1 Your instructor has found several items left behind in the classroom. He/she doesn't know which items belong to whom, but has organized the items in three groups; **aquí**, **allí**, and **allá**. Create groups of three and everyone in your group should identify the item(s) that belong to them. See how many items your group can identify that belong to someone outside the group. Use the appropriate demonstrative adjectives based on the locations of the items.

Modelos   *Este libro es mi libro.*
Aquella mochila es mi mochila.
Estos zapatos son mis zapatos.
¿Saben de quién es aquella botella de agua?
¿Saben de quién son estas cámaras?

Step 2 Now that you have identified as many of the items as you can with the help of your group, you will need help to figure out the rest of the items. Leave your group and find a new partner. Discover all the items he/she knows and tell all the ones you know. Use the correct demonstrative adjectives based on the spatial relationships between you and the objects.

Modelos   *¿Sabes de quién es este libro?*
Sí, este libro es de Jane.
¿Sabes de quién son esos zapatos?
Sí, esos zapatos son de Julio.

Gramática

C6-13 ¿Cómo va a hacerlo?

Step 1 In groups of three, take turns using adverbs to describe an animal from the list. You do not need to write them down, but you should keep a tally of how many adverbs your group came up with.

gato	gallina *(hen)*	elefante	león	tigre	tortuga	perro

Modelo *Un gato camina rápidamente y duerme tranquilamente.*

Step 2 With your group, look at the following activities. Think of some famous people and choose an activity or two. Discuss how they would complete the activities. Be sure to use adverbs to describe how the action would be completed.

caminar	dormir	cantar una canción	hablar español	estudiar español
jugar	comer un taco	correr	leer libros	conducir un coche

Modelos *Adele canta suavemente. Ella lee libros rápidamente.*
LeBron James juega bien. Él no come tacos despacio.

Step 3 Now find a different classmate and read your sentences to each other. Remember not to give the names of the famous people since your partner will try to guess to whom each sentence refers!

Modelo *Esta persona canta suavemente. ¿Es Adele o es James Brown?*

C6-14 Un viaje

Step 1 You and a classmate are speaking about past trips or vacations. Compare your favorite or most recent trips with your partner's. Topics you may want to compare and discuss: **destinos, hoteles, actividades, transporte, personas, comida, fechas, el tiempo.**

Step 2 With a new partner, relate all that you remember about your previous partner's vacation or trip. You can include information and comparisons about yourself and your favorite or most recent trip.

C6-15 Tres amigos Carmen, Concha, and Pablo are good friends and plan to take a trip together. They are chatting via text message to discuss what they want to do. They need help to confirm their plans and decide what they are going to do.

Step 1 Your instructor will assign you one of the three friends. Find a classmate who has been assigned the same person. Read all the messages from your person. Get a clear idea of what he or she wants from this trip. Then, complete the chart by listing all the key points (*puntos clave*).

Nombre:	Comida	Hoteles	Actividades	Transporte	Fechas
Puntos clave					

Student A: Mensajes de Carmen

No me importa compartir una habitación y una cama en el hotel. Somos amigos desde hace mucho tiempo. :)

Cuando vamos a la playa podemos llevar comida y hacer un picnic tranquilo.

Prefiero pagar menos dinero por el hotel y tener más dinero para ir de compras.

Me interesa el museo de arte y el museo de historia. Quiero verlos con calma.

Quiero ir a la playa para tomar el sol, leer mi libro y estar tranquila.

No es necesario tener un coche en la ciudad. Podemos caminar durante el día y tomar un taxi por la noche. :)

Yo trabajo de lunes a jueves, pero tengo la posibilidad de no trabajar un jueves y un lunes. Un fin de semana es una opción buena para mí.

Vocabulario/Gramática

Student B: Mensajes de Concha

La playa es muy bonita y debemos pasar todo el día ahí al sol.

Yo quiero un hotel buenísimo con piscina y todo. De verdad no tengo ganas de compartir una cama y yo creo que debemos tener habitaciones separadas, si es posible.

Yo quiero ir a muchas tiendas y comprar muchas cosas. $$:)

Hay un palacio grande y elegante que está afuera de la ciudad. Tenemos que alquilar un coche para ir a verlo.

Mi prima tiene su cumpleaños el martes pero los otros días puedo viajar.

No quiero hacer un picnic. Yo prefiero comer en un restaurante elegante o en un café al lado de la playa.

Yo también quiero ir a los museos, especialmente al museo de arte.

Student C: Mensajes de Pablo

Debemos salir por la noche y bailar mucho. :)

Yo no quiero pagar mucho dinero por el hotel.

Los museos son muy interesantes y también quiero ver la catedral.

Me encantan los picnics, los restaurantes, los cafés y los bares. Me gusta comer. :)

Solo tengo cinco días de vacaciones pero yo puedo elegir los días. Prefiero ir un fin de semana porque sábado y domingo no cuentan como días de vacaciones.

Podemos ir a la playa pero no quiero estar tranquilo ahí. Yo quiero nadar, jugar al volibol y explorar la costa. :)

Hay bicicletas en la ciudad que podemos usar. Solo tienes que pagar un poco de dinero y puedes usar una todo el día. Va a ser divertido.

Step 2 Form groups of three, one student representing each person: Carmen, Concha, and Pablo. Each of you should give an overview of your assigned person based on the information you know.

Step 3 After everyone has shared an overview of his/her person, discuss the following topics and work together to decide what the friends are going to do together on their trip. Are there things they are going to do separately?

1. ¿Cuántas habitaciones van a necesitar? ¿cuántas camas?
2. ¿Qué van a comer? ¿Dónde van a comer?
3. ¿Qué actividades deben hacer juntos? ¿Qué actividades deben hacer solos?
4. ¿Qué días pueden realizar el viaje juntos?
5. Describan a los amigos. ¿Cómo es Carmen? ¿Cómo es Concha? ¿Cómo es Pablo?

Step 4 Share your ideas, perceptions, and suggestions about the friends and their trip with the rest of the class. Do you agree with what the other students are saying?

Lectura

C6-16 ## Antes de leer

Step 1 Working with a partner, make a list of adventures you have had or would like to have in the future. Some examples might include speaking at the UN, eating ants in Colombia, climbing the Aconcagua, watching a game, or running a marathon in another part of the world.

Step 2 Include additional information, such as where and when these adventures happened or would happen, whether you embark on them alone or with friends or family, and whether it's a personal challenge or a family tradition, or even something you saw in a movie that made a lasting impression.

Step 3 Share your adventures with the class and group each one according to its type (sports, hobbies, challenges, leisure). Did you find some overlap within the class?

C6-17 ## Los altibajos *(Ups and downs)*

Step 1 With your partner, make a list of five things that can go wrong during a trip despite careful planning. For example: no AC in a tropical location, rude waiters, ridiculously expensive tours, or no good coffee shop in a city.

Step 2 Now, work together to make another list of the five best things that have happened to you while traveling. Perhaps it was an unexpected detour that lead to a magical place, a celebrity sighting, or being upgraded to first class on your flight.

12 signos de que eres adicto a los viajes

María Eugenia Mayobre

Ayer fue publicado un divertido artículo titulado "24 signos de que eres completamente adicto a viajar" *(24 Signs You Are Completely Addicted To Travel)*. El artículo ofrece una lista de veinticuatro síntomas, y creo que los tengo casi todos. Aquí traduzco doce de esos síntomas para que puedas detectar si sufres del mismo mal que yo. Te advierto, no hay tratamiento ni vacuna *(vaccine)* contra este vicio. ¡Afortunadamente!

1. Te pasas el día soñando con tu próximo viaje.

2. Te emocionan los viajes más que prácticamente cualquier otra cosa.

3. Pasas horas y horas curioseando blogs y websites de viajes.

4. Te estresas cuando pasa mucho tiempo entre un viaje y otro.

5. No te imaginas viviendo en la misma ciudad toda tu vida.

6. Puedes vivir solo con una maleta. De hecho, lo prefieres.

7. Precisamente por eso, eres experto empacando.

Lectura

8. Puedes dormir prácticamente en cualquier lugar.

9. Nada te da tanta felicidad como embarcarte en una nueva aventura.

10. Piensas en tu próximo viaje incluso cuando estás viajando.

11. Ves cada parte de la vida como una posible aventura.

12. En el fondo, sabes que nunca te liberarás *(will never be free)* de esta adicción a explorar… y no te importa.

Si además de esto siempre tienes un mapa al alcance de la mano, tienes una lista inmensa de lugares que quieres visitar y posees pocas pertenencias porque cada vez que tienes unos ahorritos te los gastas en viajar (yo digo que "invierto en recuerdos" si alguien me pregunta por qué no tengo casa propia ni objetos de valor), entonces tu diagnóstico está más que claro. ¡Bien por ti!

Source: www.encuentroslejanos.com/post/93442090622

C6-18 ¿Eres adicto a los viajes?

Step 1 With a new partner, review and discuss the signs of travel addiction from the reading. Decide whether each one applies to you, and if it does, how?

Step 2 Based on your findings, rate each other's level of addiction to travel and write up five statements tailored to your partner's preferences, based on the reading above. For example, if one of you does not like to travel much, you might write: **Es importante viajar por lo menos una vez al año.**

Step 3 Share your statements with the class and find out what your classmates' average level of travel "addiction" is.

Museos, arte y la gran ciudad

El fin de semana pasado fui a Madrid con mi amiga Paula. Paula tiene algunos amigos que viven cerca de la estación de Atocha. Ella se quedó con (*stayed with*) sus amigos y yo me quedé en un hotel barato. Hicimos muchas cosas juntos. Llegamos el viernes temprano. Después de pasar por el hotel, fuimos al museo más importante de España, El Prado. A mí me encanta el arte y me fascinan los artistas españoles clásicos, como Goya y Velázquez. A Paula le gusta más el arte moderno. Entonces después de la visita al Prado, ella fue a visitar el museo Reina Sofía que tiene arte de los siglos XX y XXI. Las pinturas de Dalí y Picasso son las favoritas de Paula. Por la noche cenamos con los amigos de ella. Comimos mucha comida rica. A mí me gustó la tortilla de patatas y el jamón ibérico.

Hoy fuimos al Palacio Real, la Gran Vía, la Puerta del Sol y la Plaza Mayor. En el palacio, el guía nos contó sobre la historia de la familia real. La Gran Vía es la calle principal de Madrid. Es grande y tiene muchos edificios hermosos. En la Gran Vía hicimos compras. Yo compré muchas cosas ☺ pero Paula no compró casi nada. En la Puerta del Sol compramos unos helados y miramos a las personas en la plaza. Fuimos a la Plaza Mayor por la noche. Me gustó ver a los *Street Performers*. Son muy divertidos e interesantes. Después de comer tapas, Paula y sus amigos me acompañaron a mi hotel. Luego ellos tomaron el metro a casa.

Estoy cansada porque caminamos muchísimo hoy, pero me gusta España y fue divertido pasar tiempo en Madrid. Es una ciudad grande y hermosa. Creo que voy a tener que regresar para explorar más.

Mi viaje As a class, discuss the Spanish-speaking cities you wrote about in your own blog entries, including what you can see and do there. Have students describe the photos they posted and talk about activities that can be done in that city. If your class were given the opportunity to take a field trip together, which destination would you agree on?

Síntesis: Vocabulario

En el hotel   *At the hotel*

el aire acondicionado   *air conditioning*

el albergue   *hostel, inn*

el ascensor   *elevator*

la habitación   *room*

la habitación doble   *double room*

la habitación de fumadores / de no fumadores   *smoking / non-smoking room*

el hostal   *hostel*

el hotel de cinco estrellas   *five-star hotel*

el/la huésped   *guest*

la piscina   *swimming pool*

la recepción   *reception desk*

la reservación   *reservation*

la sala de entrada   *vestíbulo*

Verbs like *gustar*

aburrir   *to bore*

caer bien (mal)   *(not) to like someone*

encantar   *to love (something)*

faltar   *to lack (something)*

fascinar   *to fascinate*

importar   *to be important*

interesar   *to be interesting*

molestar   *to bother*

parecer   *to appear. seem to be*

En el aeropuerto   *At the airport*

desembarcar   *to get off the plane*

embarcar   *to board*

hacer un tour   *to take a tour*

viajar   *to travel*

la aduana   *customs*

el aeropuerto   *airport*

el asiento de pasillo   *aisle seat*

el asiento de ventanilla   *window seat*

el avión   *airplane*

el boleto, billete   *ticket*

el centro de información   *information center*

clase turista   *coach*

el destino   *destination*

el equipaje   *luggage*

la escala   *layover*

la línea aérea   *airline*

la maleta   *suitcase*

el mapa   *map*

el pasaporte   *passport*

la playa   *beach*

primera clase   *first class*

la puerta de embarque   *departure gate*

la salida   *departure*

el sello / la estampilla   *stamp*

el sitio   *site*

la tarjeta postal   *postcard*

el turista   *tourist*

las vacaciones   *vacation*

un viaje   *a trip*

el vuelo   *flight*

Adjetivos demostrativos
Demonstrative adjectives

aquel / aquellos / aquella / aquellas

ese / esos / esa / esas

este / estos / esta / estas

¿Qué tiempo hace?
What's the weather?

Está lloviendo.   *It's raining.*

Está nevando.   *It's snowing.*

Está nublado.   *It's cloudy.*

Hace buen tiempo.   *It's nice (good) weather.*

Hace calor.   *It's hot.*

Hace fresco.   *It's cool.*

Hace frío.   *It's cold.*

Hace mal tiempo.   *It's bad weather.*

Hace sol.   *It's sunny.*

Hace viento.   *It's windy.*

llover (ue)   *to rain*

nevar (ie)   *to snow*

Síntesis: Vocabulario

grados centígrados
degrees Celsius

grados Fahrenheit   *degrees Fahrenheit*

el invierno   *winter*

el otoño   *fall, autumn*

la primavera   *spring*

el verano   *summer*

conocer (a)   *to know*

saber   *to know (something)*

Adverbios   *Adverbs*

abajo   *below*

ahí   *there*

allá   *over there*

allí   *there*

aquí   *here*

arriba   *above*

cerca   *near*

lejos   *far*

así   *thus, like this*

bien   *well*

despacio   *slowly*

difícilmente   *difficultly*

fácilmente   *easily*

horriblemente   *horribly*

lentamente   *slowly*

mal   *poorly*

perfectamente   *perfectly*

rápidamente   *quickly*

rápido   *quick, quickly*

solamente   *only*

solo   *alone*

ahora   *now*

antes   *before*

ayer   *yesterday*

después   *after*

hoy   *today*

mañana   *tomorrow*

primero   *first*

siempre   *always*

tarde   *late*

temprano   *early*

más   *more*

menos   *less*

mucho   *a lot, much*

poco   *a little*

Síntesis: Gramática

Verbs like *gustar*

There are a number of verbs in Spanish that follow the same structure as the verb **gustar.** When you use a verb like **gustar** with one or more verbs in the infinitive, use the **él, ella, usted** form of the verb. For example:

> **Me aburre** tomar el sol: prefiero nadar.
> *Sunbathing bores me: I prefer to swim.*

> **Me molesta** viajar en avión.
> *Traveling by plane bothers me.*

To use a verb like **gustar** with a **singular** noun, use the **él, ella, usted** form of the verb. For example:

> **Me encanta** esta habitación.
> *I love this room.*

> **Me parece** bien este hotel.
> *This hotel seems fine to me.*

To use verbs like **gustar** with a **plural** noun, use the **ellos, ellas, ustedes** form of the verb. For example:

> **Me fascinan** las piscinas grandes.
> *Big swimming pools fascinate me.*

> **Me faltan** las llaves de las habitaciones.
> *I'm missing the keys to the rooms.*

Verbs that are similar to **gustar** are used with indirect object pronouns to indicate to whom or for whom something is done. For example:

> **me** aburre
> *it bores me*

> **te** aburre
> *it bores you*

> **le** aburre
> *it bores him, her, or you*

> **nos** aburre
> *it bores us*

> **os** aburre
> *it bores you*

> **les** aburre
> *it bores them or you*

To clarify **le** and **les,** use the preposition **a** plus a noun, name of a person, or subject pronoun.

> **A Ana** le aburre.
> *It bores Ana. (It is boring to Ana).*

You can also use the preposition **a** plus a noun or pronoun for emphasis.

> **A nosotros** nos aburre.
> *It bores us. (It is boring to us).*

Síntesis: Gramática

Use **a mí** to emphasize **me** and **a ti** to emphasize **te.**

> **A ti** te aburre pero **a mí** no me aburre.
> *You are bored but I am not bored. (It is boring to you, but it is not boring to me).*

The preterite tense of regular verbs

To conjugate regular verbs in the preterite tense, start with the infinitive, drop the **-ar, -er,** or **-ir,** and add the appropriate ending to the stem of the verb.

trabajar *to work*

yo **trabajé**	nosotros(as) trabaj**amos**
tú trabaj**aste**	vosotros(as) trabaj**asteis**
él / ella / usted trabaj**ó**	ellos / ellas / ustedes trabaj**aron**

> Anoche **trabajé** en el restaurante.
> *Last night I worked in the restaurant.*

Regular **-er** and **-ir** verbs in the preterite have identical endings:

comer *to eat*

yo com**í**	nosotros(as) com**imos**
tú com**iste**	vosotros(as) com**isteis**
él / ella / usted com**ió**	ellos / ellas / ustedes com**ieron**

> Ayer **comieron** enchiladas de queso.
> *Yesterday they ate cheese enchiladas.*

vivir *to live*

yo viv**í**	nosotros(as) viv**imos**
tú viv**iste**	vosotros(as) viv**isteis**
él / ella / usted viv**ió**	ellos / ellas / ustedes viv**ieron**

> El año pasado **vivieron** en Puerto Rico.
> *Last year they lived in Puerto Rico.*

¡OJO! Notice that the **yo** and **él, ella, usted** forms of **-ar, -er,** and **-ir** verbs in the preterite have accent marks.

Demonstratives

Demonstrative adjectives and demonstrative pronouns are used to point out the locations of people or things in relation to the speaker.

Just like all adjectives in Spanish, demonstrative adjectives agree in number and gender with the nouns they modify. To indicate that someone or something is close to you, use these demonstrative adjectives:

	Singular	Plural
Masculine	**este** *this*	**estos** *these*
Feminine	**esta** *this*	**estas** *these*

> **Esta** chica es mi amiga, Yolanda.
> *This girl is my friend, Yolanda.*

Síntesis: Gramática

¡**OJO!** Demonstrative adjectives always come before the nouns they modify.

To indicate that someone or something is a little farther away from you, use these demonstrative adjectives:

	Singular	Plural
Masculine	**ese** *that*	**esos** *those*
Feminine	**esa** *that*	**esas** *those*

Esos libros son de mi hermana.
Those books are my sister's.

To indicate that someone or something is at a distance from you, use these demonstrative adjectives:

	Singular	Plural
Masculine	**aquel** *that (over there)*	**aquellos** *those (over there)*
Feminine	**aquella** *that (over there)*	**aquellas** *those (over there)*

Aquel hombre es el profesor de historia y **aquella** mujer es su esposa.
That man over there is the history professor and that woman over there is his wife.

Demonstrative adjectives can be used as pronouns. Like other pronouns, a demonstrative pronoun takes the place of a noun. And like demonstrative adjectives, demonstrative pronouns indicate the locations of people or things in relation to the speaker. For example:

No me gusta ese libro. Voy a leer **este.**
I don't like that book. I'm going to read this one.

No voy a comprar esos dulces; prefiero **aquellos.**
I'm not going to by those sweets; I prefer those over there.

¡**OJO!** Just like all pronouns in Spanish, demonstrative pronouns agree in number and gender with the nouns they replace.

Saber and conocer

The verbs **saber** and **conocer** both mean *to know* in English. In the present tense, both verbs have irregular **yo** forms, but follow a regular **-er** pattern in all other forms.

saber *to know*	
yo **sé**	nosotros(as) sab**emos**
tú sab**es**	vosotros(as) sab**éis**
él / ella / usted sab**e**	ellos / ellas / ustedes sab**en**

conocer *to know*	
yo **conozco**	nosotros(as) conoc**emos**
tú conoc**es**	vosotros(as) conoc**éis**
él / ella / usted conoc**e**	ellos / ellas / ustedes conoc**en**

Síntesis: Gramática

The verb **saber** is used to talk about:

- knowing facts or information.

  Sé que Quito es la capital de Ecuador.
  I know that Quito is the capital of Ecuador.

- knowing *how to do* something; having a skill.

  Juan **sabe** tocar el piano.
  Juan knows how to play the piano.

Notice that **saber** is followed by an infinitive when you want to express that someone knows how to do something.

The verb **conocer** is used to talk about:

- knowing a person.

  ¿**Conoces** a mi primo Alberto?
  Do you know my cousin Alberto?

- knowing or being familiar with a place.

  Conozco Roma. Voy todos los veranos.
  I know (I am familiar with) Rome. I go every summer.

Conocer is also used in the preterite to express that you met someone for the first time.

Ayer **conocí** a tu hermana en una fiesta.
I met your sister at a party yesterday.

¡**OJO!** Whenever you are saying that you know a *person,* use **conocer** followed by the preposition **a.** This is often referred to as the *personal **a**.*

Capítulos 5 y 6

Imagine that you work in tourism for a Spanish-speaking city and you will be participating in the annual **Feria de turismo.** You'll be asked to complete tasks in this role, such as conducting a survey to gather tourist information, preparing a proposal, and giving a presentation about your city. You'll use the grammar and vocabulary you've learned in Chapters 5 and 6 to do this.

Project Components

Activity	Points
UP3-1 Encuesta	20 points (10 individual / 10 group)
UP3-2 Propuesta	5 points (group)
UP3-3 Presentación	30 points (20 individual / 10 group)
UP3-4 Blog	20 points (group)
UP3-5 Análisis	25 points (individual)

UP3-1 Encuesta

Step 1 Since you are a tourism specialist, your employer has asked you to create a survey to find out what the general public looks for when deciding on a travel destination. Think of five relevant questions for your survey. Questions may cover accommodation, restaurants, modes of transportation available, activities and excursions, historic sites, museums, and other interesting tourist spots. These questions should be general and not specific to your project city.

Step 2 Get into a group of three and share your questions with each other. As a group, agree on the five most important questions to include in the survey. Each of you should write out all five questions for use in later steps. Proof them together and ask your instructor to check them as well.

Step 3 Now find a partner from another group, ask each other your survey questions, and record the answers. Interview at least three people.

Step 4 After recording all the results, return to your original group and compare and discuss the results in Spanish. Use **gustar** and similar verbs to make statements: **Cuatro estudiantes prefieren…**

UP3-2

Propuesta Now that you've completed your market survey, your group must agree on a city to promote and create a proposal in English for your presentation. Include the following information.

1. Name of the Spanish-speaking city you would like to present on and why your group chose this city; list two other Spanish-speaking cities as backup options

2. Three important topics from the survey that you would like to focus on as a group; these three topics should be featured in your presentation

3. List of what each person will research, who will write about each topic, and who will present what

4. Schedule for one or two group discussions; set dates, time, and places

Assign one person in your group to email the proposal to your instructor and all the members of the group.

Proyecto 3: Feria de turismo

UP3-3

Presentación The day of the **Feria de turismo** is coming up! Your group needs to present your city as an attractive tourist destination to the tourism committee. Here are some guidelines to remember when planning your presentation.

1. Each group member should present for an equal period of time.

2. No presentation should exceed 5–7 minutes. Rehearse the complete presentation before coming to class and make sure it does not go over seven minutes.

3. In addition to the blog post you will create in UP3-4, each group should include six photographs that highlight aspects of the city you are presenting on. These six images may be shared as part of a PowerPoint or other visual presentation.

4. Note cards with basic information may be used, but do not read entire sentences from them; you want to engage your audience. See below for sample topics and descriptions in Spanish.

5. Use **usted** commands to highlight must-see attractions: **Visite las ruinas de Tikal.**

6. Remember that you are trying to sell the city you are presenting. Be persuasive and creative and keep your audience interested and awake!

Sample topics

- Una descripción de la ciudad: *Hay una oficina turística en el centro, pero el aeropuerto está muy lejos del centro.*

- Medios de transporte

- Actividades y eventos en la ciudad o fuera de la ciudad

- Lugares para comer: ¿Hay restaurantes y supermercados? ¿Qué tipo de comida hay?

- Atracciones turísticas: museos, sitios de interés, restaurantes, edificios interesantes y otros aspectos que pueden ser útiles para turistas

- Costumbres y hábitos de los habitantes de la ciudad: **Generalmente la gente toma la siesta al mediodía.**

- Lugares para hospedarse: precio, lugar, en el centro, cerca de sitios de interés

UP3-4

Blog With your group, prepare a blog post to promote your city. Post your blog for the class on the day of your presentation. Try to include the following points.

Introduction to city	Activities and Events	Sites of interest
Transportation	Food	Places to stay
Contact information		

UP3-5

Análisis For each presentation by another group you will need to analyze the quality of the information and delivery. Pay close attention and make appropriate comments to submit in writing.

La tecnología

Objectives: In this chapter you will learn to

- Narrate in the past and express basic opinions
- Talk about technology, means of communication, social networking, and blogs
- Talk about events in the past, use direct object pronouns, and differentiate between **por** and **para**
- Use the preterite of regular and irregular verbs, direct object pronouns, and **por** and **para**

Vocabulario/Gramática

C7-1

El fin de semana With a partner, talk about what you did over the weekend. Make note of what your partner says so that you can share it with the rest of the class.

Modelo ¿Este fin de semana hiciste tu tarea en la computadora?
Sí, este fin de semana hice mi tarea en la computadora.

1. ¿Este fin de semana trabajaste? ¿Dónde trabajaste?
2. ¿Hiciste una actividad divertida? ¿Qué hiciste?
3. ¿Viste una película? ¿Qué película viste?
4. ¿Con quién estuviste este fin de semana? ¿Qué hicieron?
5. ¿Qué comiste el sábado? ¿Qué comiste el domingo?
6. ¿Te conectaste al Facebook con tu teléfono celular? ¿Para qué otras cosas usaste tu celular?

C7-2

Tecnología: presente y pasado

Step 1 With a partner, create a list of all the technology you used this week to communicate.

Modelo —*¿Qué tecnología usaste esta semana?*
—*Esta semana usé mi computadora.*

Step 2 Now discuss each item on your list. Talk about the people with whom you communicated. Talk about the reasons for the interactions.

Modelo Teléfono: *Hablé con mi tía por teléfono porque el domingo fue su cumpleaños.*

Step 3 Imagine what technology was like when your parents or grandparents were your age. Compare how you communicated via technology this week and how you think they did (or did not) in the past.

Modelo *Ayer hablé con mi mamá por webcam. En el pasado mi mamá habló con su madre por teléfono regular o en persona. Mi abuela escribió cartas* (letters) *a su madre.*

Vocabulario

C7-3   Exposición de tecnología

Step 1   Imagine you and a classmate are planning to attend a technology fair to see all the latest, must-have technology gadgets and accessories. What do you think you will see there? What brands and companies will be there? What are some current items that interest you? Why do you think they are popular or interesting? Have a 5–10 minute conversation in Spanish on this topic.

Modelos   *Los teléfonos inteligentes son muy populares ahora. Me gustan las aplicaciones de los ejercicios y las vidas activas.*

Para mí los accesorios son importantes. Quiero un teléfono con personalidad: por eso el casco (case) *es de Hello Kitty.*

Step 2   You both entered your name in a drawing at the exposition. One of you won $100 to spend on technology, accessories, and technology-related things represented at the exposition. Discuss what you can buy with $100.

Modelo   *Me interesa un reloj nuevo. ¿Con cien dólares puedo comprar uno?*

Step 3   Another name was drawn and one of you just won $1,000 to spend on technology, accessories, and technology-related things represented at the exposition. Discuss what you can buy with $1,000.

Modelo   *Me gusta mucho la tableta nueva. Creo que voy a comprar dos. ¿Quieres una?*

Step 4   Imagine it has been a few days since the exposition and you are telling a friend what happened. With a new partner, tell what you saw, did, and bought at the exposition.

Modelo   *La semana pasada yo fui a la exposición de tecnología. Yo fui con mi amigo. Él ganó cien dólares, pero yo gané mil dólares. Yo decidí comprar dos tabletas. Una para mí y otra para mi amigo.*

C7-4   Medios de comunicación

Step 1 With your classmates, make a list of all the ways you have communicated with people in the past two weeks.

Step 2 Read the following situations and discuss how you would communicate.

Modelo   Son las 12 de la noche y tienes algo para decirle a tu madre.
Yo voy a enviarle un mensaje de texto a mi mamá.

1. Es el cumpleaños de un amigo que vive en otro estado.

2. Tu abuela está en casa enferma.

3. Tu mejor amigo no está en la fiesta.

4. Estás pensando en tu novio(a).

5. Los vecinos hacen mucho ruido *(noise)*.

6. Tienes una pregunta importante para tu profesor.

7. Tienes algo para decirle a tu compañero(a) de cuarto.

C7-5   ¿Hace cuánto tiempo?

Step 1 List three things that you haven't done for a while and three more things that you have been doing for a while.

For each one, think of the relevant expression of time that you need to use and create a sentence.

Modelos   *Hace dos semanas que no veo a mis padres.*
Hace dos años que yo hago yoga.

Step 2 With a partner, take turns reading your sentences and indicating your own experiences.

Modelo   Student A: *Hace tres meses que estudio español.*
Student B: *Hoy hace un año que estudio español.*

C7-6A

En la oficina **A** The storage room at your workplace is filled with many things. Some of them haven't been used in a long time. Your supervisor has given you and a coworker the assignment of taking an inventory of all the items. In your inventory, you need to find out who is / was the owner of each item on your list, how long it has been in the office, and how long it has been since it was last used. When you complete step 1, go to C7-6B to work with your partner on steps 2–4.

Step 1 You and your coworker have been working hard taking inventory and learning about the items in the storage room. Work together to fill in any information you don't know. Some of the information you both know, some of it only you know, and some only your partner knows.

Modelo   Student A: *¿De quiénes son los cables?*
Student B: *Son de Juan. ¿Hace cuánto tiempo que están en la oficina?*
Student A: *Hace más o menos cinco años. ¿Sabes cuánto tiempo hace que no los usamos?*
Student B: *Hace tres años que no los usamos.*

Student A

Objeto / Cosa	¿De quién es?	¿Hace cuánto que está en la oficina?	¿Hace cuánto que no usamos el objeto?
muchos libros	todos	por lo menos cinco años	
dos teclados		no sabemos	no sabemos
tres monitores grandes y viejos		más de diez años	veintitrés meses
ratones	todos		
caja de cables	no sabemos	mucho tiempo	siete años
diez tabletas nuevas		seis meses	seis meses
vasos de plástico	todos	unos meses	
una fotografía de todos los empleados		dos años	dos años
papel			
una silla rota (*broken*)	la supervisora		cuatro meses
muchos discos compactos		siete años	
una pintura hermosa	no sabemos	mucho tiempo	mucho tiempo

Gramática/Vocabulario

C7-6B

En la oficina B

The storage room at your workplace is filled with many things. Some of them haven't been used in a long time. Your supervisor has given you and a coworker the assignment of taking an inventory of all the items. In your inventory, you need to find out who is / was the owner of each item on your list, how long it has been in the office, and how long it has been since it was last used.

Step 1 You and your coworker have been working hard taking inventory and learning about the items in the storage room. Work together to fill in any information you don't know. Some of the information you both know, some of it only you know, and some only your partner knows.

Modelo   Student A: *¿De quiénes son los cables?*
Student B: *Son de Juan. ¿Hace cuánto tiempo que están en la oficina?*
Student A: *Hace más o menos cinco años. ¿Sabes cuánto tiempo hace que no los usamos?*
Student B: *Hace tres años que no los usamos.*

Student B

Objeto / Cosa	¿De quién es?	¿Hace cuánto que está en la oficina?	¿Hace cuánto que no usamos el objeto?
muchos libros		por lo menos cinco años	mucho tiempo
dos teclados	no sabemos	no sabemos	
tres monitores grandes y viejos	Paco, Pedro y Anita	más de diez años	
ratones		ocho años	3 años
caja de cables		mucho tiempo	
diez tabletas nuevas	no sabemos		
vasos de plástico			una semana
una fotografía de todos los empleados	todos	dos años	
papel	todos	poco tiempo	lo usamos todos los días
una silla rota (*broken*)		tres años	
muchos discos compactos	no sabemos		no sabemos
una pintura hermosa	no sabemos	mucho tiempo	mucho tiempo

Step 2 Now that you have completed the form, your supervisor has asked you to put the items into three piles. In the first one, include things the office should keep. In the second, include items that should be recycled, and in the third, things that should be donated to a local school. Discuss the items and write down which piles they should go to; you will need this for the next step.

1. Cosas para la oficina	2. Cosas para reciclar	3. Cosas para donar (donate)

Modelo   Student A: *¿Qué debemos hacer con los cables de Juan?*
            Student B: *Hace 3 años que no los usamos y ahora Juan no trabaja aquí.*
            Student A: *¿Debemos reciclarlos o donarlos?*
            Student B: *Son muy viejos. Debemos reciclarlos.*
            Student A: *Estoy de acuerdo. ¿Qué más tenemos?*

Step 3 Look at the three piles of items. Prepare a verbal report for the next office meeting. You need to tell why you put the items in each group. Why did you choose items to stay in the office? Why should we recycle certain items? Why is it a good idea to donate items to a school?

Modelos   *Hace dos años que no usamos las sillas viejas. Debemos donarlas a la escuela. No las usamos pero están en buenas condiciones. Los estudiantes pueden usarlas.*
            Los platos deben estar en la oficina. Los usamos todos los días.

Step 4 Now form groups of four students. With your partner, present the results of your inventory and the suggestions for what to do with the items. Listen to the report from the other pair. Then discuss which items you added to the same groups and which ones ended up in different groups. Why did some items end up in the same groups while others did not?

Gramática

C7-7

Encuesta: Los hábitos estudiantiles To help cover your college costs, you are working as a resident assistant this year. You and the other resident want to create a questionnaire to find out how long residents have been doing some things and how long it has been since they have done others.

Step 1 Work together to create a seven-question survey to find out how long a student has been doing something or how long it has been since they did something. You may find the vocabulary about **quehaceres (Capítulo 4)** useful while creating your questions.

Modelo   *¿Cuánto tiempo hace que no lavas los platos?*
         ¿Cuánto tiempo hace que estudias aquí?

Step 2 Before asking residents the questions, you and the other resident assistant decide to ask each other the questions. Take turns asking the questions and fine-tune them as needed.

Modelo   Student A: *¿Cuánto tiempo hace que no lavas los platos?*
         Student B: *Hace dos días que no lavo los platos.*
         Student B: *¿Cuánto tiempo hace que estudias aquí?*
         Student A: *Hace tres años que estudio aquí.*

Step 3 Now that you have your questions ready, find a new partner and ask your questions. Then switch roles. Once you've each had a turn, find a new partner. Speak with as many classmates as possible in the time allowed. Note in writing the responses you get.

Step 4 Return to your original partner. Compare and discuss the results of the survey questions. Discuss the questions you had to answer. Add any questions that you would like to include in your own survey.

Gramática

C7-8 **¿Qué hiciste?** In groups of three, take turns asking and answering these questions. Compare what you say with what the people in your group say. Use the direct object pronouns as needed.

Modelo   Student A: *¿Leyeron (ustedes) el libro* El Hobbit*?*
              Student B: *Sí lo leí. Me gusta mucho.*
              Student C: *No, no lo leí. Prefiero las películas.*

1. ¿Terminaron la tarea ayer?
2. ¿Cuántas veces por día miran el Snapchat?
3. ¿Leyeron los libros de Harry Potter?
4. ¿Cuándo vieron la película *El Rey León (Lion King)*?
5. ¿Cuántas veces por semana miran o leen las noticias?
6. ¿Dónde cenaron anoche?
7. ¿Estudiaron los objetos directos?

C7-9 **Un trabajo como asistente** There is a job opening for a professional assistant. They are looking for someone who is hard-working and has experience with social media and online promotion. You have applied for the job and have an interview soon.

Step 1 Your friend has agreed to help you get ready for the interview. He/she has prepared a few possible questions about social media. Read the questions together. Write a follow-up question for each of the original questions; you both should write the questions down. Note that you aren't answering the questions yet.

Modelo   Pregunta: *¿Usas Facebook regularmente?*
              Pregunta adicional: *¿Hace cuánto tiempo que lo usas?* OR *¿Para qué lo usas?*

Gramática

1. ¿Cuándo compraste tu teléfono inteligente? _____

2. ¿Hace cuánto que usas Twitter? _____

3. ¿Cuándo enviaste tu primera fotografía por Snapchat? _____

4. ¿Sabes usar la aplicación de WhatsApp? _____

5. ¿Cómo prefieres ver los programas de televisión? _____

6. ¿Te gusta leer las noticias? _____

Step 2 Imagine you are at the job interview. One of you should ask the questions as if you were conducting the interview. The other will answer the questions as best you can. Then switch roles and repeat the interview.

Modelo   Student A: *¿Usas Facebook regularmente?*
         Student B: *Sí, lo uso todos los días.*
         Student A: *Muy bien. ¿Para qué lo usas?*
         Student B: *Lo uso para conectarme con mis amigos y mi familia.*
         Student A: *Perfecto. ¿Cuándo compraste tu teléfono?*
         Student B: *Lo compré hace un año y medio.*

Step 3 In a real interview, you will usually not know the questions beforehand. Find a new partner and answer his/her questions as best you can. Then ask him/her your questions.

Gramática

C7-10

Las oraciones With a partner, use the columns to create sentences. One of you will begin the statement with an element from each of the first two columns. The other will complete the statement with elements from the last two columns. Take turns beginning the statements. Pay close attention to your use of **por** and **para.**

Modelo   Student A: *Me gusta comer cereal...*

              Student B: *... por la mañana.*

              Student B: *Quiero trabajar...*

              Student A: *... para Google.*

Columna A	Columna B	Columna C	Columna D
Me gusta	viajar	por	(nombre de una persona)
Tengo que	trabajar	para	(medio de comunicación)
Quiero	hablar		(medio de transporte)
	terminar la tarea		(nombre de una compañía)
	chatear		(destino o lugar)
	enviar mensajes		(tiempo)
	caminar		
	comprar un regalo		

Gramática

C7-11 Compañero(a) de cuarto

Step 1 With a partner, imagine that you are new roommates. Use the following questions to get to know each other better. Write down your partner's responses for the next step.

Modelo   Student A: *¿Por cuánto tiempo vas a estudiar en el cuarto?*
Student B: *Voy a estudiar por dos horas por la tarde.*

1. ¿Qué cosas necesitamos para el cuarto?

2. ¿Cuántas horas por día vas a estar en el cuarto?

3. ¿Normalmente prefieres estudiar por la mañana?

4. ¿Para ti es importante mantener el cuarto limpio? ¿Por qué?

5. ¿Normalmente cuántas horas duermes por la noche?

6. ¿…?

Step 2 After answering all the questions, discuss the results and decide whether it is a good idea for you two to be roommates. Be prepared to share some reasons with the whole class.

Step 3 With your partner, create three to five more questions. Then with a new partner, ask and answer the new questions. Return to your partner and compare the responses.

Gramática

Un viaje

Step 1 Jorge sent the following message to a friend. With a partner, read the message out loud in Spanish, without speaking in English or looking up words. Mark all the uses of **por** and **para**. Then answer the questions together.

> Hace seis meses que conozco a mi novia. Nos conocimos por Internet. Para mí, ella es la más guapa de todas. Ella es muy especial y por eso quiero comprarle un regalo especial. Creo que voy a invitarla a un viaje. Vamos a ir a Hawái por una semana. Vamos a viajar por avión. Espero no pagar mucho por los billetes. Otra preocupación es que ella trabaja para una compañía internacional y no sé si ella va a tener tiempo libre para ir de vacaciones. Yo sé que para ti Hawái es uno de tus destinos favoritos. En la isla quiero caminar por la playa y nadar en el océano. ¿Tienes otras recomendaciones para el viaje a Hawái?

1. Mencionen tres ejemplos del uso de **por**. ¿Por qué usó **por**?
2. Mencionen tres ejemplos del uso de **para**. ¿Por qué usó **para**?
3. ¿De qué habla Jorge? ¿Qué información es más importante?
4. ¿Cuáles son algunos problemas que les pueden ocurrir a Jorge y a su novia?

Step 2 Josefina just came back from a trip with her boyfriend. She sent the following post card to her aunt telling about her trip. With a partner, read her postcard out loud. Mark all the times she used **por** and **para**. Then answer the questions.

Hola tía:

Hace ocho meses que conozco a mi novio Jorge. Nos conocimos por un sitio web. Él es alto, guapo y no tiene pelo. Fuimos a Hawái por dos semanas. Usamos muchas formas de transporte. Viajamos en avión, en taxi, en barco y en bicicleta, pero para mí la mejor parte fue cuando caminamos por la playa. Me encanta la playa. Para mí, el viaje fue necesario porque yo trabajo mucho. Por suerte tuve una semana de vacaciones para usar.

Un abrazo,

Josefina

1. Mencionen un ejemplo del uso de **por** o **para.** ¿Por qué usó **por** o **para**?

2. ¿Qué pasó con las preocupaciones de Jorge?

Step 3 Imagine that Jorge and Josefina have been together for three years. Below you will see the start of a conversation they are having about where to go and what to do for their anniversary. With your partner, create the rest of the conversation.

JORGE: Hace tres años que nos conocimos por Internet. :)

JOSEFINA: Sí, te quiero mucho. Debemos hacer algo para celebrarlo.

JORGE: ¿Quieres ir a Hawái de nuevo?

JOSEFINA: Me gustó el viaje a Hawái, pero no. Debemos…

Mutaciones

José Emilio Pacheco

En el centro de la ciudad se levanta una estatua que cambia de forma. Por las noches representa a Diana, durante el día asume la figura de Apolo. Si viste los atributos de Marte anuncia la guerra—tan claro y obvio es su simbolismo. Nadie se atreve a contemplarla más de un segundo, pues si ve en ella la imagen de Thánatos sabe que a las pocas horas encontrará la muerte. Quizá la estatua solo existe en la imaginación de quienes creen verla. Pero hay fotografías de sus innumerables mutaciones. En otros tiempos hubo incluso quienes osaron tocarla y, antes de morir, nos legaron su testimonio. Sea como fuere, la estatua plural obsesiona a los habitantes de la ciudad. El rey quiso demolerla. El Consejo de Ancianos vetó la orden ya que, de acuerdo con la leyenda, cuando la estatua sea destruida se va a acabar el mundo.

Photoshot Images/Newscom

C7-13

With a partner, review and discuss the reading in Spanish. Decide whether you believe the story and explain why or why not.

Mi teléfono nuevo

El fin de semana pasado, fui al centro comercial para comprar un teléfono celular (o, como se dice aquí en España, un móvil). La razón principal para comprar un móvil nuevo es que mi móvil de los EEUU cuesta mucho aquí en Europa. Recibí la cuenta la semana pasada y tuve que pagar mucho dinero.

En la tienda hablé con una chica que se llama Juani. Ella sabe mucho sobre los teléfonos y las opciones. Después de hablar de todas las opciones, yo elegí un móvil que era muy barato. Juani me dio el formulario para rellenar. Lo rellené *(filled out)* con toda la información necesaria. Se lo di a Juani y ella me pidió el pasaporte. El problema fue que lo dejé en casa. Tuve que volver a casa para buscarlo.

Salí de la tienda de teléfonos y vi a mi profesora de historia. Ella me saludó y hablamos unos minutos. Yo le conté la situación, que no tenía el pasaporte, y ella me dijo que debía ir a casa a buscarlo. Después, vi a unos amigos de la universidad. Ellos acababan de comprar unos libros. Ellos me los querían mostrar *(wanted to show them)* y luego, hablamos unos minutos. Cuando por fin llegué a mi apartamento vi una nota: "Llama a tu mamá". Tuve que llamarla y hablamos casi media hora por teléfono. (¡Va a costar mucho dinero!)

Después de todo eso, tuve que correr para llegar a la tienda de teléfonos antes de la hora de cerrar. Pero, me alegra mucho decir… tengo mi teléfono nuevo y voy a usarlo mucho. ☺

El blog de Bella

C7-14

Lo que me pasó When Bella went to buy her new cell phone, she didn't know she would need her passport and had to go home to find it. For your blog entry, write about a recent experience purchasing or forgetting something. State when and where it happened, and mention any people who were involved. (100–200 words)

_____

_____

_____

_____

_____

_____

_____

_____

_____

_____

C7-15

Get together with the classmates whose blogs you reviewed online. Take turns reading your blog entries and asking the questions you've prepared. After the group has heard the answers, the activity should be repeated with the next person reading and answering questions.

Síntesis: Vocabulario

La tecnología   *Technology*

alta definición   *high definition (HD)*

el cable   *cable*

la computadora   *computer*

la computadora portátil   *laptop*

la conexión   *connection*

digital   *digital*

inalámbrico   *wireless*

el monitor   *monitor*

el móvil   *cell phone (Spain)*

el ordenador   *computer (Spain)*

el ratón   *mouse*

la memoria USB   *flash drive*

la tableta   *tablet*

el teclado   *keyboard*

el teléfono celular   *cell phone*

la televisión   *television*

el wifi   *wifi*

colgar   *to post*

conectar   *to connect*

descargar / bajar   *to download*

enviar   *to send*

grabar   *to record, to save*

guardar   *to save*

hacer clic / doble clic   *to click / double click*

instalar   *to install*

subir   *to upload*

Medios de comunicación
Methods of communication

chatear   *to chat*

enviar un mensaje de texto   *to send a text message*

hablar por teléfono   *to speak on the phone*

el buzón   *inbox* (also *mailbox*)

el contrato   *contract*

el mensaje de voz   *voicemail*

prepago   *prepaid*

la tarifa   *rate*

la tarjeta   *card*

Redes sociales   *Social networks*

el estatus   *status*

las redes sociales   *social networks*

comentar   *to comment*

editar   *to edit*

poner   *to put, to place, to post*

publicar   *to publish, to post*

Síntesis: Gramática

Preterite of irregular verbs

The verbs **dar, ver, hacer,** and **tener** are irregular in the preterite, which means that they don't follow the same pattern of conjugation as regular -**ar** and -**er** and verbs. Notice that the preterite endings of **dar** and **ver** are the same.

dar *to give*	
yo **di**	nosotros(as) **dimos**
tú **diste**	vosotros(as) **disteis**
él / ella / usted **dio**	ellos / ellas / ustedes **dieron**

ver *to see*	
yo **vi**	nosotros(as) **vimos**
tú **viste**	vosotros(as) **visteis**
él / ella / usted **vio**	ellos / ellas / ustedes **vieron**

hacer *to make*	
yo **hice**	nosotros(as) **hicimos**
tú **hiciste**	vosotros(as) **hicisteis**
él / ella / usted **hizo**	ellos / ellas / ustedes **hicieron**

tener *to have*	
yo **tuve**	nosotros(as) **tuvimos**
tú **tuviste**	vosotros(as) **tuvisteis**
él / ella / usted **tuvo**	ellos / ellas / ustedes **tuvieron**

Hace + expressions of time

The verb **hacer** can be used to say how long something has been going on or to tell how long ago something happened.

To say how long something has been going on, or to indicate the amount of time that has passed since something started, use the following construction:

Hace + *amount of time* + **que (no)** + *verb in the present*

Hace diez años **que** estudio español.
I have studied Spanish for ten years.

Hace dos meses **que** no voy al cine.
I have not gone to the movies in two months.

To ask how long something has been going on, use:

¿**Cuánto tiempo hace que** + *verb in the present*?

¿Cuánto tiempo **hace que** estudias español?
How long have you been studying Spanish?

To say how long ago something happened, use the following construction:

verb in the past + *hace* + **an amount of time**

Conocí a Lupita **hace** cuatro años.
I met Lupita four years ago.

Síntesis: Gramática

You can also choose to place **hace** at the beginning of the sentence by using the following construction:

hace + **amount of time** + *que* + **verb in the past**

Hace cuatro años **que** conocí a Lupita.
I met Lupita four years ago.

To ask how long ago someone did something, use:

¿Cuánto tiempo hace que + *verb in the preterite*?

¿Cuánto tiempo **hace que** conociste a Lupita?
How long ago did you meet Lupita?

Direct object pronouns

A direct object is the person or thing that **receives** the action of a verb. It answers the question *who?* or *what?* For example, in the following sentence:

Carlos habla **español.**
Carlos speaks Spanish.

The verb is *to speak.* **What** is spoken? Spanish. Therefore, *Spanish* is the direct object.

Here's another example:

Vi a **María** en la plaza.
I saw María in the plaza.

The verb is *to see.* **Who** is seen? María. Therefore, *María* receives the action of the verb: she is the direct object.

A direct object pronoun is a word that takes the place of a direct object. In English, we use *me, you, him, her, it, us,* and *them.* Direct object pronouns in Spanish are as follows:

Direct object pronouns			
Singular		**Plural**	
me	*me*	**nos**	*us*
te	*you* (informal)	**os**	*you* (informal)
lo	*it, him, you* (formal)	**los**	*them, you* (formal)
la	*it, her, you* (formal)	**las**	*them, you* (formal)

The third-person direct object pronouns (**lo/la, los/las**) agree in gender and number with the direct objects they replace.

¿Ves **la televisión** por las noches? *Do you watch TV at night?*
No, no **la** veo nunca. *No, I don't watch it ever.*

The direct object pronoun can always be placed before the conjugated verb. If the conjugated verb is followed by an infinitive or if the verb is in the present progressive, you have the option of placing it before the conjugated verb or attaching it to the end of the infinitive or present participle; for example:

Ana **te** quiere ver. / Ana quiere ver**te.**
Ana wants to see you.

Laura **nos** está llamando. / Laura está llamándo**nos**.
Laura is calling us.

Notice how **llamándonos** has an accent mark. To maintain the original stress of the present participle, an accent mark is required when attaching a direct object pronoun.

Síntesis: Gramática

When using direct object pronouns with negative commands, place the pronoun directly before the verb. For example:

> Este pescado no está bueno. No **lo** comas.
> *This fish isn't good. Don't eat it.*

When using direct object pronouns with affirmative commands, attach the pronoun to the end of the verb. For example:

> Estas palabras de vocabulario son importantes; **estúdialas.**
> *These vocabulary words are important; study them.*

Notice how **estúdialas** has an accent mark. When you attach the direct object pronoun to an affirmative command, you often have to add an accent mark to maintain the original stress of the command.

Grammar summary: Por and Para

Both **por** and **para** are commonly used Spanish prepositions that can sometimes be translated as *for.* Which one you use depends on the meaning you want to convey.

Here is a list of their most common uses.

Por to indicate:	
Reason / Cause	Recibió un multa **por** conducir muy rápido. *He received a ticket for driving very fast.*
Period of time	**Por** la mañana estudié **por** tres horas. *In the morning I studied for three hours.*
Motion / General direction (through, along, around, by)	Pasaron **por** el parque. *They walked through the park.*
On behalf of	Yo puedo trabajar **por** ti si estás enfermo. *I can work for you if you are sick.*
In exchange for	Ellos pagaron cinco mil dólares **por** su coche. *They paid five thousand dollars for their car.*
By means of	Viajan **por** avión porque es más rápido. *They travel by plane because it is faster.*

There are a number of fixed expressions that use the preposition **por:**

por ejemplo	*for example*	**por fin**	*finally*
por eso	*that's why*	**por lo menos**	*at least*
por favor	*please*	**por supuesto**	*of course*

Síntesis: Gramática

Para to indicate:

Intended recipient / Beneficiary	El regalo es **para** mi hermana. *The gift is for my sister.*
Specific time / Deadline	La tarea es **para** el martes. *The homework is for Tuesday.*
Destination	El autobús sale **para** Cali a las dos. *The bus leaves for Cali at two.*
In the employ of	Mi padre trabajó **para** una compañía grande. *My father worked for a big company.*

In order to *(with an infinitive)*	**Para** enseñar a niños, necesitas mucha paciencia. *To teach children, you need a lot of patience.*
Opinion *(with a noun or pronoun)*	**Para** Carolina, los libros de ficción son más interesantes. *For Carolina, fiction books are more interesting.*

When the personal pronoun **yo** or **tú** comes after **por** or **para,** use **mí** or **ti.** For example: **por mí, por ti, para mí, para ti.**

Profesiones y carreras

Objectives: In this chapter you will learn to

- Talk about professions, majors, and job qualifications
- Narrate in the past
- Indicate ongoing and completed actions in the past
- Use stem-changing verbs in the preterite and indirect object pronouns

Vocabulario

C8-1

Los estudios y los trabajos With a partner, find out what three real or imaginary family members studied and what jobs they do now.

Modelo   *¿Qué estudió tu madre?*
Mi madre estudió química.
¿En qué trabaja?
Ella es farmacéutica.

C8-2

Consejero(a) y estudiante

Step 1 Look at the following cued conversation between an academic advisor and a student. With a partner, follow the instructions to ask and answer the questions.

Student A (Consejero(a))	Student B (Estudiante)
1. Greet Student B.	2. Respond to Student A's greeting politely.
3. Ask what professions interest Student B and why.	4. Respond to Student A with two or three professions and why they interest you. (**Me interesa… porque…**)
5. Give advice based on Student B's response. (**… es buena profesión si te interesa…**)	6. Ask Student A what classes you should take to pursue your first choice.
7. Answer Student B and provide additional advice.	8. Ask Student A one or two follow-up questions.
9. Answer the questions and wish Student B luck. (**¡Suerte!**)	10. Say thank you and goodbye to Student A.

Step 2 Imagine that you are meeting with an academic advisor on campus to discuss your path to graduation and your career plans. Play the role of advisor while your classmate plays the student; then switch roles. When you are the student, either choose the career that you really want to pursue, or pretend to be interested in another profession.

C8-3

Trabajos You and your classmates need to collect information about work: past, present, and future.

Step 1 Ask and answer the following survey questions. Start with the first question and ask the second or third follow-up questions only when appropriate. Write down the basic answers to each question for the next step. Speak with as many classmates as time allows.

Modelo Student A: *¿Qué trabajo quieres hacer en el futuro?*
Student B: *Quiero trabajar en un hospital. Quiero ser médico.*
Student A: *¿Por qué quieres hacer este trabajo?*
Student B: *Quiero hacer este trabajo porque…*

1. ¿Qué trabajos tuviste en el pasado? ¿Cuál fue el mejor trabajo y cuál fue el peor? ¿Por qué?

2. ¿Trabajas ahora? ¿Qué trabajo haces? ¿Te gusta tu trabajo?

3. ¿Qué trabajo quieres tener en el futuro? ¿Por qué quieres ese trabajo?

4. ¿Qué aspectos o elementos son importantes para ti cuando buscas un trabajo?

Step 2 Return to the first classmate you interviewed. Compare and contrast the answers each of you has gathered from other classmates. Prepare four statements about work based on the survey results.

Modelo *Muchos estudiantes quieren ser médicos porque quieren ayudar a las personas.*

Step 3 Present your statements to the class and comment and react to the other statements being presented. Try to make some connections or generalizations to share with the class.

C8-4 **¿Quién?** You and a partner are working in a human resources department for a large company and you have been tasked with reviewing several résumés.

Step 1 Read the two job descriptions below to learn about the qualifications and requirements.

> **Puesto 1:** Necesitamos un supervisor para nuestra división de producción. Tiene que saber usar programas básicos en la computadora. Debe ser bueno con los números. Tiene que dirigir a un grupo de personas. Preferimos una persona que se haya graduado de una universidad.

> **Puesto 2:** Necesitamos un supervisor para nuestra división de atención al cliente. Tiene que saber usar programas básicos en la computadora, especialmente para hacer llamadas con clientes. Debe ser bueno con los idiomas, especialmente inglés y español. Hay la opción de trabajar por la noche.

Step 2 With a partner, review the excerpts from the three résumés below. The names have been withheld, but you should use the information you have to discuss each person and get a general idea of what that person is like.

CV 1

Correo electrónico:	elcapitan1@capit.net
Educación:	Se graduó de la Universidad de Arizona en contabilidad y después estudió negocios en la Universidad de Oviedo (España).
Experiencia laboral:	cinco años en una empresa internacional, dos años como supervisor de un equipo de seis personas
Autodescripción:	trabajador, organizado, líder

Vocabulario

CV 2

Correo electrónico: escritora22@gege.net
Educación: Se graduó en periodismo y comunicación de la Universidad de Río.
Experiencia laboral: un año en *El País*, tres años escribiendo blogs
Autodescripción: creativa, dedicada, honesta

CV 3

Correo electrónico: chica.chicana123@yaha.net
Educación: Está estudiando marketing en la Universidad de Mesa. Va a graduarse en un mes.
Experiencia laboral: Trabajó para un restaurante por cuatro años. Trabaja ahora en un centro de llamadas; es supervisora de las llamadas en español.
Autodescripción: buena compañera, simpática

Step 3 You need to decide who goes on to have an actual interview. Based on the résumés, choose one candidate who will not move on to the interview. Explain your rationale in 2–3 sentences.

Step 4 With your partner, decide whether you are going to put the remaining candidates forward for one or both positions. Explain your rationale in making the decision.

Step 5 Think about the candidate who did not move on to the interview process. Discuss what kind of job he/she would succeed at and tell why. Write a brief job description and share with the class.

Gramática

C8-5 In groups of two or three, use verbs from the bank to make at least one statement and ask each other and answer questions about what celebrities or other well-known people did in the past.

ir	decir	estar	pagar	hablar	pedir
divertirse	trabajar	dar	reírse	comer	

Modelo *Bill Gates pagó mucho dinero por su casa.*
¿Dónde estuvo Jennifer Lawrence el fin de semana pasado?
Estuvo en California. Trabajó en su película nueva.

C8-6 ¿Dónde está mi bicicleta? You are an intern working with the campus police. As part of your job you assist during investigations. There were two bikes reported missing this morning. You recorded the information from one of the thefts.

Step 1 Review your notes below in preparation to meet with a colleague who interviewed the other victim. Be ready to compare and contrast the crimes.

Apuntes del testimonio de Andrea

Andrea salió de su casa en su bicicleta a las 8:30.

Ella llegó al Café de Betty a las 8:45. No tenía su cadena *(chain)*. Por eso, dejó su bici cerca de la puerta del café.

Pidió un café y se sentó cerca de la ventana.

Tomó su café y leyó un libro para su clase de literatura.

Estuvo en el Café de Betty hasta las 9:25 cuando se fue a clase, pero no pudo encontrar su bicicleta.

Llamó a la policía para denunciar el robo de su bicicleta y se fue a su clase en la biblioteca.

Dijo que su bicicleta es azul, nueva y de la marca *(brand)* Schwinn. El asiento *(seat)* es negro y tiene un poco de blanco. La bicicleta tiene una pegatina *(sticker)* de dos gatos rosados.

Cuando salió de clase, ella vio su bicicleta al lado de la puerta.

Llamó de nuevo a la policía (a las 10:45) para decir que encontró su bicicleta. Llevó la bicicleta a su casa.

Gramática

Apuntes del testimonio de Manuel

Manuel salió del Café de Betty a las 9:00 más o menos.

Tomó su bicicleta y se fue a la universidad.

Cuando llegó a la universidad se dio cuenta *(he realized)* de que no tenía su cadena *(chain)*.

Dejó su bicicleta cerca de la puerta de la biblioteca y se fue a su clase.

Estuvo en clase hasta a las 11:00. Salió y no pudo encontrar su bicicleta.

Una persona le dijo que vio a una chica en una bicicleta azul.

Llamó a la policía a las 11:05 para denunciar el robo de su bicicleta.

Dijo que su bicicleta es azul y está en buenas condiciones. Tiene una botella blanca para agua.
El asiento *(seat)* es negro. Es de la marca *(brand)* Schwinn.

Step 2 Your supervisor wonders whether there is a connection between the two bike thefts. Work with your partner to share and summarize the information you have regarding both cases. Together, make note of things you think are connected, important, and key to the investigation.

Step 3 You and your partner must come up with two theories about the two bikes. Your supervisor has asked you to piece together a possible sequence of events and to answer the following questions.

¿Qué tienen en común los dos casos?

¿Qué tienen en común las dos bicicletas?

¿Cómo podemos distinguir entre las dos bicicletas?

¿Qué pasó con las dos bicicletas?

¿Dónde está la bicicleta de Manuel?

¿Dónde está la bicicleta de Andrea?

Step 4 Based on the combined information and answers to the questions, create an explanation of what happened to the two bikes. What questions should you ask Andrea and Manuel to confirm your conclusion? Write one or two questions for each person. Where should you start looking for Manuel's bike?

C8-7 La cita Imagine that Andrea and Manuel met and went out to dinner last weekend. Using the word bank, and knowing that they both had their bikes stolen, decide what you think happened on their date. Keep in mind that you are telling a story with a beginning, middle, and end. Be prepared to share your story with the class.

| dar | pagar | repetir | vestirse | reírse | conducir | venir | ver |
| ir | pedir | servir | divertirse | poner | decir | estar | |

C8-8 La niñez

Step 1 With a partner, brainstorm vocabulary in Spanish related to your childhood.

Step 2 Now separate the words into two lists: one list should be nouns and the other verbs and activities.

Step 3 Using the two lists, ask each other about what activities you used to do as children. Include questions about what places you visited. Use the imperfect tense as needed.

Modelo   Student A: *¿Cuándo eras niño, jugabas a muchos deportes?*
          Student B: *Cuando yo era niño jugaba al fútbol y al béisbol.*

Step 4 Compare what you said and what your partner said. What do you have in common? What differences did you discover? Share some of your childhood experiences with the class.

C8-9 Amigos Now work with a new partner to make statements about what you and your friends used to do and what you do now that is different.

Modelos   *Mis amigos y yo jugábamos a muchos deportes, pero ahora solo jugamos al tenis.*
           Comíamos mucha comida rápida, pero ahora yo como comida vegetariana.

C8-10

Un cuento para niños

Step 1 With a partner, read the beginning of the story. Fill in the blank spaces with various adjectives describing the characters, the lake, and the island where they live.

> Había una vez tres amigos: un caballo, un burro y una vaca. Vivían en una isla
> _____ en el medio de un lago _____. El caballo era _____.
> El burro era _____. La vaca era _____.

Step 2 Now brainstorm verbs for the story. Add a few more verbs to the list below. Once you have finished the list, talk about how each verb would change in meaning if you used it in the preterite or the imperfect.

Verbos: tener, estar, decir, saber, _____

Step 3 Begin writing your story. Use the verbs from your list (you can add more if needed) and continue to tell the story. Be sure to use the imperfect and preterite of verbs appropriately as you narrate. Choose one person to be the scribe, but work together and be creative. Once you have a good start, pass your story on to another pair to read the story and add two or three sentences. Keep going until you have your story back again. Read the story and give it a conclusion. Be prepared to share your story with the class.

C8-11

El candidato ideal With a partner, describe the ideal candidate for each of the following jobs.

Modelo   arquitecto: *Un arquitecto tiene que ser creativo y motivado.*

1. médico(a)
2. contador(a)
3. profesor(a) de español
4. veterinario(a)
5. periodista
6. mecánico(a)
7. ¿…?

Gramática

C8-12 Un puesto

Step 1 You and two other classmates form a committee in charge of conducting job interviews. Choose one of the following jobs and create seven questions for the applicants to answer. Your questions should be in a variety of tenses. Everyone in the group needs to have a copy of the questions.

> un(a) secretario(a)
>
> un(a) maestro(a) de la escuela secundaria
>
> un(a) dentista
>
> un(a) supervisor(a) de un restaurante

Modelo   *¿Dónde estudiaste?*

Step 2 Now find a partner who was not part of your original group. One of you should act as the interviewer and the other as the person seeking the job. The interviewer should explain what job is being offered. The interviewee should adjust his or her answers based on the job opening. After conducting the interview, switch roles and repeat.

Modelo   Dentista
         Student A: *¿Dónde estudiaste?*
         Student B: *Estudié en la Universidad de…*

Step 3 Return to your original group and compare the results of the interviews. Choose one person who you think best answered the questions. Write three reasons that explain why the committee recommends that person to move on to the next round of interviews.

Lectura

El carpintero

Eduardo Galeano

Orlando Goicoechea reconoce las maderas por el olor, de qué árboles vienen, qué edad tienen, y oliéndolas sabe si fueron cortadas a tiempo o a destiempo y les adivina los posibles contratiempos.

Él es carpintero desde que hacía sus propios juguetes en la azotea de su casa del barrio de Cayo Hueso. Nunca tuvo máquinas ni ayudantes. A mano hace todo lo que hace, y de su mano nacen los mejores muebles de La Habana: mesas para comer celebrando, camas y sillas que te da pena levantarte, armarios donde a la ropa le gusta quedarse.

Orlando trabaja desde el amanecer. Y cuando el sol se va de la azotea, se encierra y enciende el video. Al cabo de tantos años de trabajo, Orlando se ha dado el lujo de comprarse un video, y ve una película tras otra.

No sabía que eras loco por el cine —le dice un vecino.

Y Orlando le explica que no, que a él el cine ni le va ni le viene, pero gracias al video puede detener las películas para estudiar los muebles.

C8-13 ¿Innato o adquirido?

Step 1 With a partner, review and discuss Orlando's talent for woodwork as it is presented in the short story. Based on what you have read, do you think his ability is innate or acquired? Provide an explanation for your decision.

Step 2 Now make a list in Spanish of activities and professions that you believe can be mastered through continuous practice, and a second list of activities and professions that require natural talent or ability, without which no amount of practice will lead to success. Provide reasons for each item on each list.

Step 3 Share your lists and reasons and discuss any differences of opinion to reach a final verdict or two defined positions in the class.

La señorita del anillo

Ayer hablé con mi amigo Juan sobre su trabajo nuevo. Él empezó la semana pasada. Le gustan sus compañeros de trabajo y está listo para los desafíos nuevos. Me hizo pensar en el trabajo que yo tenía cuando estaba en la escuela secundaria.

Yo trabajaba para un restaurante. Yo tenía que hacer muchas cosas ahí. Era un restaurante pequeño de una familia y solo había cuatro trabajadores: yo, la madre, el padre y su hijo. Además de ser camarera, yo tenía que limpiar las mesas, barrer el suelo y sacar la basura todos los días. Nunca tuve que lavar los platos. Eso fue el trabajo del hijo. Yo recuerdo que un día mientras barría el suelo, yo encontré un anillo *(ring)*. El jefe me dijo que teníamos que esperar para ver si alguien lo reclamaba. Un día pasó y nadie lo reclamó. Otro día pasó y nada. Pero el tercer día entró una mujer en el restaurante y ella buscaba un anillo. Ella nos contó que el anillo era de su abuela y que estaba muy contenta de tenerlo de nuevo. Yo me sentía muy feliz también. No me gustaría perder un anillo especial así.

Ekaterina43/ ShutterStock.com

C8-14 **Mi experiencia** In groups of three or four, share the blog posts that you wrote online and ask each other questions to ensure you have understood them. After you have all had a chance to share and discuss, vote for your favorite blog and present it to the class.

Síntesis: Vocabulario

Profesiones y carreras
Professions and careers

el/la abogado(a)   *lawyer*

el actor / la actriz   *actor / actress*

el/la arquitecto(a)   *architect*

el/la artista   *artist*

el/la asistente   *assistant*

el/la autor(a)   *author*

el/la barbero(a)   *barber*

el/la bibliotecario(a)   *librarian*

el/la bombero(a)   *firefighter*

el/la camarero(a)   *waiter / waitress*

el/la científico(a)   *scientist*

el/la contador(a)   *accountant*

el/la dentista   *dentist*

el/la diseñador(a) gráfico(a)   *graphic designer*

el/la empleado(a)   *employee*

el/la enfermero(a)   *nurse*

el/la farmacéutico(a)   *pharmacist*

el/la gerente   *manager*

**el hombre / la mujer de
  negocios**   *businessperson*

el/la ingeniero(a)   *engineer*

el/la jefe(a)   *supervisor*

el/la juez/a   *judge*

el/la maestro(a)   *teacher*

el/la mecánico(a)   *mechanic*

el/la médico(a)   *doctor*

el/la peluquero(a)   *hair stylist*

el/la periodista   *journalist*

el/la policía   *police officer*

el/la profesor(a)   *professor*

el/la programador(a)   *computer programmer*

el/la veterinario(a)   *veterinarian*

Irregular preterite verbs

andar   *to walk*

conducir   *to drive*

dar   *to give*

decir   *to tell*

divertirse   *to have fun*

dormir   *to sleep*

estar   *to be*

ir   *to go*

medir   *to measure*

morir   *to die*

pagar   *to pay*

pedir   *to ask for*

poner   *to put, to place*

preferir   *to prefer*

reírse   *to laugh*

repetir   *to repeat*

saber   *to know*

servir   *to serve*

venir   *to come*

ver   *to see*

vestirse   *to dress oneself*

Concentraciones   *Majors*

la administración de empresas   *business
  administration*

la biología   *biology*

las ciencias de la computación   *computer
  science*

las ciencias físicas   *physical science*

las ciencias políticas   *political science*

las ciencias sociales   *social sciences*

la comunicación   *communications*

la criminología   *criminal justice*

el derecho   *law*

la economía   *economics*

la educación   *education*

la enfermería   *nursing*

las finanzas   *finance*

la historia   *history*

la ingeniería   *engineering*

Síntesis: Vocabulario

las lenguas/los idiomas *languages*

la literatura *literature*

el marketing/el mercadeo *marketing*

los negocios *business*

el periodismo *journalism*

la psicología *psychology*

las relaciones públicas *public relations*

Cualificaciones *Qualifications*

la comunicación interpersonal *interpersonal communication*

de confianza *reliable*

creativo(a) *creative*

escribir bien *to write well*

la experiencia *experience*

hablar bien *to speak well*

honesto(a) *honest*

la iniciativa *initiative*

motivado(a) *motivated*

organizado(a) *organized*

las relaciones públicas *public relations*

saber escuchar *to know how to listen*

ser un(a) líder *to be a leader*

trabajar bien con otros *to work well with others*

Síntesis: Gramática

Irregular preterite: Spelling changes in the preterite

Verbs that end in **-car, -gar,** and **-zar** have spelling changes in the **yo** form of the preterite.

Infinitive	Preterite
buscar *to look for*	yo bus**qué**
pagar *to pay*	yo pa**gué**
organizar *to organize*	yo organi**cé**

Irregular preterite: Stem-changing verbs in the preterite

In the preterite, **-ar** and **-er** verbs *do not* have stem changes. Only **-ir** verbs that have stem changes in the present tense also have stem changes in the preterite.

There are two types of stem-changing verbs in the preterite: **o > u** and **e > i.**

Verbs like **dormir** are **o > u** stem-changing verbs.

dormir (o > u) *to sleep*	
yo **dormí**	nosotros(as) **dormimos**
tú **dormiste**	vosotros(as) **dormisteis**
él / ella / usted **durmió**	ellos / ellas / ustedes **durmieron**

Notice that the endings are the same as those of regular **-ir** verbs in the preterite, but the stem changes from **o** to **u** in the **él / ella / usted** and **ellos / ellas / ustedes** forms only.

Verbs like **pedir** are **e > i** stem-changing verbs.

pedir (e > i) *to ask for*	
yo **pedí**	nosotros(as) **pedimos**
tú **pediste**	vosotros(as) **pedisteis**
él / ella / usted **pidió**	ellos / ellas / ustedes **pidieron**

Notice that the endings are the same as those of regular **-ir** verbs in the preterite, but the stem changes from **e** to **i** in the **él / ella / usted** and **ellos / ellas / ustedes** forms only.

More irregular verbs in the preterite

You have already seen several irregular verbs in the preterite, such as **ser, ir, estar, dar, ver, hacer,** and **tener.**

Some irregular verbs in the preterite share the same endings. For example, the following verbs share the same irregular endings in the preterite as **estar, tener,** and **hacer:**

	andar	poder	poner
yo	anduve	pude	puse
tú	anduviste	pudiste	pusiste
él / ella / usted	anduvo	pudo	puso
nosotros(as)	anduvimos	pudimos	pusimos
vosotros(as)	anduvisteis	pudisteis	pusisteis
ellos / ellas / ustedes	anduvieron	pudieron	pusieron

Síntesis: Gramática

	querer	saber	venir
yo	quise	supe	vine
tú	quisiste	supiste	viniste
él / ella / usted	quiso	supo	vino
nosotros(as)	quisimos	supimos	vinimos
vosotros(as)	quisisteis	supisteis	vinisteis
ellos / ellas / ustedes	quisieron	supieron	vinieron

Notice that there are no accent marks on irregular verbs in the preterite.

Some verbs that are irregular in the preterite have similar conjugation patterns, which makes it easier to learn them. When the verbs **conducir, decir,** and **traer** are conjugated in the preterite, they have similar irregular stems that end in **j.**

	conducir	decir	traer
yo	conduje	dije	traje
tú	condujiste	dijiste	trajiste
él / ella / usted	condujo	dijo	trajo
nosotros(as)	condujimos	dijimos	trajimos
vosotros(as)	condujisteis	dijisteis	trajisteis
ellos / ellas / ustedes	condujeron	dijeron	trajeron

Notice that the **ellos / ellas / ustedes** ending for verbs whose stems end in **j** is **-eron.**

The imperfect: Regular verbs

To conjugate regular **-ar** verbs in the imperfect, drop the **-ar** and add the appropriate ending to the stem.

trabajar *to work*

yo trabaj**aba**	nosotros(as) trabaj**ábamos**
tú trabaj**abas**	vosotros(as) trabaj**abais**
él / ella / usted trabaj**aba**	ellos / ellas / ustedes trabaj**aban**

Notice that the **nosotros / nosotras** ending for regular **-ar** verbs in the imperfect (**-ábamos**) has an accent mark on the first **a.**

To conjugate regular **-er** and **-ir** verbs in the imperfect, drop the **-er** or **-ir** and add the appropriate ending to the stem. Regular **-er** and **-ir** verbs have identical endings in the imperfect.

comer *to eat*

yo com**ía**	nosotros(as) com**íamos**
tú com**ías**	vosotros(as) com**íais**
él / ella / usted com**ía**	ellos / ellas / ustedes **comían**

vivir *to live*

yo viv**ía**	nosotros(as) viv**íamos**
tú viv**ías**	vosotros(as) viv**íais**
él / ella / usted viv**ía**	ellos / ellas / ustedes viv**ían**

Notice that all of the endings for regular **-er** and **-ir** verbs have accents on the **i.**

Síntesis: Gramática

Irregular verbs in the imperfect

There are only three irregular verbs in the imperfect: **ser, ir,** and **ver.**

	ser	ir	ver
yo	era	iba	veía
tú	eras	ibas	veías
él, ella, usted	era	iba	veía
nosotros(as)	éramos	íbamos	veíamos
vosotros(as)	erais	ibais	veíais
ellos, ellas, ustedes	eran	iban	veían

Notice that the **nosotros / nosotras** endings for irregular verbs in the imperfect have accent marks.

Indirect object pronouns

An indirect object tells *to whom* or *for whom* something is being done. For example, in the sentence:

> Le di un consejo a **mi hermano.**
> *I gave advice to my brother.*

To whom did I give advice? To my brother. Therefore, **mi hermano** is the indirect object.

Indirect object pronouns are used to refer to indirect objects. Here are the indirect object pronouns in Spanish:

Indirect object pronouns			
Singular		**Plural**	
me	*me*	**nos**	*us*
te	*you (informal)*	**os**	*you (informal)*
le	*him, her, you (formal)*	**les**	*them, you (formal)*

Always use the indirect object pronoun when indicating *to whom* or *for whom* something is done, even if the *indirect object* is mentioned. For clarification or emphasis, the preposition **a** plus a noun or pronoun can be added to a sentence. For example:

> Tomás: Norma, ¿qué **le** diste **a** Ricardo?
> Norma: **Le** di un libro de Isabel Allende.
> Tomás: *Norma, what did you give Ricardo?*
> Norma: *I gave him a book by Isabel Allende.*

In this example, **le** is the *indirect object pronoun* and Ricardo is the *indirect object* that clarifies **le.**

An indirect object pronoun agrees with the indirect object it refers to. For example:

> **Le** recomendamos el restaurante a **Marco.**
> *We recommended the restaurant to Marco.*

> **Les** recomendamos el restaurante a **Marco y Amanda.**
> *We recommended the restaurant to Marco and Amanda.*

Síntesis: Gramática

Indirect object pronouns, just like direct object pronouns, can always be placed before the conjugated verb. If the conjugated verb is followed by an infinitive or if the verb is in the present progressive, you have the option of placing it before the conjugated verb or attaching it to the end of the infinitive or present participle. For example:

> Esteban **me** va a mandar un email. / Esteban va a mandar**me** un email.
> *Esteban is going to send me an email.*

> Carmen **nos** está comprando helado. / Carmen está compr**ándonos** helado.
> *Carmen is buying us ice cream.*

Notice how **compr ándonos** has an accent mark. To maintain the original stress of the present participle, an accent mark is required when attaching an indirect object pronoun.

When using indirect object pronouns with negative commands, place the pronoun directly before the verb.
For example:

> Soy vegetariano. Por favor, no **me** prepares chuletas de cerdo.
> *I am a vegetarian. Please don't make me pork chops.*

When using indirect object pronouns with affirmative commands, attach the pronoun to the end of the verb.
For example:

> Necesito estudiar para el examen. Présta**me** tu libro, por favor.
> *I need to study for the exam. Lend me your book, please.*

Note that an accent mark is often needed to maintain the correct stress when attaching an indirect object pronoun to an affirmative command.

Capítulos 7 y 8

For this project, you'll imagine that you are evaluating candidates for a job. You will also play the role of job candidate. You'll practice comparing and contrasting credentials, talking about past experiences, and speaking in a professional manner. You'll use the grammar and vocabulary you've learned in Chapters 7 and 8 to do this.

Project components

Activity	Points
UP4-1 Descripción del puesto	20 points (individual)
UP4-2 Preguntas para la entrevista	20 points (individual)
UP4-3 Solicitud	15 points (individual)
UP4-4 Evaluación de los candidatos	10 points (individual / group)
UP4-5 Entrevista de trabajo	15 points (individual)
UP4-6 Selección del candidato	20 points (individual)

Descripción del puesto In groups of three or four, form a candidate search committee. Each committee will write a job description in Spanish, of approximately 150 words, for one of the jobs listed below. Committee members will work together in class to complete this step and then have one member post the description. Be sure to include all committee member names for reference and specify the job title when you post your description.

- Empleado(a) en un banco
- Reportero(a) para un periódico local
- Instructor(a) de español
- Diseñador(a) de videojuegos
- Alto(a) ejecutivo(a) de una compañía
- Agente de viajes

 Preguntas para la entrevista Now that you have posted the job opening, your committee will need to prepare interview questions. In your group, prepare six questions, at least two of which use the past tense to ask about past experiences, including successes and challenges (**desafíos**). Have one committee member post the questions. In addition to your six questions, every committee should be prepared to ask candidates why they believe they are qualified for the position: **¿Por qué cree que usted es el mejor candidato para este puesto?**

UP4-3 **Solicitud**

> **Step 1** **Carta de presentación** *This step should be completed online.*

> Now shift gears to play the role of job candidate. Reply to the job description of your choice with a one-page cover letter (170–200 words) in Spanish that summarizes why you feel you are

qualified. Introduce yourself in the letter. Be sure to describe your past experience and mention any technical skills.

Step 2 | Currículum vitae

Write a one-page résumé in Spanish that lists your qualifications and previous work experience. For the purposes of this project only, you may choose to create a persona with imaginary credentials for the job for which you will be applying. Organize your résumé using the guidelines provided in UP4-7. Send a copy of your résumé and letter of introduction to the committee offering the job of your choice.

UP4-4 Evaluación de los candidatos   Each committee member will critique one applicant's résumé prior to the interview. Use the résumé review form provided on the next page.

UP4-5 Entrevista de trabajo   To prepare for the interview, each candidate should receive the interview questions for his/her job of choice. Each committee will then conduct interviews and each student will participate as an interviewee. Interviews should last no more than three minutes per candidate.

Committee members should take notes during the interview to assess whether the applicant is qualified for the position. Each committee member will have to select and rank his/her top two candidates and complete the candidate assessment form.

Speaking in English is not allowed during the interview and may result in disqualification.

UP4-6 Selección del candidato   Each committee will prepare a one-paragraph written summary that details the reasons for choosing its candidate. One committee member should announce the selected candidate and present the summary to the class.

Résumé critique form

Your name: _____   Name of applicant: _____

Although you will be reading all of your applicants' résumés, you will review one in more depth and complete the following critique. Make sure that your responses are constructive.

1. ¿Es el contenido del currículum *(résumé)* fácil de leer y comprender? ¿Por qué sí o por qué no?

_____

_____

_____

2. ¿Qué hizo el (la) candidato(a) (experiencia pasada) para estar preparado(a) para este puesto?

_____

_____

_____

3. ¿Es profesional el formato del currículum? ¿Es apropiado para el puesto *(job position)*?

_____

_____

_____

4. ¿Qué podría hacer el (la) candidato(a) para mejorar su currículum?

_____

_____

_____

5. ¿Qué hace que este(a) candidato(a) sea mejor / peor que los demás?

_____

_____

_____

Proyecto 4: Metas profesionales

UP4-7 Résumé guidelines Use the guidelines below to write your résumé. Remember that it should catch the eye of your potential employer. Not only do you need to make sure your content is flawless, but also your format and layout are very important and should look professional. You can find an appropriate example online to follow and you should use complete sentences when possible. Your résumé should be a minimum of one page and not exceed two pages. Remember that this portion of the project is 50% of your project grade (take it very seriously).

Nombre Include your name, address, phone, and email. Double check all your contact information to make sure it is correct.

Objetivo This section should include what the objective of this résumé is, i.e., the job you are applying for. It should be the shortest section and not exceed a couple of sentences. *(Use present tense)*

Resumen de cualificaciones This section should include your qualifications for the job, any skills you may have, and reasons why you would be good for the job. You should write an entry / description for each of the appropriate points listed below. *(This section should have a mixture of tenses when and where appropriate: present, preterite, etc.)*

- description of yourself using several adjectives
- what makes you qualified for the job you are seeking
- skills and talents you possess that are important for this job
- projects you have done
- technologies you know
- publications you have authored / published
- key strengths

Experiencia profesional This section should include your work experience. You should use the present perfect tense to detail what you have done in your past jobs. Use the present tense when talking about your current job, position, and responsibilities. For each employer (include at least three to four employers) you should include the following:

- current or past employers (contact info) and dates
- positions / jobs you have held
- responsibilities
- job accomplishments

Educación y credenciales This section should include your educational background and any certifications and/or credentials you have that are applicable to the position you are seeking. You should include: name of the institution(s), dates, and degrees / programs currently enrolled in or received. You may also include any training, certifications, and/or credentials that you have completed.

Intereses y logros Use this section to share anything you feel will distinguish you from the competition. The key points here are:

- description of your interests
- your accomplishments in life *(use preterite or present perfect)*

Candidate Assessment Form

1. Escribe los nombres de tus dos candidatos favoritos:
   _____
   _____

2. Describe a los dos candidatos y da tu impresión de cada uno durante la entrevista (mínimo cuatro frases por candidato(a)).
   _____
   _____
   _____
   _____

3. ¿Qué experiencia tuvo cada candidato(a) que le preparó para el trabajo?
   _____
   _____
   _____
   _____

4. Compara a los dos candidatos entre ellos y con el resto (mínimo cuatro frases en total).
   _____
   _____
   _____
   _____

5. Explica cuál de los dos es tu favorito(a) y por qué.
   _____
   _____
   _____
   _____

Las películas

Objectives: In this chapter you will learn to

- Discuss visual arts, popular culture, movies, and TV
- Narrate ongoing and completed past actions

- Use double object pronouns and employ various uses of **se**

Rido/Shutterstock.com

C9-1 Entrevista

Step 1 With a partner, ask each other about a recently released movie you saw. Ask questions to complete the chart. Once you have the information from one classmate, find a new classmate and repeat.

	compañero(a)	compañero(a)	compañero(a)
película (título)			
cuándo			
clase de película			
actores / actrices principales			
historia / se trata de			
recomendación			

Modelo   Student A: *¿Qué película viste?*
                Student B: *Vi la película…*

Step 2 In groups of three or four, share the titles of the movies that you and your partner recently watched. Vote on whether the movies are good or bad. Write down what you think makes a movie good or bad. Think of several examples of both and explain why you like them or dislike them.

1. ¿Qué elementos tiene una película buena? _____

2. ¿Qué elementos tiene una película mala? _____

3. ¿Cuáles consideras que son películas buenas? ¿Por qué? _____

4. ¿Cuáles consideras que son películas malas? ¿Por qué? _____

Gramática

C9-2 La última vez

Step 1 You are working with a classmate on a survey for your communications class. You need to create an additional question and follow-up questions for all six questions.

Modelo   ¿Qué le diste a tu madre para su cumpleaños?
           ¿Dónde *lo / la / los / las compraste*?

1. ¿A quién escribiste el último mensaje de texto que enviaste? ¿Cuándo _____?
2. ¿Cuál fue el último libro que leíste? ¿Dónde _____?
3. ¿Cuál fue el último regalo que recibiste? ¿Quién _____?
4. ¿Quiénes fueron los últimos amigos que viste? ¿Cuándo _____?
5. ¿Cuál fue la última cosa que compraste? ¿Dónde _____?
6. _____

Step 2 With a new partner, take turns asking and answering the questions. Note the responses.

Modelo   Student A: *¿Qué le diste a tu madre para su cumpleaños?*
           Student B: *Le di un libro.*

           Student A: *¿Dónde lo compraste?*
           Student B: *Lo compré por Internet.*

Step 3 Return to your first partner and share the responses to the survey.

Modelo   *María le dio un libro a su madre. Lo compró por Internet.*

C9-3 Póster de la película   In groups of three or four, share images of two movies and react to each by addressing the following questions.

1. ¿Viste la película?
2. ¿Cuantas estrellas le das a la película?
3. ¿Por qué te gustó o por qué no te gustó la película?
4. ¿Qué pasa en la película?

Gramática

C9-4 Los anuncios

Step 1 In the Spanish-speaking world, many ads and signs use forms of a verb with **se.**
With a partner, discuss each sign below and decide who wrote it, why, and where it is found:
¿Quién? ¿Por qué? ¿Dónde? Be creative and write down your ideas.

Modelo   **Se venden tomates.**

¿Quién *escribió el anuncio?*

Lo escribió una mujer con un jardín grande.

¿Por qué *lo escribió?*

Tiene muchos tomates y quiere venderlos.

¿Dónde *está?*

El anuncio está enfrente de su casa.

Step 2 Choose three of the following places or situations and create a sign or ad accordingly.
Use **se** in your sign and be creative. Be prepared to share your signs with the class.

Enfrente de un cine

En la ventana de un dentista

Una persona que no sabe dónde está su mascota *(pet)*

Enfrente de un restaurante

Gramática

Una persona quiere empezar un negocio

En la puerta de la clase de español

Step 3 Now create your own original sign. Think of who needs the sign and why they need it. Decide where the sign would be found. Write your new sign and one of your signs from **Step 2** on the board.

Step 4 With your partner, read all the signs on the board. Guess where you would find each sign, and who would write it and why.

C9-5 Cosas viejas

Step 1 You and your two roommates are moving and decided to sell several items before the move. You each sold different items and interacted with different people. In groups of three, ask each other questions to gather information about the price of each item, who bought the items, and, in some cases, to whom the items were given.

Modelo   la mesa

¿Quién compró la mesa?   *El señor Ruiz la compró.*
¿Por cuánto dinero la vendimos?   *La vendimos por $200.*
¿A quién se la dio?   *Se la dio a su hija.*

Gramática

Student A

cosa para vender	precio	compró...	dio a...
televisión	$200		sus hijos
dos sillas		Carlos	sus compañeros de cuarto
el sofá amarillo			
platos		la señora Gómez	
mesa	$35		
monitor viejo		(nadie)	(a nadie)
escritorio		Susana	su esposo
cuadro antiguo			
bicicleta	$225		

Student B

cosa para vender	precio	compró...	dio a...
televisión		el señor Fernández	sus hijos
dos sillas	$38		
el sofá amarillo		Felipe	(a nadie)
platos	$12		
mesa		María	
monitor viejo	$10		
escritorio			su esposo
cuadro antiguo		mi amigo Tom	su novia
bicicleta			

Gramática

Student C

cosa para vender	precio	compró...	dio a...
televisión			
dos sillas			
el sofá amarillo	$50	Felipe	
platos		la señora Gómez	(a nadie)
mesa			su hermana
monitor viejo			
escritorio	$75	Susana	
cuadro antiguo	$25		su novia
bicicleta		(nadie)	(a nadie)

Step 2 Once everyone in your group has all the information about the sales, answer the following questions.

1. ¿Cuánto dinero recibieron en total? ¿Cuánto recibieron por persona?

2. ¿Qué van a hacer con su parte del dinero?

3. ¿Qué cosas no vendieron? ¿Por qué piensan que nadie las compró?

4. ¿Qué pueden hacer con las cosas que nadie compró?

C9-6A Compañeros de cuarto

Step 1 David and Jorge are roommates. They have different habits and schedules. One of you has information about David on this page and one of you has information about Jorge in activity C9-6B on the next page. Your goal is to fill in the gaps in the charts for each roommate to form a complete schedule. Ask each other questions to figure out what the other roommate did or was doing at different times last Friday using the preterite or imperfect as needed.

Modelo   Student A: *¿Qué hizo Jorge a las 4:00?*
            Student B: *A las 4:00 Jorge empezó a estudiar.*
            Student B: *¿Qué hacía David a las 3:00?*
            Student A: *A las 3:00 David trabajaba en el garaje.*

Estudiante A: Horario de David

¿Cuándo?	¿Qué hacía?	¿Qué hizo?
5:00 de la mañana	David (dormir) en su cuarto.	
8:00		David (preparar) y (comer) desayuno.
10:00		David (salir) para ir al gimnasio.
Mediodía	David (estudiar) en la biblioteca.	
12:30	David (estar) en clase.	
2:00		David (empezar) a trabajar en el garaje.
4:00	David (limpiar) la cocina.	
7:00		David (llegar) a casa.
8:30	David (prepararse) para salir con amigos.	
9:00		David (salir) con sus amigos.
Medianoche		David (regresar) a casa.

Gramática

C9-6B Compañeros de cuarto

Step 1 David and Jorge are roommates. They have different habits and schedules. One of you has information about Jorge on this page and one of you has information about David in activity C9-6A on the previous page. Your goal is to fill in the gaps in the charts for each roommate to form a complete schedule. Ask each other questions to figure out what the other roommate did or was doing at different times last Friday using the preterite or imperfect as needed.

Estudiante B: Horario de Jorge

¿Cuándo?	¿Qué hacía?	¿Qué hizo?
5:00 de la mañana		Jorge (llegar) a casa.
8:00	Jorge (dormir) en el sofá.	
10:00	Jorge (ducharse) en el baño.	
Mediodía		Jorge (llamar) a David para hacerle una pregunta.
12:30		Jorge (comer) la pizza de David.
2:00	Jorge (escribir) mensajes a su novia.	
4:00		Jorge (estudiar).
7:00	Jorge (escuchar) música en su cuarto.	
8:30		Jorge (poner) la televisión.
9:00	Jorge (estudiar) y (mirar) la tele en la sala.	
Medianoche	Jorge (salir) con sus amigos.	

Step 2 Once you have all the spaces filled, recreate the events from last Friday. Take turns telling what happened at each time of day.

Modelo   (5:00) *David dormía en su cuarto cuando Jorge llegó a casa.*

Step 3 Decide which of the following statements would most likely apply to David and which to Jorge. Give examples to justify your reasoning. Then state which person you would like to have as a roommate and why you would be a good match.

1. Es un buen estudiante.
2. Le interesa ver la televisión y películas.
3. Trabaja por la noche.
4. Es activo y le gustan los deportes.

C9-7 Antes y ahora

Step 1 In groups of three, find out what you have in common with your group members by asking and answering the following questions about when you were high school students. You should take turns asking the questions but everyone should answer. Find three things your group has in common that you can share with the class.

Cuando eran estudiantes en la escuela secundaria:

¿Qué programas de televisión veían?

¿Cuáles eran sus películas favoritas? ¿Por qué?

¿Qué música escuchaban?

¿Trabajaban? ¿Qué tipo de trabajo tenían?

¿Estudiaban mucho o poco?

¿Qué actividades hacían con sus amigos y familia?

Step 2 Find out whether things have changed for your group members since high school. Ask about current situations and preferences for: *programas de televisión, películas, música, trabajo, estudios y actividades.*

Step 3 With your group, answer the following questions. Base your answers on your conversations from the previous steps and your personal experiences. Be prepared to report your ideas to the class.

1. ¿Qué música, películas y programas de televisión son populares entre los estudiantes de la escuela secundaria?

2. ¿Qué música, películas y programas de televisión son populares entre los estudiantes universitarios?

3. ¿Todavía a ustedes les gustan las mismas películas, los mismos programas y la misma música que antes? ¿Cuáles son? ¿Por qué les gustan? ¿Por qué no les gustan?

4. Pensando en el trabajo, los estudios y las actividades, ¿qué diferencias hay en la vida de estudiantes típicos de la escuela secundaria y estudiantes típicos universitarios?

Gramática

C9-8 Un cuento y charadas

Step 1 You and your partners need to create a basic story that you will later act out in the form of charades. Use the form below to help prepare your story. Decide who the characters are (people, animals, and/or things) and what they are like. Then write down the key events and actions for each character.

Modelo   Nombre y descripción *Alberto es alto. Tiene el pelo negro. Él...*
        ¿Qué hacía? *Alberto comía un helado. Paseaba en el parque.*
        ¿Qué hizo? *Alberto vio a María. Él saludó a María.*

Nombre y descripción de la persona	¿Qué hacía?	¿Qué hizo?

Step 2 Find another group. Play charades by acting out your story without words. Continue acting out each part of the story until they correctly guess what your characters are like and what they did or were doing in the story.

Modelo   *Es un hombre alto y tiene mucho pelo. Tiene pelo blanco. No, pelo negro. Comió un helado. Caminaba. Vio algo.*

Step 3 Once they have correctly guessed the elements of your story, reenact your story, but this time verbally narrate your story as you act it out. Then watch the other group perform their story while you guess. Then watch and listen as they narrate and act out their story.

C9-9 En el museo de arte As a campus ambassador, you have been assigned to work with
the art museum on campus. The museum wants to enhance the visitor's experience for
children who speak Spanish. You and another campus ambassador have been asked to help
create flyers that Spanish speakers can use while at the museum.

Step 1 The museum curator has asked you and your partner each to identify one work of art
by a Hispanic artist that the curator should feature when she speaks to school groups visiting
the museum. Answer her questions about the works. First, answer her questions about the
works found below. Then create four questions of your own that you will use in the next step.

1. ¿Qué cosas y colores hay en la obra de arte?

2. ¿Es nueva o antigua?

3. Piensa en una palabra para describirla.

Step 2 A group of Spanish speakers are visiting the museum. The flyer is not ready yet, but
the curator wants you to test the questions on real people. Find a new partner and ask the
questions. Then switch roles and answer his/her questions. Repeat with a new partner as
many times as time allows. Make note of the answers.

Step 3 With your original partner, address the curator's concerns.

¿Todos los visitantes respondieron con la misma respuesta?

¿Qué respuestas / comentarios fueron más originales? Denme unos ejemplos.

¿Qué preguntas fueron las más difíciles para contestar? ¿Por qué?

Solo hay espacio para cinco preguntas en español. ¿Cuáles son las que me
recomiendan? ¿Por qué?

¿Podemos usar estas cinco preguntas con varias obras de arte o solo con una obra
en específico?

La música de Latinoamérica

Los sonidos, danzas y estilos musicales de América Latina tienen raíces africanas, precolombinas, criollas y europeas. Estas culturas se fusionaron y dieron origen a nuevos géneros *(types)* característicos de cada zona, que, a su vez y con el paso del tiempo, se combinaron con otros géneros para seguir creando estilos y ritmos.

El reguetón es ejemplo de esto: nace en la comunidad jamaiquina de Panamá y combina reggae con hip hop, pero le debe su nombre a Puerto Rico. Algo parecido pasa con **la salsa,** que nace en Nueva York, con influencia de Cuba y Puerto Rico, y los aportes del son cubano y el jazz de los Estados Unidos.

El pop latino: El éxito del pop latino en el mundo se debe al carisma de cantantes como Shakira, Juanes, Marc Anthony, Jennifer Lopez, Ricky Martin y Gloria Estefan, pero también a la adaptación de la rica tradición de la música latinoamericana que se fusiona con el pop para volverse más accesible al público internacional. Carlos Vives llevó **la cumbia** y **el vallenato** colombiano a las listas de las estaciones de radio con sus canciones pegadizas *(catchy),* donde se mezcla la música tradicional con el rock y el pop.

El son: La música de Cuba volvió a disfrutar un momento de gloria internacional a fines de los 90, impulsando *(inspiring)* el renacimiento del son y de **la trova.** Esto ocurrió gracias al álbum del grupo Buena Vista Social Club, producido por el guitarrista Ry Cooder en un viaje a Cuba. El director de cine Wim Wenders registró *(captured)* todo el proyecto en un documental que recibió varios premios y una nominación al Óscar.

La bachata, de República Dominicana, muestra influencias del son y del bolero. El cantante y compositor Romeo Santos, nacido en Nueva York, modernizó el género y lo llevó a la escena de la música internacional como líder de la agrupación *Aventura*. En 2009 fue invitado a cantar en la Casa Blanca para el presidente Barack Obama.

El tango nació en el Río de la Plata: su origen exacto es tema de discusión eterno entre Argentina y Uruguay. Lo cierto es que desde el principio fue una danza urbana con raíces africanas, gauchescas y europeas. La escena tanguera se revolucionó en el siglo XXI tras la aparición del tango eléctronico con el grupo Bajofondo. Gustavo Santaolalla, uno de los fundadores del proyecto, es compositor de música de películas y ganador de dos premios Óscar consecutivos por mejor banda sonora.

C9-10   La música de mi país

Step 1 With a partner, choose a band or singer that you both admire and would choose to represent your country's music in any part of the world.

You need arguments to support your choice: consider their image, the type of music they play, the lyrics from their most popular songs, some anecdote that you remember or their attitude towards politics, environment, gender issues, etc.

Step 2 Now write a brief paragraph declaring that singer or band the most emblematic musician from your country; list your reasons and find a tag line to further support your choice.

Step 3 Share your text with the class. Find out whether there are points in common with your classmates: compare which aspects each of you tried to highlight. Can you convince the others? Try to advertise your "nomination" for Best Band / Singer!

Una película buena

Ayer fuimos a ver una película. Para mí a veces es difícil entender lo que dicen los actores cuando hablan rápido, pero no fue así con esta película. ¡Me encantó! Se trató de una chica y un chico y de cómo ellos se conocieron. Antes de conocer a la chica, el chico era tímido y se vestía con ropa vieja. Todos los días, él no hacía nada más que estudiar y jugar en su computadora. Ella era muy popular y no era muy simpática. Ella siempre llevaba ropa cara y de moda. Ella tenía muchos amigos guapos y ricos. Los dos chicos asistieron a la misma clase de química. Ella no era buena estudiante pero él entendía muy bien la clase. Ellos no tenían mucho en común, pero un día él le ayudó a ella a estudiar para la clase. Él le compró un libro a ella. A ella no le gustaban los libros pero ese día empezó a sentir algo por él. Al final ellos se enamoraron y fueron muy felices. Ella le compró mucha ropa a él y se la dio antes de ir a un baile de la escuela. Así, al final de la película el chico se veía muy guapo. Mi amigo Juan dice que esta es una de las peores películas que ha visto. A él le gustan las películas de acción. A mí me gustan las películas de acción también, pero a veces me gusta ver una película romántica cómica. ¿Qué tipos de películas te gustan a ti?

C9-11 Mi blog

Step 1 In groups of three, read aloud the blog entries you each created for Bella's Blog in MT for this chapter. Then react to each other's favorite programs and movies. Do you like the same ones? Have you seen your classmates' favorites before? Do you like the actors in them?

Modelo   Student A: *Mi película favorita es* Deadpool *de Ryan Reynolds. Me gusta la película porque…*

Student B: *A mí me encanta Ryan Reynolds. Es muy guapo y un buen actor.*

Student C: *A mí me gusta su película* La Proposición *más que* Deadpool.

Step 2 Based on your previous discussion and blog entries, create a five-question survey related to movies or television programs. Everyone in the group needs to have a copy of the same questions for the next step.

Modelo   1. ¿Cuál es tu película de acción favorita?
2. ¿Qué películas viste de Ryan Reynolds?
3. ¿...?

Step 3 Leave your group and find a new partner. Ask and answer each other's questions. Write down your partner's responses. If there is time, interview another person.

Step 4 Once you have finished asking and answering the questions, return to your group and compare the survey results. Prepare five sentences to share with the class based on the results.

Modelo   *En nuestra clase, la película* Avengers *es muy popular. A muchas personas les gustan las películas de* La guerra de las galaxias.

Síntesis: Vocabulario

En el cine   *At the movies*

el actor   *actor*
la actriz   *actress*
el argumento / la trama   *plot*
el cine   *movie theater*
el/la crítico(a)   *critic*
el/la director(a)   *director*
el documental   *documentary*
el drama   *drama*
los efectos especiales   *special effects*
la escena   *scene*
el guion   *script*
el presupuesto   *budget*
el/la productor(a)   *producer*
el/la protagonista   *protagonist*
los subtítulos   *subtitles*
doblado(a)   *dubbed*
filmar / rodar   *to film*
se trata de…   *it is about …*

Clases de películas   *Types of movies*

la comedia   *comedy*
los dibujos animados   *cartoons*
el misterio   *mystery*
el musical   *musical*
la película   *movie*
la película de acción   *action movie*
la película de ciencia ficción   *science fiction movie*
la película de horror / terror   *horror movie*
la película romántica   *romantic movie*

La televisión   *Television*

el anuncio / el comercial   *comercial*
el cable   *cable*
el episodio   *episode*
las noticias   *news*
el programa de realidad   *reality show*
el programa de televisión   *television program*
la telenovela   *soap opera*
la temporada   *TV season*
en vivo   *live*
cambiar el canal   *to change the channel*
grabar   *to record*
transmitir   *to broadcast*
ver   *to see or to watch*

La música   *Music*

la música clásica   *classic music*
la música country   *country music*
la música pop   *pop music*
el rock   *rock / rock and roll*

Otras palabras   *Other words*

la canción   *song*
el/la cantante   *singer*
el concierto   *concert*
el espectáculo   *show*
la letra   *lyrics*
el/la músico(a)   *musician*
la obra de teatro   *play*
aplaudir   *to applaud*
cantar   *to sing*
hacer cola / hacer fila   *to wait in line*
tocar   *to play a musical instrument*

El arte   *Art*

el artista   *artist*
el dibujo   *drawing*
el diseño   *design*
la escultura   *sculpture*
la estatua   *statue*
el estilo   *style*
el museo   *museum*
la pintura   *painting*
crear   *to create*
dibujar   *to draw*
pintar   *to paint*
sacar fotos / tomar fotos   *take pictures*

Síntesis: Gramática

Double object pronouns

Indirect object pronouns and direct object pronouns are often used in the same sentence. The indirect object pronoun *always* comes *before* the direct object pronoun. For example:

Mi papá **me** compró **un perro** ⟶ Mi papá **me lo** compró.
My father bought me a dog. ⟶ *My father bought it for me.*

When using double object pronouns, if **le** or **les** comes before **lo, la, las,** or **los,** it has to be changed to **se** in order to avoid awkward pronunciation. For example:

La maestra le dio chocolate. ⟶ La maestra **se** lo dio.
    IO   DO   IO DO

The teacher gave him chocolate. ⟶ *The teacher gave him it.*

Ayer les escribí una carta. ⟶ Ayer **se** la escribí.
    IO   DO   IO DO

They wrote them the letter yesterday. ⟶ *They wrote them it yesterday.*

Double object pronouns can always be placed before a conjugated verb. If a conjugated verb is followed by an infinitive or if the verb is in the present progressive, you also have the option of attaching them to the end of the infinitive or present participle. For example:

Mi hermana me los va a comprar para mi cumpleaños.
My sister is going to buy me them for my birthday.

Mi hermana va a comprármelos para mi cumpleaños.
My sister is going to buy me them for my birthday.

Mi hermana está comprándomelos para mi cumpleaños.
My sister is buying me them for my birthday.

Remember, if you attach double object pronouns to an infinitive or present participle, you need to add an accent mark to maintain the original stress.

When using double object pronouns with a negative command, place them directly before the verb. For example:

No me lo traigas ahora, por favor.
Don't bring it to me now, please.

When using double object pronouns with an affirmative command, attach the pronoun to the end of the verb. For example:

Tráemelo ahora, por favor.
Bring it to me now, please.

Remember, if you attach double object pronouns to an affirmative command, you have to add an accent mark to maintain the original stress of the command.

Uses of *se*

Se accidental

In Spanish, the pronoun **se** can be used to indicate an unintentional action. To talk about unplanned or accidental occurrences, use the following formula:

se + indirect object pronoun + verb *(third person)*

Síntesis: Gramática

For example:

> **A Carlos se le rompió** su teléfono.
> *Carlos broke his phone.*

> ¿**Se te perdieron** las llaves?
> *Did you lose the keys?*

The subject is the thing that gets broken, forgotten, or lost (**el teléfono, las llaves**) and the indirect object pronoun refers to the person to whom it happened (**Carlos, te**).

Remember, if the subject is a verb in the infinitive, the verb is always in the third-person singular. For example:

> Lo siento, **se me olvidó** hacer la tarea.
> *I am sorry, I forgot to do the homework.*

Here are some verbs commonly used with **se** to indicate accidental occurrences:

> **acabar**   to finish / to end, to run out of
> **caer**   to fall down / to drop
> **olvidar**   to forget
> **perder**   to lose
> **romper**   to break

Se impersonal

Another common use of the pronoun **se** is in impersonal expressions. Impersonal expressions are used when you can't or don't want to specify exactly who is doing an action. In English we use a word such as *one, they,* or *people* as the subject of the sentence. In Spanish, the pronoun **se** is placed in front of the **third-person singular** form of a verb. For example:

> En Perú **se come** bien.
> *In Peru they eat well.*

> ¿Dónde **se estudia** aquí en la universidad?
> *Where does one study here in the university?*

The impersonal **se** can also be used when asking for directions. For example:

> ¿Cómo **se va** al museo?
> *How does one get to the museum?*

Se pasivo

The **passive** voice is when the **action** of the sentence is emphasized and the subject is de-emphasized. To express the passive voice in Spanish, use what is called the passive **se**.

To use the passive **se** with a singular noun, put the pronoun **se** in front of the **third-person singular** form of a verb and then add the singular noun. For example:

> **Se habla español** aquí.
> *Spanish is spoken here.*

Síntesis: Gramática

To use the passive **se** with a plural noun, put the pronoun **se** in front of the **third-person plural** form of a verb and then add the plural noun. For example:

Se compran libros usados en la librería.
Used books are bought in the bookstore.

Preterite and Imperfect

In Spanish, the preterite and imperfect are both used to describe past events. Which one you use depends on the meaning that you want to convey.

The preterite is used to express completed actions: in other words, actions that had a clear beginning and ending. For example:

Ayer **llegué** a casa a las seis, **comí** con la familia, **bañé** a los niños y **me dormí** a las nueve.
Yesterday I arrived home at six, ate with the family, bathed the kids, and fell asleep at nine.

The imperfect is used to express ongoing and habitual actions in the past.

En la universidad siempre **comía** en la cafetería, **salía** con amigos y **me acostaba** tarde.
In college, I always used to eat in the cafeteria, go out with friends and go to bed late.

The imperfect is often used to describe a person, place, or thing in the past. For example:

¿Cómo **eras** de niña?
What were you like as a girl?

Era muy tímida.
I was very shy.

The imperfect is also used to say what time it was or to tell how old someone was. For example:

Eran las cuatro y media.
It was four thirty.

Mi padre **tenía** veinte años.
My father was twenty years old.

The imperfect is used with the word **mientras** *(while)* to talk about two simultaneous actions that happened in the past. For example:

Esteban **dormía mientras** Natalia **estudiaba.**
Esteban was sleeping while Natalia was studying.

In Spanish, sometimes you use the preterite and imperfect in the same sentence. For example, when there is an on-going action interrupted by another action, the **imperfect** is used for the action in progress and the **preterite** is used for the action that is interrupting. The word **cuando** *(when)* is often used in these sentences. For example:

> Mis padres **miraban** la tele **cuando sonó** el teléfono.
> *My parents were watching television when the phone rang.*

Here are some expressions that are generally used with the **preterite** to indicate that the past action is completed.

anoche	*last night*
ayer	*yesterday*
anteayer	*the day before yesterday*
el (lunes) pasado	*last (Monday)*
la semana pasada	*last week*
el mes pasado	*last month*
el año pasado	*last year*
una vez / dos veces	*one time, once / two times, twice*

Here are some expressions that are generally used with the **imperfect** to indicate that the past action does **not** have a clear beginning or ending.

a menudo	*frequently*
a veces	*sometimes*
generalmente	*generally*
normalmente	*normally*
siempre	*always*
todos los años	*every year*
todos los días	*every day*
todos los meses	*every month*
todas las semanas	*every week*

La moda

Objectives: In this chapter you will learn to

- Express opinions and subjective reactions
- Talk about hypothetical situations
- Discuss clothing and style
- State indirect commands and opinions using the subjunctive
- Talk about the future

imageBROKER/Alamy Stock Photo

Vocabulario/Gramática

C10-1 Ropa de viaje

Step 1 With a partner, look at the following travel destinations. Write a suggestion or recommendation for what clothing your partner should take on the trip. Have half of your recommendation be logical and half illogical. If time allows, create additional situations.

Modelo   Miami, el 4 de julio

Sugiero / Recomiendo que lleves un traje de baño y pantalones cortos porque va a hacer calor.

1. Alaska, el 1 de enero
2. El gran cañón en Arizona, en verano
3. Buenos Aires, Argentina, en julio y agosto
4. Cancún, México, en otoño
5. Chicago, en 14 de febrero
6. Las montañas, en primavera
7. Europa, en las vacaciones de verano
8. ¿…?

Step 2 With a new partner, share your recommendations and react to each one. Tell why it is logical or illogical.

Modelo   Miami, el 4 de julio

Student A: *Recomiendo que lleves un traje de baño y pantalones cortos.*
Student B: *Es lógico porque hace calor.*

C10-2A

En el armario de Eva y Paola A

Step 1 Half the class will use this activity and half of the class will work with C10-2B. If you are chosen for this activity, look at Paola's closet and answer the following questions in complete sentences.

1. ¿Qué zapatos tiene? ¿Cómo son los zapatos?

   _____

   _____

   _____

2. ¿Qué estilo tiene la persona?

   _____

   _____

   _____

3. ¿Cómo es la persona? ¿Qué le interesa?

   _____

   _____

   _____

El armario de Paola

C10-2B En el armario de Eva y Paola **B**

Step 1 Half the class will use this activity and half of the class will work with C10-2A. If you are chosen for this activity, look at Eva's closet and answer the following questions in complete sentences.

1. ¿Qué zapatos tiene?
   ¿Cómo son los zapatos?
   _____
   _____
   _____

2. ¿Qué estilo tiene la persona?
   _____
   _____
   _____

3. ¿Cómo es la persona? ¿Qué le interesa?
   _____
   _____
   _____

El armario de Eva

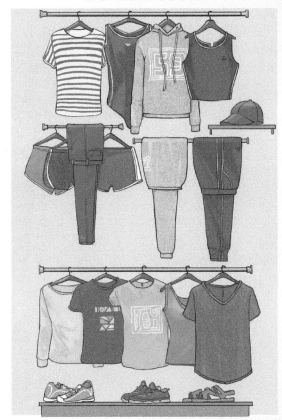

Vocabulario/Gramática

Step 2 Work with a partner. You have seen Eva's closet and your partner has seen Paola's closet: help organize the clothing according to whom you think it belongs to. Give reasons why you think each item of clothing belongs to that person. What does the clothing tell you about the owner?

Modelo   *¿De quién es la camiseta?*
         Creo que la camiseta es de Eva. Eva tiene muchas camisetas porque hace mucho ejercicio.

	Eva	Paola
zapatos de tacón alto	☐	☐
sudadera vieja	☐	☐
vestido moderno	☐	☐
blusa elegante	☐	☐
traje de baño	☐	☐
zapatos de tenis	☐	☐
falda	☐	☐
botas negras	☐	☐
sandalias	☐	☐
pantalones cortos	☐	☐

Step 3 Eva and Paola have been invited to two different events and they need your help preparing their clothing. Eva has been invited to a three-day professional conference with a formal awards ceremony and dinner. Paola has been invited to go camping by a lake where they will hike and canoe. Based on what you and your partner know about their closets, recommend what they should and should not do clothing-wise. Give reasons for your recommendations. Some useful words: **llevar, comprar, poner, traer, usar.**

Modelo   *Recomendamos que Eva compre… porque…*
         Sugerimos que Paola no use… porque…

C10-3 La ropa

Step 1 You and your partner are working as wardrobe experts. You have a college-student client who has a new job and needs your advice. In order to find out about his/her current style preferences and clothing needs, create five questions addressing some of the following topics: **prendas, preferencias, dónde, cuánto dinero, marcas, cantidad, colores.**

Modelo *¿Qué ropa llevas cuando estás en la universidad?*

Step 2 With a new partner, imagine you're the client. Answer his/her questions. Then switch roles and ask your questions. Write down the answers.

Step 3 With your original partner, discuss the information you have collected. Make three or four clothing-related recommendations for your client about his/her new job. You may want to include fabrics, colors, styles, articles of clothing, and when and where to wear them. Be creative and use a variety of verbs. Some useful verbs are: **comprar, vender, llevar, usar, donar, lavar, etc.**

Modelo *Sugerimos que lleves tu blusa de seda los fines de semana.*
Recomendamos que compres…

Step 4 Share your recommendations with the client. Then listen to and react to his/her recommendations.

Vocabulario

C10-4 La ropa de los estudiantes

Step 1 Find a partner and ask the following questions. Then find a new partner and repeat. Your goal is to speak with at least three or four classmates. Write down the key information for each person you interview.

¿De qué está hecha tu ropa?

¿De qué marca es la ropa que llevas hoy?

¿En qué país fue hecha tu ropa?

¿Qué accesorios tienes hoy?

Step 2 With your last partner, answer the following questions based on the information you have gathered.

¿Qué materiales son más comunes o populares en la clase?

¿De qué marca es la ropa que llevan los estudiantes de la clase hoy?

¿En qué países fue hecha la ropa?

¿Qué accesorios son populares en la clase?

Step 3 With your partner, prepare three statements based on clothing. What does our clothing tell us about us? Be prepared to share your ideas with the whole class.

Gramática

C10-5 ¿Qué quieres?

Step 1 With a partner, write five things you want someone to act out.

Modelo *Quiero que escribas un mensaje con tu teléfono.*

Step 2 Leave your partner and form a group of four or five students. Whisper one of your sentences to a group member. He/she has to silently act it out until the rest of the group correctly guesses. In order for it to be guessed correctly, it needs to follow the model below.

Modelo *Él/Ella quiere que tú escribas un mensaje con tu teléfono.*

C10-6 ¿Qué ropa deben llevar?

Step 1 Use the following sentences to take turns with a partner suggesting what each celebrity should wear.

Modelo *Sugiero que Sofía Vergara lleve un vestido negro, zapatos de tacón alto y un collar de diamantes en los Óscar.*

1. Beyoncé va a cantar en un concierto internacional.
2. Jennifer Lawrence va a estar sola en casa.
3. Justin Bieber va a promocionar ropa como modelo.
4. Kevin Durant va a jugar baloncesto.
5. Jimmy Fallon y Justin Timberlake van a estar en la televisión.
6. Martha Stewart va a cocinar en la cocina.

Step 2 Share and compare your suggestions with your group from **C10-5**. Then, invent two or three more situations for one of the celebrities and recommend clothing and accessories. Be prepared to present your ideas to the class.

C10-7 Promociones de prendas

Step 1 You have the job of marketing clothing. To get started, work with a partner. Look at the image and answer the following questions.

iordani/Shutterstock.com

1. ¿De qué está hecha la ropa? _____

2. ¿Quién va a comprar las cosas de la foto? _____

3. ¿Dónde podemos venderlas? _____

4. ¿Qué precio es aceptable? _____

Step 2 Now you need to get creative and sell the clothing line to the rest of the company. You need to create a twenty- to thirty-word blurb promoting your clothing. You will then present your blurb to the class and vote on which blurb is the most convincing.

Modelo   *La ropa está hecha de materiales reciclados y producida en fábricas que funcionan con energía renovable. Los tejidos son resistentes, pero también cómodos y elegantes.*

Gramática

C10-8   ¿Tú qué crees?

Step 1 With a partner, read the following statements. State whether you believe them, or doubt they are true. Then explain your reasoning.

Modelo   Mi abuelo tiene 120 años.
          Dudo que tu abuelo tenga 120 años. 120 años es mucho.
          Shakira vive en Barcelona.
          Creo que Shakira vive en Barcelona.

1. El edificio más alto del mundo está en Buenos Aires.

2. La capital de Honduras se llama Tegucigalpa.

3. En España no bailan el flamenco.

4. En México, D.F., comen más tortillas que en Bogotá.

5. En Sudamérica no existen los pingüinos.

6. Haití y Puerto Rico comparten *(share)* una frontera.

7. Bolivia tiene playas en la costa atlántica.

8. Los chilenos beben mucho pisco.

Step 2 With your partner, create three additional statements similar to the ones from the previous step. Both of you should write them down.

Step 3 Find a new partner and take turns reading your new statements and reacting to them.

Gramática

En el futuro

Step 1 Add three well-known people to the chart below and predict their futures. Then make predictions for your partner and yourself as well. Be prepared to share your predictions with the class.

Modelo   *En cinco años Brad Pitt tendrá más hijos. En diez años será un hombre viejo en una película. En quince años no actuará en películas.*

Nombre	En cinco años	En diez años	En quince años
tú			
tu compañero(a)			

Step 2 Form a new group and, without saying the people's names, share your predictions. Have the other people in your group see whether they can guess each person based on the predictions.

C10-10   ¿Será?

Step 1 You and your partner are looking at the following items of clothing. You have learned that the future tense can be used to speculate in addition to talking about the future. Use the future tense and the chart as a guide to ask speculative questions about each item. Write simple answers in the spaces provided.

Modelo Student A: *¿De quién será ese traje?*
Student B: *Será de George Clooney.*

1.

2.

3.

4.

5.

6.

Gramática

Pregunta	camisa	zapatos	pantalones	vestido	calcetines	corbata
how much it costs						
what is it made of						
who wears it						
where you can buy it						
who it belongs to						

Step 2 Look at the information you added to the chart and prepare answers to the following questions. Be prepared to report to your class.

1. ¿Cuál es la prenda de ropa más cara? ¿Cuál es la más barata? ¿Por qué?

2. ¿Cuánto es el máximo que pagarías por cada prenda?

3. ¿Puedes comprar todas las cosas en el mismo lugar? ¿Dónde?

4. ¿De qué están hechas las prendas? ¿Pueden estar hechas de otros materiales? Den unos ejemplos.

Gramática

C10-11 Recomendaciones

Step 1 The following people need advice. With a partner, read each situation and work together to write your recommendation about the best action(s) to take. Be prepared to share your ideas with the class.

Modelo   Paco tiene mucha hambre y no tiene comida en su casa.
Sugiero que vaya al supermercado y compre comida.

Eduardo tiene una cita y no tiene ropa limpia.

El coche de Anita es viejo y está en malas condiciones. Ella tiene cinco mil dólares en el banco.

Mary y Rosa quieren viajar a Perú pero no tienen mucho dinero.

Un estudiante quiere recibir una nota buena en su clase de español.

Hoy es lunes y tu amiga tiene un examen el martes y otro el miércoles.

Antonio y Saúl saben una palabra en inglés pero no la saben en español.

Marta tiene una entrevista importante con una compañía internacional mañana.

Step 2 Share your recommendations with the class, and as others share theirs, vote whether you agree or disagree. While you listen, decide which recommendations you think are the best, most creative, and most logical.

Gramática

C10-12 ¿Qué harían?

Step 1 In groups of three or four, write down the names of four famous people. Consider including some of the following: **políticos, cantantes, deportistas, actores, personas de negocios, artistas.** Read the following hypothetical situations and ask a related question about what your first person would do in each one. Everyone in the group should tell what they think the famous person would do. Once you finish with one famous person, move on to the next person.

Modelo   *Ellen DeGeneres:* Un amigo especial va a visitarla.
               ¿Qué haría Ellen con su mejor amigo?
               Ellen planearía una broma (joke) *y sorprendería a su amigo.*

1. Tiene hambre.
2. Es el/la nuevo(a) presidente(a) de los Estados Unidos.
3. Quiere comprar ropa nueva.
4. Ha perdido *(lost)* todo su dinero.
5. Tiene que viajar a otro país.
6. Va a tener una entrevista en la televisión.

Step 2 Now choose two of the famous people and write two new hypothetical situations for them. Tell what they would do differently.

Modelo   *Ellen DeGeneres y Paris Hilton: Han recibido mucho dinero que no necesitan.*
               Paris compraría ropa nueva y haría una fiesta grande con muchas personas, pero Ellen daría dinero a personas que lo necesitan.

Gramática

C10-13 ¿Qué harías?

Step 1 With a partner, ask each other what you would do in the following situations. Write down what your partner says.

Modelo   Ganas la lotería.
          Yo viajaría por todo el mundo.

1. Encuentras una maleta llena de dinero.

2. Tu mejor amigo(a) se va de viaje y nunca más vas a verlo(la).

3. Un terremoto destruye tu casa.

4. Tu familia decide mudarse a Argentina.

5. Pierdes tu computadora.

6. Te llaman para hacer una película en Hollywood.

7. Te despiertas tarde y tienes poco tiempo antes de clase.

Step 2 With a new partner, compare what your previous partners said. Did they say they would do similar things or did they have different ideas? Prepare at least four comparative statements.

Modelo   Ganas la lotería.
          Juan viajaría por todo el mundo, pero Antonio compraría un coche nuevo.

Gramática

C10-14 Un viaje con amigos

Step 1 You and your classmates are making the initial plans for a trip. You all have come up with several ideas of where you would like to go. Look at the list and discuss what you would do in each place. Add a few more places and tell what you would do while there.

Lugares: Las Vegas, el parque nacional de Yellowstone, la ciudad de Nueva York, San Francisco, Los Ángeles, (…)

Modelo *¿Qué haríamos en Boston?*
En Boston visitaríamos muchos sitios históricos. Veríamos un partido de béisbol en Fenway Park. Cenaríamos cerca de Harvard. Podríamos…

Step 2 Based on your conversation in **Step 1**, choose one destination. You will travel together, but still have some questions to answer. Work together to address the following concerns about a trip to that location.

¿Cómo viajaríamos al destino? ¿Tendríamos que pagar mucho dinero?

¿Cuántas noches nos quedaríamos?

¿Cuánto dinero necesitaríamos para el hotel?

¿Dónde y qué comeríamos?

¿Qué actividades específicas haríamos?

¿Qué ropa llevaríamos / necesitaríamos?

Step 3 Prepare a few statements explaining why your group decided to travel to that destination.

Los diseñadores hispanos más famosos

Los hispanos han tenido una gran influencia en el mundo de la moda. Hagamos un repaso de los diseñadores que han logrado sobresalir y marcar su estilo.

Francisco Rabaneda y Cuervo, mejor conocido como **Paco Rabanne**, nació en 1934 en España. Su madre trabajó como costurera [titular] con Balenciaga. Rabanne creó bisutería y botones de plástico para las grandes casas de la moda de la época: Balenciaga, Nina Ricci, Maggy Rouff, Philippe Venet, Pierre Cardin, Courrèges y Givenchy.

Ágatha Ruiz de la Prada llegó al mundo de la moda para quedarse cuando presentó en Madrid en 1981 su primera colección para dama, […] un gran éxito [que] la motivó a abrir su primer estudio en la capital española y a empezar a participar en desfiles tanto en Madrid como en Barcelona.

Isabel Toledo había mantenido un perfil más bajo a nivel internacional, hasta el día que Barack Obama tomó posesión como presidente de los Estados Unidos y Michelle salió de su brazo luciendo un conjunto en lana y encaje color limón, diseñado y confeccionado por ella.

La diseñadora **Gabriela Perezutti,** quien ahora radica en Nueva York, explora y plasma sus raíces uruguayas en sus creaciones. Perezutti lanzó con éxito una línea de ropa femenina y de calzado llamada Candela y planea incursionar en el comercio electrónico con el lanzamiento de su página. Además, ha presentado sus creaciones en la semana de la moda en Nueva York con mucha aceptación.

Excerpted from: http://www.univision.com/noticias/los-disenadores-hispanos-mas-famosos-fotos

C10-15 **La lista** Do you agree with this list? Can you think of other well-known Hispanic designers? Do a search and decide whether names should be added to this list.

C10-16 **Los requisitos** What does it take to be a fashion designer?

Step 1 Individually, make a list of the skills you believe a designer should develop to find a place in the fashion industry.

Modelo —*Para ser diseñador(a), la persona tiene que saber...*

—*Es importante/necesario que...*

—*Uno debe poder...*

Step 2 Work in groups. Discuss your lists and try to agree on the most important skills.

Modelo —*Creo que es muy importante poder / saber...*

—*Es cierto, pero también tiene que....*

—*(No) Estoy de acuerdo.*

Step 3 Compare your final list with those of the other groups. What was missing in each list? What points did the groups have in common?

El blog de Bella

Este fin de semana voy a ir de compras con María y sus amigas. Estoy animada porque yo necesito y también quiero ropa nueva. Vamos a ir a varias tiendas en el centro de la ciudad. Creo que voy a comprar unas camisas y un vestido. Dudo que vayamos a gastar *(spend)* mucho dinero pero si tengo que elegir entre comprar las camisas o un vestido, voy a comprar el vestido. Necesito un vestido nuevo porque voy a asistir a la boda de mis amigos Pedro y Ana. Espero que encontremos un vestido económico porque yo realmente quiero llevar un vestido nuevo en la boda. ☺

No solo vamos a ir de compras, también vamos a visitar el museo de bellas artes. A María le gusta mucho el arte de Fernando Botero y hay una exhibición de su arte en el museo. Él es un artista famoso colombiano. Creo que va a ser una experiencia interesante. Después de ir al museo, vamos a comer en un restaurante de comida mexicana. Yo voy a pedir enchiladas y creo que María va a pedir tacos. Vamos a divertirnos mucho este fin de semana.

Artepics/Alamy Stock Photo

El blog de Bella

C10-17 Tu Blog: Optimista y pesimista

Step 1 In groups of three, read your blog entries about your plans for the weekend. The person reading should pause often to let the other two react. One person is the **optimista** and one is the **pesimista**. If you are the optimist, you need to react favorably to all the plans. If you are the pessimist, you need to be doubtful about all the plans. With each reading, change roles between pessimist and optimist.

Modelos Lector: *Vamos a comer en un restaurante elegante.*
      Optimista: *Creo que van a comer mucha comida rica.*
      Pesimista: *Dudo que vayan a tener dinero suficiente.*
      Lector: *Voy a visitar a mis abuelos en Florida.*
      Pesimista: *No creo que tus abuelos quieran verte.*
      Optimista: *Espero que lo pases muy bien con tus abuelos.*

Step 2 As a group, discuss when is it good to be an optimist and when is it appropriate to be a pessimist. Choose two cases or situations for both. Be prepared to tell the class why your group thinks this way.

Síntesis: Vocabulario

Prendas de ropa   *Articles of clothing*

el abrigo   *coat*

la blusa   *blouse*

las botas   *boots*

los calcetines   *socks*

la camisa   *shirt*

la camiseta   *t-shirt*

la corbata   *tie*

la falda   *skirt*

la gorra   *cap*

el impermeable   *rain coat*

el jersey   *sweater*

los pantalones   *pants*

los pantalones cortos   *shorts*

el saco   *jacket or sports coat (Latin America)*

las sandalias   *sandals*

el sombrero   *hat*

la sudadera   *sweatshirt, sweats*

el suéter   *sweater*

el traje   *suit*

el traje de baño   *swimsuit*

el vestido   *dress*

los zapatos   *shoes*

los zapatos de tacón alto   *high-heeled shoes*

los zapatos de tenis   *tennis shoes / athletic shoes*

los bluyines / los jeans / los pantalones de mezclilla *(denim)* **/ los tejanos / los vaqueros**   *jeans*

Los accesorios   *Accessories*

los aretes   *earrings*

la bolsa   *bag*

el brazalete / la pulsera   *bracelet*

la bufanda   *scarf*

la cartera   *wallet*

el collar   *necklace*

las gafas de sol   *sunglasses*

los guantes   *gloves*

¿De qué está(n) hecho(s)?
What is it (are they) made of?

está hecho(a) de…   *it is made of…*

están hechos(as) de…   *they are made of…*

el algodón   *cotton*

el cuero   *leather*

la lana   *wool*

el lino   *linen*

la piel   *leather / skin / fur*

el poliéster   *polyester*

la seda   *silk*

a cuadros   *plaid / checkered*

de lunares   *polka-dotted*

de solo un color   *solid-color*

estampado(a)   *printed*

rayado(a)   *striped*

De compras   *Shopping*

comprar   *to buy*

hacer compras   *to shop*

ir de compras   *to go shopping*

llevar   *to wear, to carry*

pagar   *to pay*

probar   *to try / taste, to try on clothing*

quedarse   *to stay, to remain, (in the case of clothing) to fit*

Síntesis: Gramática

The subjunctive

The indicative and the subjunctive are grammatical moods. Conjugating verbs in the present subjunctive is very similar to forming formal commands. To conjugate all verbs (except **o → ue** and **e → ie -ir** stem- changing verbs) in the present subjunctive, start with the present indicative **yo** form of the verb, drop the **-o**, and add **-er** endings for **-ar** verbs and **-ar** endings for **-er** and **-ir** verbs. For example:

hablar *to speak*

yo **hable**	nosotros(as) **hablemos**
tú **hables**	vosotros(as) **habléis**
él / ella / usted **hable**	ellos / ellas / ustedes **hablen**

tener *to have*

yo **tenga**	nosotros(as) **tengamos**
tú **tengas**	vosotros(as) **tengáis**
él / ella / usted **tenga**	ellos / ellas / ustedes **tengan**

vivir *to live*

yo **viva**	nosotros(as) **vivamos**
tú **vivas**	vosotros(as) **viváis**
él / ella / usted **viva**	ellos / ellas / ustedes **vivan**

Expressing indirect commands or suggestions

You can express commands indirectly by using verbs of influence and desire. These verbs convey a sense of wanting someone else to do something or hoping that something happens. Here are several common verbs of influence and desire.

desear	*to wish*
esperar	*to hope*
necesitar	*to need*
pedir	*to ask for*
preferir	*to prefer*
querer	*to want*
recomendar	*to recommend*
rogar	*to beg*
sugerir	*to suggest*

In Spanish, when the main clause contains a verb of influence or desire and there is a change in subject, the verb in the dependent clause is always in the subjunctive. For example:

Yo quiero   que   ella **haga** la tarea.
main clause   dependent clause

The main clause has a verb of influence or desire (**quiero**) and there is a change in subject from **yo** to **ella,** so the verb in the dependent clause is in the subjunctive (**haga**). Notice that the conjunction **que** joins the two clauses.

When there is **no** change of subject in a sentence, an **infinitive** follows the verb of influence or desire. For example:

I want to do the homework
Quiero **hacer** la tarea.

Síntesis: Gramática

Sometimes in Spanish, impersonal expressions are used to convey influence and desire. Impersonal expressions are expressions that don't refer to specific people. The understood subject is *it*. Here are some common impersonal expressions that convey influence and desire.

es importante	*it is important*
es mejor	*it is better*
es necesario	*it is necessary*

Expressing opinions

In Spanish, the subjunctive can be used to express opinions. When the **main clause** contains an expression of doubt or denial, the verb in the **dependent clause** is in the subjunctive. Here are several common verbs that express doubt or denial.

dudar	*to doubt*
no creer	*not to believe*
no estar seguro (de)	*not to be sure (that)*
negar	*to deny*
no pensar	*not to think*

When the main clause contains a verb of doubt or denial and there is a change in subject, the verb in the dependent clause is always in the subjunctive. For example:

Yo dudo   que   Miguel **trabaje** en verano.
main clause   _dependent clause_

The main clause has a verb of doubt or denial (**dudo**) and there is a change in subject from **yo** to **Miguel,** so the verb in the dependent clause is in the subjunctive (**trabaje**). Notice that the conjunction **que** joins the two clauses.

Here are some common impersonal expressions that convey doubt and denial:

no es cierto	*it is not true / certain*
es dudoso	*it is doubtful*
es imposible	*it is impossible*
no es posible	*it is not possible*
no es seguro	*it isn't certain*
no es verdad	*it is not true*

When the main clause does **not** express doubt or denial, the indicative is used. Here are some ways to express certainty in Spanish.

creer	*to believe*
es cierto	*it is true / certain*
es evidente	*it is obvious*
es verdad	*it is true*
no dudar	*not to doubt*
no negar	*not to deny*
pensar	*to think*

Es cierto   que   Miguel **trabaja** en verano.
main clause   _dependent clause_

Síntesis: Gramática

The main clause expresses certainty (**es cierto**) and there is a change in subject from **es** to **Miguel,** so the verb in the dependent clause is in the indicative (**trabaja**).

The future

In Spanish, one of the ways to express that something will happen in the future is to use the future tense. To conjugate a regular verb in the future tense, just add the appropriate ending to the infinitive. All -**ar, -er,** and -**ir** verbs take the same endings in the future tense. Here are the endings:

	Future tense endings
estudiar- comer- vivir-	-é
	-ás
	-á
	-emos
	-éis
	-án

El próximo semestre, **estudiaré** en España.
Next year, I will study in Spain.

Nosotros **comeremos** en un restaurante este fin de semana.
We will eat in a restaurant this weekend.

El año que viene, mi hermano **vivirá** en Puerto Rico.
Next year, my brother will live in Puerto Rico.

Here are some common verbs that have irregular stems in the future tense. Their endings are the same as those for regular verbs.

decir	dir-	
haber	habr-	
hacer	har-	-é
poder	podr-	-ás
poner	pondr-	-á
querer	querr-	-emos
saber	sabr-	-éis
salir	saldr-	-án
tener	tendr-	
venir	vendr-	

Se lo **diré** mañana.
I will tell him it tomorrow.

Habrá más gente la semana que viene.
There will be more people next week.

In Spanish, you can also use the future to speculate about the present. When used in questions, it conveys the idea of *to wonder.* For example:

¿Qué hora **será**?
I wonder what time it is.

When used in statements, the future tense gives a sense of probability.

Serán las dos y media.
It is probably two thirty.

Síntesis: Gramática

The conditional

In Spanish, one of the ways to express that something would happen is to use the conditional. Just like regular verbs in the future tense, a regular verb in the conditional is formed by adding the appropriate ending to the infinitive. All **-ar, -er,** and **-ir** verbs take the same endings in the conditional tense. Here are the endings:

	Conditional endings
hablar- leer- vivir-	-ía
	-ías
	-ía
	-íamos
	-íais
	-ían

La próxima vez **hablaría** con el profesor.
The next time I would speak with the professor.

Ellos **leerían** más pero nunca hay tiempo.
They would read more, but there is never time.

Viviríamos en la ciudad pero es caro.
We would live in the city, but it is expensive.

The same verbs that are irregular in the future are also irregular in the conditional. Notice that these are the same irregular stems that are used in the future tense. Irregular conditional verbs take the same endings as regular verbs.

decir	dir-	
haber	habr-	
hacer	har-	-ía
poder	podr-	-ías
poner	pondr-	-ía
querer	querr-	-íamos
saber	sabr-	-íais
salir	saldr-	-ían
tener	tendr-	
venir	vendr-	

¿Qué **harías** con un millón de dólares?
What would you do with a million dollars?

Para llegar a tiempo, **saldría** temprano.
To arrive on time, I would leave early.

In Spanish, you can also use the conditional to speculate about the past. When used in questions, it conveys the idea of *to wonder* when referring to something in the past. For example:

¿Qué hora **sería?**
I wonder what time it was.

When used in statements, the conditional gives a sense of probability when referring to the past.

Serían las dos y media.
It was probably two thirty.

You can also use the conditional to soften a request.

Querría un café.
I would like a coffee.

Capítulos 9 y 10

For this project, imagine that you are studying film. You'll talk about favorite films and actors, and be given certain scenarios that film students might face, such as coming up with ideas for new films and deciding what characteristics make a good film. You'll use the grammar and vocabulary you've learned in Chapters 9 and 10 to do this.

Project components

Activity	Points
UP5-1 Lluvia de ideas	5 points (group)
UP5-2 Descripción Step 1	15 points (individual)
Step 2	5 points (group)
UP5-3 Actores favoritos	25 points (individual)
UP5-4 Película favorita	15 points (individual)
UP5-5 Análisis	10 points (group)
UP5-6 Sugerencias	15 points (individual)
UP5-7 Conclusiones	10 points (individual)

UP5-1 Lluvia de ideas *(Brainstorming)* You are part of the creative team working for a movie studio. The studio is in the process of reviewing proposals for new films and has asked your team to draft some ideas for movies and potential protagonists. In groups of three or four, discuss and decide on the following information in Spanish. Each of you should take notes for later use.

- the genre of movie would you like to create
- where will it take place and in what time period
- descriptions of two or three main characters including three or four adjectives for each
- main plot description to provide the gist of the storyline

UP5-2 Descripción

Step 1 Using the information from your group brainstorm, write a paragraph of 100–150 words to present your movie idea and a film title to your supervisor.

Step 2 Read what the other members of your group wrote. Agree on a favorite description and revise for any spelling or grammar corrections and repost as your group's **Descripción.**

UP5-3 Actores favoritos

Step 1 The studio has asked everyone to choose a favorite actor to select a cast for the film. Write about the actor or actress of your choice. Explain what you like about this person. You should include the following.

- Información general: ¿De dónde es? ¿Qué edad tiene? ¿Cuánta experiencia tiene? ¿Su estado civil *(marital status)*? ¿Cómo es su familia? ¿Dónde vive?
- ¿Qué tipo de personajes prefiere interpretar este actor o actriz?
- ¿Cuáles son algunas de sus películas más populares?
- ¿Qué cualidades artísticas o personales tiene esta persona? ¿Cómo es?

Step 2 Now think of a scene you like from one of his/her movies and write a few sentences to describe it. You should include:

- preterite and imperfect verbs
- the title of the movie
- a basic description of the physical scene
- what people were wearing in the scene
- any other important details

UP5-4 **Película favorita** You're now tasked with enhancing the studio's website with staff picks for the best movies of all time. You need to create a one- to two-minute audio or video recording in which you talk about your favorite movie. Include the following information.

- basic information about the movie
- list of main actors and their roles
- a plot overview

UP5-5 **Análisis** Back in your groups, read another group's description from **UP5-2 Descripción, Step 2.** As a group, discuss and then explain what you think is important, good, or relevant to the success of the movie and what would be required, important, and/or necessary qualities of the protagonists and other characters. Each of you should write five to eight sentences and submit them individually.

Modelos   *Es importante que la película…*
Es necesario que…
Es bueno que el protagonista…
Es importante que la protagonista sea una actriz que…

UP5-6 Sugerencias You now need to provide some suggestions based on the discussion you had with your group in **UP5-5 Análisis.**

- Express your opinion of the group's proposed movie. Include at least one critical appraisal (something you would change or do not like) and at least one praising assessment (something you like).

- Suggest male and female actors for the different roles and explain why each is suitable for the role.

- Make a list of five things that you suggest or recommend the actors do to prepare for the job and explain why they should do it.

    Modelo *Sugiero que Hugh Jackman haga mucho ejercicio porque tendrá que correr y saltar para escapar de los zombies. Recomiendo que Salma Hayek aprenda chino porque en la película viajará a Pekín.*

UP5-7 Conclusiones Read what your classmates wrote in **UP5-6 Sugerencias** about your movie description. React to their comments by writing four sentences. What you write can be a general reaction or you can react to specific suggestions. You can agree or disagree with the suggestions your peers made.

El cuerpo

Objectives: In this chapter you will learn to

- Describe symptoms and visiting a medical clinic
- Talk about exercise routines and healthy lifestyles
- Express emotions, hopes, and wishes
- Use conjunctions to connect sentences
- State what you have done and what has happened

C11-1 El cuerpo

With a partner, read each situation and determine which parts of the body need to be used.

Modelo Marta tiene que sacar la basura.
Ella va a usar las manos para sacar la basura y abrir la puerta. Ella necesita los pies para caminar.

1. Elena va a cantar karaoke con sus amigas.
2. Tienes que conducir tu coche.
3. Queremos montar en nuestras bicicletas.
4. Martin tiene que escribir una composición para una clase.
5. Quieres hablar con tu madre por teléfono.
6. Fred quiere aprender español.

C11-2 Nuestro mundo

Step 1 The world and our lives are full of positive things as well as elements we would like to improve or change. With a partner, ask each other questions about things in the world today or in your life that make you happy, sad and hopeful. Create a list of those things to use in Step 2.

Cosas alegres: _____

Cosas tristes: _____

Cosas preocupantes: _____

Cosas que dan esperanza: _____

Step 2 Based on the information from the previous step, write several sentences about the good things in the world and in your lives. Write several sentences about what is sad or worrisome in the world.

Modelo   *Es bueno que tengamos la oportunidad de ser estudiantes.*
          Es triste que las escuelas reciban poco dinero.

Step 3 With new partners, in groups of three, share your feelings and ideas from the previous step. React to what your group members say; do you feel the same or differently? Overall is your group more optimistic or pessimistic? Prepare three statements to share with the class telling what you and your group hope and desire for the world.

Modelo   *Esperamos que los maestros reciban más dinero.*
          Ojalá haya menos conflictos y guerras en el mundo.

C11-3 Una persona única

Step 1 In groups of three, draw a person together on a single sheet of paper by taking turns using the subjunctive to indicate which part of the body should be drawn. The next student should draw it and pass the paper to the third student in the group with instructions for what should be drawn next. Work as quickly as you can until you have a complete person.

Modelo   Student A: *Quiero que dibujes una nariz grande.*
          Student B: *Recomiendo que dibujes los pies.*
          Student C: *Quiero que dibujes…*

Step 2 Now that you have completed the drawing, add a name and write four sentences describing your person physically and telling something he/she likes. What makes him/her unique?

Modelo   *Manolo es grande, musculoso y guapo. Tiene el pelo azul oscuro y los ojos pequeños pero penetrantes. Sé que le gustan los gatos porque tiene doce en casa.*

Step 3 Pass your paper to another group. Look at the person and read the description. Then, use the subjunctive to create three sentences about what your group thinks the person hopes or wishes. Be creative and write your sentences on the same paper.

Modelo   *Manolo espera que el gimnasio esté abierto hoy para levantar pesas.*
Quiere que los gatos no coman toda la comida.
Para él es importante que su ropa sea moderna y atractiva.

Step 4 Pass your paper to another group. Look at the new person and read the description. Then, on the same paper, write two or three sentences about what your group thinks the person dislikes, is bothered by, or considers sad.

Modelo   *A Manolo le molesta que los gatos duerman en su cama.*
Es triste que Manolo no tenga un perro.

Step 5 Give the paper back to the original group. Read and react to what has been added to the description of your person. Then prepare to present your person to the class and tell what makes him/her a unique individual.

Gramática

C11-4 ¿Cómo reaccionas?

Step 1 You are chatting with your new roommate and several topics have come up. Some of them interest you, but others do not interest you as much. You want to make a good impression and come across as a responsible and friendly roommate. With a partner, state how you would respond to each of the different topics. Use the word bank as a guide.

espero	me alegro de	me molesta	odio	(no) me gusta	ojalá

1. Tu compañero(a) no tiene tarea, pero tú tienes mucha tarea.
2. La abuela de tu compañero(a) va a visitarlo(la).
3. Ustedes hablan de la gente maleducada.
4. Tú tienes que leer mucho para una clase difícil.
5. Ustedes hablan de hacer ejercicio y de ir al gimnasio.
6. Ustedes hablan de los vegetales y las frutas.
7. Tú tienes familia que vive cerca pero la familia de tu compañero(a) vive lejos.

Step 2 As a class, report how you reacted to each situation (with a positive statement or a negative statement). Is there a pattern to the way the class reacted? Why?

Vocabulario

C11-5 Síntomas

Step 1 Alberto is not feeling well. With a partner, read each of his complaints and then think of some possible problems that could be affecting him.

Modelo   Alberto: Me duele la garganta
Él tiene una infección y…

1. Estoy congestionado. _____

2. Me duele mucho el tobillo. _____

3. Tengo mucho calor. _____

4. Tengo náuseas y estoy un poco mareado. _____

Step 2 Alberto is feeling better in some cases (items 2 and 4) and still not well in other cases (items 1 and 3). Write four sentences expressing your sympathy or pleasure accordingly. Some useful expressions are: *Me alegro de que, espero que, es triste que, (no) me gusta que, ojalá.*

Modelo   *Me alegro de que no te duela la garganta. / Me alegro de que no tengas una infección de la garganta.*

C11-6 Encuesta de la salud

Step 1 Work with a partner to create 6 questions for the health survey below. Following are some topics and key words you may use in your questions.

la comida, el ejercicio, dormir (calidad, horas), la salud, la medicina, los médicos, los hospitales, los accidentes

Modelos   *¿Vas al médico todos los años? ¿Haces ejercicio? ¿Qué comida comes regularmente?*

Vocabulario

Encuesta

Pregunta	Respuesta
1.	1.
2.	2.
3.	3.
4.	4.
5.	5.
6.	6.

Step 2 Find a new partner and take turns asking and answering the questions. Record your partner's answers to the questions and then react to each one. Some useful expressions for your reactions are:

me alegro de que, no es bueno que, ojalá, espero que, me gusta que, etc.

Modelo   Student A: *¿Qué comida comes regularmente?*
Student B: *Yo como muchas frutas y vegetales. No como mucha carne.*
Student A: *Me alegro de que comas muchas frutas. Es importante para la salud.*

Step 3 Based on your partner's answers, think of a few things he/she can do to improve or can continue doing to have a healthy lifestyle.

Modelo   *Sugiero que duermas más. Recomiendo que sigas comiendo fruta todos los días.*

Vocabulario/Gramática

C11-7 En nuestra clase

Step 1 Your instructor will ask the whole class several questions. Raise your hand for the appropriate answers. Then fill in the total number of respondents for each answer.

1. Ir al médico todos los años: sí _____ / no _____

2. Sentirse: bien _____ / más o menos _____ / mal _____

3. Ser un persona activa: muy _____ / más o menos _____ / no muy _____

4. Comer comida: no carne _____ / solo comida saludable _____ / todo tipo de comida _____

5. Tener alegría en la primavera: sí _____ / no _____

Step 2 Once all the numbers are ready, review them with a partner. Make a statement(s) about your class for each of the five topics.

Modelo *Hay tres personas en la clase que no comen carne, pero la mayoría comen todo tipo de comida.*

Step 3 You and your partner should find another pair to work with. Look at your statements and decide whether you think the students in your class are like other college students or whether you are exceptional. Be prepared to share and justify your ideas with the whole class.

Vocabulario/Gramática

C11-8A Una visita al médico **A**

Step 1 Elena is visiting the doctor's office today. With a partner, ask and answer questions to complete the chart with information about Elena's, Marta's, and the doctor's hopes and concerns. The last column will not be used in this step.

Modelo Elena / esperar que
Student A: *¿Qué espera Elena?*
Student B: *Elena espera que el doctor Gómez esté en la oficina.*

Student A	Esperar que	Molestar que	Alegrarse de que	Gustar que	Querer que	Es impor-tante que	Dudar que
Elena (paciente)		Haber mucha gente esperando	El doctor no cobrar mucho dinero		El doctor le dar medicina		
Marta (enfermera)	Elena llegar			Elena no necesitar medicina		Comer almuerzo	
Doctor Gómez		Elena no comer bien	Elena no tener fiebre y no tener tos		Marta buscar la información de Elena		

Step 2 The last column is still empty. With your partner, imagine what each person would doubt. Write your ideas in the spaces. Be prepared to share what you added and why you think it is appropriate.

Step 3 In groups of three or four students, share what you added in the last column and tell why you added it. Compare and contrast the things added and choose the best ones to share with the whole class.

Vocabulario/Gramática

C11-8B Una visita al médico **B**

Step 1 Elena is visiting the doctor's office today. With a partner, ask and answer questions to complete the chart with information about Elena's, Marta's, and the doctor's hopes and concerns. The last column will not be used in this step.

Modelo Elena / esperar que
Student A: *¿Qué espera Elena?*
Student B: *Elena espera que el doctor Gómez esté en la oficina.*

Student B	Esperar que	Molestar que	Alegrarse de que	Gustar que	Querer que	Es impor-tante que	Dudar que
Elena (paciente)	El doctor Gómez estar			Marta trabajar ahí		Poder leer revistas *(magazines)*	
Marta (enfermera)		La gente ser maleducada	Elena estar mejor		El doctor Gómez permitirle ir a comer		
Doctor Gómez	No haber muchas personas hoy			Marta ser buena compañera del trabajo		Elena comer bien, hacer ejercicio todos los días	

Step 2 The last column is still empty. With your partner, imagine what each person would doubt. Write your ideas in the spaces. Be prepared to share what you added and why you think it is appropriate.

Step 3 In groups of three or four students, share what you added in the last column and tell why you added it. Compare and contrast the things added and choose the best ones to share with the whole class.

Vocabulario/Gramática

C11-9 ¿Qué me recomiendas?

Step 1 Your best friend is studying abroad and having a hard time, not with the language, but with his/her health. With a partner, take turns reading what she/he has to say. Recommend a course of action for each situation.

Modelo   Me duele la cabeza
            Recomiendo que tomes dos aspirinas y te relajes.

1. Me corté el dedo con una botella sucia.
2. El doctor me dice que tengo que comer menos dulces.
3. Tengo que guardar cama por tres días y estoy aburrido(a).
4. Me lastimé el brazo.
5. Mi corazón está palpitando muy rápido.
6. Me caí y se me rompieron dos dientes.
7. Tengo fiebre y me duele el cuerpo.
8. Estoy mejor y mis amigos quieren salir hoy.

Step 2 Now rank your friend's symptoms from the most serious to the least. Tell why you ranked them in that order. Are any of the situations serious enough for your friend to come home? Be prepared to report to the class on your rankings and ideas.

C11-10 Vidas saludables

Step 1 Working with a partner, look at the following questions from a health survey. Create additional survey questions related to health, food, and exercise.

1. ¿Qué comida saludable compras?

2. ¿Normalmente te pones la vacuna para la gripe?

3. ¿En el verano te pones protector solar?

4. ¿Dónde te gusta hacer ejercicio? ¿Por qué te gusta?

5. _____

6. _____

7. _____

8. _____

Step 2 With a new partner, imagine you are assigned to interact with the public and conduct the survey. Ask your partner the survey questions, jotting down the answers as you react to them.

Modelo   Student A: *¿Qué comida saludable compras?*
          Student B: *Compro muchos vegetales y frutas.*
          Student A: *Me alegro de que comas muchas frutas. A mí me gustan las manzanas y las peras.*

Step 3 Return to your original partner, choose three of the questions, and talk about the answers. Write a statement based on each of the three questions, telling why it is important. Be prepared to share your ideas with the class.

Modelo   *Es importante que comas comida saludable para que no te enfermes.*

Vocabulario/Gramática

Entrenador(a) y cliente

Imagine you are meeting with your personal trainer. One of you should role play the client and the other will be the trainer. As a client, you want advice and guidance on a number of issues. As a trainer, you want to help your client improve his/her physical health and lifestyle. Before starting the conversation, think about what you will need to say and how you will say it. Once you complete the conversation, switch roles and repeat.

Student A	Student B
1. You are a trainer / health expert. Greet the client.	2. You are the client meeting with your personal trainer / health expert. Greet him/her.
3. Ask the client about his/her current exercise habits; use general questions and specific targeted questions.	4. Respond by telling about your current exercise habits. Ask questions related to exercise.
5. Give a few exercise-related recommendations.	6. Tell about your current eating habits and ask several questions related to food.
7. Respond to the questions and give advice related to food.	8. React to the advice. Then, based on the advice, tell what you plan to do to live a healthy lifestyle.
9. Respond to the client's plan and give additional advice, or stress the importance of previous advice.	10. Commit to the advice you think you will actually do and then say thanks and goodbye.

Vocabulario/Gramática

C11-12 La salud en los Estados Unidos

Step 1 Health and health care are important topics in the United States. In groups of three or more students, answer the following questions. On the board, write several key points or topics for each question.

1. ¿Por qué es importante el tema de la salud para los Estados Unidos?

2. ¿Qué tipos de trabajos hay relacionados con la salud? ¿Conoces a alguien con uno de estos trabajos?

3. ¿Qué podemos hacer para vivir vidas más saludables?

Step 2 Based on the bullet points on the board, prepare a short presentation called *Salud en los Estados Unidos*. Focus on the following: suggestions, problems, examples, solutions, recommendations, importance, and effects (personal and public).

C11-13 ¿Para qué? Imagine you are accompanying a curious child, possibly a younger sibling, niece, nephew, or your own child to a medical clinic. This child wants to know what everything is and what it is used for. For the first five items, imagine you're the curious child. Ask your partner about everything. Then switch roles for remaining items.

Modelo   Receta
Student A: *¿Qué es una receta y para qué se usa?*
Student B: *Una receta es algo que el doctor te da, como pastillas. Es para ayudar a mejorarse de una enfermedad o una infección.*

1. tiritas
2. vitaminas
3. radiografía
4. vacunas

5. aspirina
6. medicina
7. antibióticos

8. yeso
9. jarabe para la tos
10. protector / crema solar

Gramática

¿Qué ha hecho Daniela?

Step 1 It is 4:15 P.M. You and a classmate are waiting for Daniela to arrive for a study group. You are wondering where she is. You check her Facebook page to see whether she has posted anything recently. Look at her earlier posts, messages, and pictures. Share with your partner all the information you have about what Daniela has done today and listen to everything your partner knows. One of you has the information for Student A and the other for Student B.

Modelo

> Me encanta la canción nueva de Enrique Iglesias. Estoy escuchándola ahora.
> 1:15 P.M.

Daniela ha escuchado la canción de Enrique Iglesias.

ILeysen/Shutterstock.com

10:11 A.M.

Tengo ganas de jugar al fútbol…

Student A:

> Buenos días. ¿Cómo has dormido? Yo he dormido muy bien.
> 7:30 A.M.

> Hola, compañeros: Quiero confirmar el grupo de estudio a las 4:00.
> 9:45 A.M.

> ¡Por fin estoy libre! jajaja Ahora puedo jugar al fútbol con mis amigos.
> 2:15 P.M.

Harald Lueder/Shutterstock.com

hace 20 min.

#yolo #amofutbol #ganamos

Student B:

hace 7 horas

#cafedebetty

> Estoy en la clase de historia.
> No debo enviar mensajes.
> Hablamos luego.

11:10 A.M.

> ¡Eres lo que comes! Entonces
> yo soy sana, limpia y rica.

hace 4 horas

> Voy a jugar al fútbol ahora. :)
> Nos vemos en la biblioteca
> a las 4:00 para estudiar.

2:30 P.M.

Step 2 Based on what you found in the messages and images, what do you think has happened to Daniela? Work together to write her a message to confirm your suspicions.

Step 3 Listen as your instructor reads Daniela's last message. Then write another message to Daniela expressing your concern, hopes, and wishes.

Gramática

C11-15A ¿Qué han hecho? **A**

Step 1 Bella and Marcela have a friend, Kristen, who will be visiting them in Spain soon. She wants to know what activities they have and have not done already. One of you will use the info about Bella in this activity and your partner will use the information about Marcela in C11-15B. Each of you should read aloud to each other the information in your activity about Bella and Marcela. Then, using what you both know, answer Kristen's questions in step 2 together.

> **Bella** Ayer fui al museo para ver obras de arte de Picasso. Después le escribí un mensaje de texto a mi amiga Anita y comimos en un restaurante que se llama La Finca de Susana. Probé el pulpo *(octopus)* y me gustó mucho. La semana pasada viajé a un castillo muy bonito y saqué muchas fotos e hice compras en el mercado. Compré un regalo para mi mamá. Hace dos semanas vi una película en español con Marcela. Entendí toda la película. Me gustaría hacer un viaje en coche para ver los pueblos pequeños.

Step 2 With your partner, work together to answer Kristen's questions.

Preguntas de Kristen

1. ¿Han visitado muchos museos? _____

2. ¿Qué han usado para comunicarse? _____

3. ¿Adónde han viajado? _____

4. ¿Qué y dónde han comido? _____

5. ¿Qué actividades han hecho recientemente? _____

Step 3 Now imagine that Kristen is halfway through her visit. She is writing home to tell her friends what she has done (and not done) so far. Be creative and write at least six sentences.

Gramática

¿Qué han hecho? **B**

Step 1 Bella and Marcela have a friend, Kristen, who will be visiting them in Spain soon. She wants to know what activities they have and have not done already. One of you will use the info about Marcela in this activity and your partner will use the information about Bella in C11-15A. Each of you should read aloud to each other the information in your activity about Bella and Marcela. Then, using what you both know, answer Kristen's questions in step 2 together.

> **Marcela** Ayer tuve clase por la mañana. Por la tarde comí chocolate con churros con mis padres. A ellos les conté sobre mi viaje a la Costa del Sol. Estuve allí hace tres semanas. No hay metro así que usé muchos taxis. Vi un partido de fútbol muy divertido. Envié muchas fotos por Snapchat y Whatsapp. Durante el día tomé el sol en la playa y por la noche salí y bailé con amigos. Me gustaría volver a la Costa del Sol. También me gustaría visitar el museo de arte moderno.

Step 2 With your partner, work together to answer Kristen's questions.

Preguntas de Kristen

1. ¿Han visitado muchos museos? _____

2. ¿Qué han usado para comunicarse? _____

3. ¿Adónde han viajado? _____

4. ¿Qué y dónde han comido? _____

5. ¿Qué actividades han hecho recientemente? _____

Step 3 Now imagine that Kristen is halfway through her visit. She is writing home to tell her friends what she has done (and not done) so far. Be creative and write at least six sentences.

Gramática

¿Qué ha hecho nuestra clase?

Step 1 For this activity, you will find out what your classmates have or have not done. To start, think of three things you have done and one thing you have never done. Next, get into a group of three to four students. In your group, present all four things as things you have done. Your partners have to guess which of your statements is not true.

Modelo   Student A: *He conocido a Jimmy Fallon.*
Student B: *Dudo que hayas conocido a Jimmy Fallon.*

Step 2 As a group, create five or more questions based on your sentences from the previous step. You will each need a copy of the questions.

Modelo   *¿Alguna vez has comido sushi?*

Step 3 Find a new partner and ask the questions. Write down the answers. Speak with as many people as time allows.

Modelo   Student A: *¿Alguna vez has comido sushi?*
Student B: *Sí, he comido mucho sushi. ¿Y tú?*
Student A: *Yo también he comido mucho sushi.*

Step 4 With your group, analyze the information you collected and prepare to present examples of what most people have in common and what are some of the less common things classmates have done. Include yourself and your group members in the statements.

Modelo   *Todos nosotros hemos comido tacos al pastor.*
Eric ha leído El Quijote, *pero nosotros no lo hemos leído.*

Lectura

C11-17 ## Antes de leer

Think about ways in which adults communicate with babies and how babies transmit their needs, ideas, and feelings to adults. Write down your conclusions and share them with the class.

C11-18 ## Lectura

Read the following story about a mother and her newborn daughter.

Tía José Rivadeneira

Ángeles Mastretta

Tía José Rivadeneira tuvo una hija con los ojos grandes como dos lunas, como un deseo. Apenas colocada en su abrazo, todavía húmeda y vacilante, la niña mostró los ojos y algo en las alas de sus labios que parecía pregunta.

—¿Qué quieres saber? —le dijo la tía José jugando a que entendía ese gesto.

Como todas las madres, tía José pensó que no había en la historia del mundo una criatura tan hermosa como la suya. La deslumbraban el color de su piel, el tamaño de sus pestañas y la placidez con que dormía. Temblaba de orgullo imaginando lo que haría con la sangre y las quimeras que latían en su cuerpo.

Se dedicó a contemplarla con altivez *(haughtiness)* y regocijo durante más de tres semanas. Entonces la inexpugnable *(impregnable)* vida hizo caer sobre la niña una enfermedad que, en cinco horas, convirtió su extraordinaria viveza en un sueño extenuado *(exhausted)* y remoto que parecía llevársela de regreso a la muerte.

Cuando todos sus talentos curativos no lograron mejoría alguna, tía José, pálida de terror, la cargó hasta el hospital. Ahí se la quitaron de los brazos, y una docena de médicos y enfermeras empezaron a moverse agitados y confundidos en torno a la niña. Tía José la vio irse tras una puerta que le prohibía la entrada y se dejó caer al suelo incapaz de cargar consigo misma y con aquel dolor como un acantilado *(cliff)*.

Ahí la encontró su marido, que era un hombre sensato y prudente como los hombres acostumbran fingir que son. La ayudó a levantarse y la regañó por su falta de cordura y esperanza. Su marido confiaba en la ciencia médica y hablaba de ella como otros hablan de Dios. Por eso lo turbaba la insensatez *(foolishness)* en que se había colocado su mujer, incapaz de hacer otra cosa que llorar y maldecir al destino.

Lectura

Aislaron a la niña en una sala de terapia intensiva. Un lugar blanco y limpio al que las madres solo podían entrar media hora diaria. Entonces se llenaba de oraciones y ruegos. Todas las mujeres persignaban *(made the sign of the cross on)* el rostro de sus hijos, les recorrían el cuerpo con estampas y agua bendita, pedían a todo Dios que los dejara vivos. La tía José no conseguía sino llegar junto a la cuna donde su hija apenas respiraba para pedirle: "No te mueras". Después lloraba y lloraba sin secarse los ojos ni moverse hasta que las enfermeras le avisaban que debía salir.

Entonces volvía a sentarse en las bancas cercanas a la puerta, con la cabeza sobre las piernas, sin hambre y sin voz, rencorosa y arisca, ferviente y desesperada. ¿Qué podía hacer? ¿Por qué tenía que vivir su hija? ¿Qué sería bueno ofrecerle a su cuerpo pequeño lleno de agujas y sondas para que le interesara quedarse en este mundo? ¿Qué podría decirle para convencerla de que valía la pena hacer el esfuerzo en vez de morirse?

Una mañana, sin saber la causa, iluminada solo por los fantasmas de su corazón, se acercó a la niña y empezó a contarle las historias de sus antepasadas. Quiénes habían sido, qué mujeres tejieron sus vidas con qué hombres antes de que la boca y el ombligo de su hija se anudaran a ella. De qué estaban hechas, cuántos trabajos habían pasado, qué penas y jolgorios *(joys)* traía ella como herencia. Quiénes sembraron con intrepidez *(fearlessness)* y fantasías la vida que le tocaba prolongar.

Durante muchos días recordó, imaginó, inventó. Cada minuto de cada hora disponible habló sin tregua en el oído de su hija. Por fin, al atardecer de un jueves, mientras contaba implacable alguna historia, su hija abrió los ojos y la miró ávida y desafiante *(defiant),* como fue el resto de su larga existencia.

El marido de tía José dio las gracias a los médicos, los médicos dieron gracias a los adelantos de su ciencia, la tía abrazó a su niña y salió del hospital sin decir una palabra. Solo ella sabía a quiénes agradecer la vida de su hija. Solo ella supo siempre que ninguna ciencia fue capaz de mover tanto como la escondida en los ásperos y sutiles hallazgos de otras mujeres con los ojos grandes.

C11-19

Los personajes *(The characters)*

In groups of three or four, describe one of the following characters or groups in the story: Tía José, her baby daughter, the father, or the doctors and nurses. Write down all the attributes you come up with; then share them with the group. How do they compare? What does this tell you about the possible meanings of the story?

Una visita a la clínica

La semana pasada me enfermé. Tenía tos y fiebre. Y mi madre no vive aquí para cuidarme. Le hablé y ella se preocupó mucho e insistió en una visita a la clínica. Yo fui el martes por la mañana. Mientras esperaba mi turno, hablé con un chico que tenía el brazo roto. Se llama Jorge y tiene diez años. Me contó todo lo que le pasó con su accidente.

A Jorge le gusta jugar al fútbol con sus amigos. Estaban jugando cuando la pelota *(ball)* voló y se quedó en un árbol grande. Jorge decidió subir al árbol para recuperar la pelota. Al pegarla *(hit it)*, él y la pelota se cayeron al suelo. A Jorge no le pasó nada, así que continuaron jugando al fútbol. Unos minutos después, Jorge chocó *(crashed into)* con dos chicos del otro equipo, se cayó y se pegó fuertemente contra la portería *(goalposts)*. Se rompió el brazo. Por suerte Jorge vive muy cerca y sus amigos lo llevaron a casa y luego a la clínica.

Después de hablar con la médica, quien me dijo que yo solo tenía un resfrío, vi a Jorge saliendo con un yeso en su brazo. Con una sonrisa grande me lo mostró y me dijo, "Bella, ¿quieres ser la primera en firmar mi yeso?" Yo firmé mi nombre y fui a la farmacia para comprar medicina. Después de unos días de descanso, mucho té y medicina, ya me siento mucho mejor. Pienso mucho en Jorge, él es una persona tan feliz. Espero que él esté bien y que todavía esté encantado de tener un yeso en el brazo. Yo estoy muy feliz de no estar enferma.

igorwheeler/Shutterstock.com

El blog de Bella

C11-20 Un accidente o una visita al médico

Step 1 In groups of three, take turns reading aloud the blog entries you wrote online. As you listen to your classmates' blogs, write down three or four questions you can ask to get more information or to clarify the story. After hearing the whole story, ask and discuss the questions.

Step 2 Analyze your group's blog entries by answering the following questions. Be prepared to share your ideas with the rest of the class.

1. ¿Qué tienen en común las entradas de su grupo? (una lista de tres o cuatro cosas)

2. ¿Piensan que las otras entradas de la clase también tienen estas cosas en común? ¿Por qué?

3. ¿Qué diferencias hay entre las entradas de su grupo? (una lista de dos o tres cosas)

Síntesis: Vocabulario

El cuerpo   *The body*

la boca   *mouth*

el brazo   *arm*

la cabeza   *head*

la cara   *face*

las cejas   *eyebrows*

el cerebro   *brain*

el codo   *elbow*

el corazón   *heart*

el cuello   *neck*

el dedo   *finger*

los dientes   *teeth*

la espalda   *back*

el estómago   *stomach*

la garganta   *throat*

el hombro   *shoulder*

el hueso   *bone*

los labios   *lips*

la lengua   *tongue*

la mano   *hand*

el músculo   *muscle*

la nariz   *nose*

el ojo   *eye*

la oreja   *ear*

el pecho   *chest*

el pie   *foot*

la pierna   *leg*

los pulmones   *lungs*

la rodilla   *knee*

la sangre   *blood*

el tobillo   *ankle*

Los síntomas   *Symptoms*

la alergia   *allergy*

el (la) doctor(a) / médico(a)   *medical doctor*

la enfermedad   *illness*

el (la) enfermero(a)   *nurse*

la fractura   *fracture*

la gripe   *flu*

la herida   *wound, injury*

la infección   *infection*

el (la) paciente   *patient*

doler (ue) [cabeza, estómago, garganta, etcétera]   *to hurt [head, stomach, throat, etc.]*

estar congestionado(a)   *to be congested*

estar mareado(a)   *to be dizzy*

estar resfriado(a)   *to have a cold*

quebrado(a) / roto(a)   *broken*

sentirse bien / mal   *to feel well / badly*

tener catarro   *to have a cold*

tener fiebre   *to have a fever*

tener tos   *to have a cough*

tener / sentir náuseas   *to feel nauseated*

torcido(a)   *twisted*

Verbos y la salud   *Verbs and health*

cortarse   *to cut oneself*

desmayarse   *to faint*

estornudar   *to sneeze*

guardar cama   *to stay in bed*

hacer ejercicio   *to exercise*

lastimarse   *to hurt oneself*

mejorarse   *to get better*

palpitar   *to palpitate*

poner   *to put on, to rub on*

respirar   *to breathe*

tener tos   *to have a cough*

tomar la temperatura   *to take one's temperature*

tragar   *to swallow*

vomitar   *to vomit*

La medicina   *Medicine*

el antibiótico   *antibiotic*

la aspirina   *aspirin*

la inyección   *injection*

el jarabe para la tos   *cough syrup*

la medicina   *medicine*

la pastilla / píldora   *pill*

el protector solar / el bloqueador solar / la crema solar   *sunscreen*

la radiografía   *x-ray*

la receta   *prescription*

la tirita   *band-aid*

la vacuna   *vaccine*

la vitamina   *vitamin*

el yeso   *cast*

Síntesis: Gramática

Subjunctive with emotions, hopes, and wishes

The structure used to express wishes or suggestions, such as **Quiero que Estelita hable español,** is also used when there is a verb or verbal expression in the main clause that indicates the speaker's emotions, hopes, or wishes about the subordinate clause. Look at the following examples:

MAIN CLAUSE (emotions, hopes, wishes)		DEPENDENT CLAUSE
Espero		
Es bueno		
Es necesario		Carlos <u>llegue</u> temprano.
Me alegro de	que	<u>hables</u> más de una lengua.
Es triste		tus padres <u>estén</u> en París.
Confío en		<u>estudies</u> chino.
Ojalá que		
No es verdad		

Irregular verbs in the subjunctive

There are several types of verbs that show irregularities when conjugated in the subjunctive. Some of the changes are the same or very similar to what you saw for the present indicative; others are different.

Verbs that require spelling changes

Because the subjunctive forms of **-ar** verbs all add the vowel **-e** after the verb stem, some **-ar** verbs have a spelling change in the last consonant in the stem in order to keep the same sound:

c → qu	atacar > ataque, ataques, ataque, etc.
g → gu	apagar > apague, apagues, apague, etc.
z → c	cazar > cace, caces, cace, etc.

Stem-changing verbs

All **-ar** and **-er** verbs that have stem changes in the present indicative have the same changes in the subjunctive. Remember that in these verbs **o > ue; u > ue;** and **e > ir.**

contar	pensar	jugar
cuente	piense	juegue
cuentes	pienses	juegues
cuente	piense	juegue
contemos	pensemos	juguemos
contéis	penséis	juguéis
cuenten	piensen	jueguen

Verbs in the **-ir** group also have the same changes as in the indicative, but the **nosotros / nosotras** and **vosotros / vosotras** forms also change: **e > i** and **o > u.**

pedir	sentir	morir
pida	sienta	muera
pidas	sientas	mueras
pida	sienta	muera
pidamos	sintamos	muramos
pidáis	sintáis	muráis
pidan	sientan	mueran

Síntesis: Gramática

Irregular verbs

There are only six verbs in Spanish that are fully irregular in the present subjunctive. These are very common verbs that you will have to use often.

dar	estar	ir	haber	saber	ser
dé	esté	vaya	haya	sepa	sea
des	estés	vayas	hayas	sepas	seas
dé	esté	vaya	haya	sepa	sea
demos	estemos	vayamos	hayamos	sepamos	seamos
deis	estéis	vayáis	hayáis	sepáis	seáis
den	estén	vayan	hayan	sepan	sean

Negative *tú* commands

Negative **tú** commands in Spanish use the same forms as the present subjunctive. Notice that the underlined forms of the verbs in the following commands are the same forms used in the subjunctive:

> No <u>hables</u> muy alto: estoy estudiando.
>
> Señora, no <u>olvide</u> cerrar la puerta, por favor.
>
> No <u>conduzcas</u> tan rápido: es peligroso.

El mundo de hoy

Objectives: In this chapter you will learn to

- Express opinions and react to current and past events
- Discuss the environment, politics, and the media
- Express doubt and disbelief
- State what has or had happened

BlueSkyImage/Shutterstock.com

Vocabulario/Gramática

C12-1 ¿Quién es?

Step 1 In groups of three, read the following clues and guess who is being described.

1. Es una persona a quien le gusta hablar. Es una persona que ha tenido mucha experiencia en el gobierno como senadora y Secretaria de Estado. Tiene un esposo que fue presidente.

2. Es una autora que vive en Escocia cuyos libros son famosos en todo el mundo y son especialmente populares entre los jóvenes. Ahora hay ocho películas que representan sus siete libros y las aventuras de un niño que se llama Harry.

3. Es una cantante famosa que ha cantado durante el Superbowl. Tiene un esposo que es cantante también. Tiene una canción que se llama 'Single Ladies'. Ha recibido varios premios: por ejemplo, muchos premios Grammy.

Step 2 Think of two additional, well-known people and write three or four clues about each of them. Your clues should be similar to the ones above. Once you have all your clues, leave your group and form a new group. Take turns telling your clues and see whether the new group can guess each person.

Vocabulario/Gramática

C12-2   Noticias del día

Step 1 Look at the following topics with a partner. Indicate your level of interest in each topic: **mucho, más o menos,** or **no mucho.**

Modelo   —*¿Cuáles de los temas te interesan?*
          —*La contaminación del aire me interesa mucho, pero la desigualdad me interesa menos.*

contaminación del aire	elecciones	crimen	manifestaciones / protestas
desigualdad	terrorismo	desastres naturales	economía
noticias	derechos humanos		

Step 2 Choose two that interest you and your partner. Write three or four reasons why the topics interest you or are important. Be prepared to share your ideas with the class.

Modelo   *No hay otro tema más importante que la contaminación del aire. Nos interesa la contaminación del aire porque somos deportistas y nos gustan las actividades al aire libre. Es un tema importante para todo el mundo.*

Step 3 Share your ideas with the class. After listening to your classmates, discuss with your partner what the topics and ideas have in common and what sets them apart. What ideas were the most original and thoughtful?

C12-3

Nuestra escuela y nuestro mundo

Step 1 You are working for your school newspaper. In preparation for next semester's publications, the editor has asked you to research local and global issues that concern the student body and faculty. Start by brainstorming with your group. Create a list of three global issues that affect your community, for example **contaminación del aire.**

Step 2 For each issue, write three or four questions that you would like to ask your classmates.

Modelo   *¿Piensas que la contaminación del aire es un problema para el campus?*
          ¿Por qué?
          ¿Qué haces para mejorar la calidad del aire?

Step 3 Conduct the interview with three to four different people. Write down the answers so you can report back to your group.

Step 4 Return to your original group and analyze the answers. Prepare to tell the editor what topics and issues would make good articles for next semester. You need to justify your recommendations with results from the interviews. Suggest a title for at least one article.

Gramática

Personas

Step 1 With a partner, take turns asking and answering the following questions. Write down your answers and your partner's answers.

Modelo   Student A: ¿Sabes quién es la persona que canta la canción "Hello"?
                Student B: *Sí, la persona que canta "Hello" es Adele.*

1. ¿Conoces a una persona que viva en Europa?
2. ¿Sabes cuál es el libro más famoso que escribió Cervantes?
3. ¿Hay alguien con quien prefieras visitar Machu Picchu?
4. ¿Sabes quién es la actriz que fue Hermione Granger en las películas de Harry Potter?
5. ¿Hay alguien en tu familia cuyo nombre sea el mismo que el tuyo?
6. ¿Sabes quién es el autor que escribió el libro *Cien años de soledad*?
7. ¿Tienes un amigo que hable español?

Step 2 With a new partner, share the answers your previous partners gave. Then compare what the two of them have in common.

Modelo   *Julia conoce a una persona que vive en Europa.*
             Julia no tiene un amigo que hable español.

Gramática

C12-5A Prácticas en el congreso **A**

Step 1 You and your classmate are working as interns for your congressperson who needs your help reaching out to the Spanish-speaking community. You have been provided with a list of resources needed. You (student A) will use the list below and your partner (student B) will use the list in activity C12-5B. Read the list together and see whether you have found all the people and things needed.

Modelo Una persona que hable francés
  Student A: *Necesitamos una persona que hable francés.*
  Student B: *Tengo un amigo que es de París.*

Lista del congresista (lo que necesita)

un periódico de América Latina
la doctora que se llama Ana
una persona que hable español
el número del alcalde de San Francisco
el experto sobre el medio ambiente

una Dr. Pepper
un sitio web sobre elecciones en Europa
los líderes de las manifestaciones de la semana pasada

Step 2 What items and people are you still missing? Decide where and how you are going to find them. Share your plan with the rest of the class.

Modelo *¿Por qué quiere hablar con la doctora Ana Hernández? Creo que él tiene problemas de espalda y la doctora es experta en eso.*

Gramática

Prácticas en el congreso **B**

Step 1 You and your classmate are working as interns for your congressperson who needs your help reaching out to the Spanish-speaking community. You have been provided with a list of resources needed. You (student B) will use the list below and your partner (student A) will use the list in activity C12-5A. Read the list together and see whether you have found all the people and things needed.

Modelo   Una persona que hable francés
          Student A: *Necesitamos una persona que hable francés.*
          Student B: *Tengo un amigo que es de París.*

Lista de tus recursos

Doctora Ana Hernández – (405)123-6789
Señor Viento y señorita Ríos – manifestación por el medio ambiente
Juan de la Vega – medio ambiente
Periódicos: *El País* de España, *El Universal* de México, *New York Times*
Tienes un amigo que es de Guatemala.

Step 2 What items and people are you still missing? Decide where and how you are going to find them. Share your plan with the rest of the class.

Modelo   *¿Por qué quiere hablar con la doctora Ana Hernández? Creo que él tiene problemas de espalda y la doctora es experta en eso.*

C12-6 Asuntos importantes

Step 1 Imagine that you and your partner(s) are on a government budget committee. Review the budget from the previous committee. Answer the following:

1. Basándose en el dinero, ¿cuáles eran los asuntos más importantes para el comité anterior? ¿Cuáles eran los asuntos menos importantes?

2. ¿Están de acuerdo con los números? Por qué? Para ustedes, ¿cuál es el asunto más importante?

Asunto	Comité anterior	Recesión	Local
Economía	70 millones		
Discriminación / Igualdad	15 millones		
Medio ambiente	10 millones		
Educación	30 millones		
Violencia doméstica / Crimen	10 millones		
Terrorismo / Guerras	55 millones		
	10 millones		

Step 2 As a group, add a seventh item to the budget. You have $10 million for that item. Write two reasons why you chose this item.

1. _____

2. _____

Step 3 Your committee has had its budget cut due to a recession. You need to cut 50 million dollars from the budget. Adjust the numbers to reflect the opinions of your group. Write your new budget in the column called *Recesión*. Be prepared to justify your budget.

Some useful words: **deber**   *should* or *ought to*
                    eliminar   *remove*
                    añadir a   *to add to*

Modelo   *Sugiero que eliminemos diez millones de dólares de la economía y que*
         añadamos el dinero a educación, porque hay muchas personas que
         necesitan una buena educación.

Step 4 Prepare to report on your budget. Write the numbers on the board and prepare to tell how much you have put in each category and give a reason.

Modelos *Hemos puesto sesenta millones en educación porque la educación*
         es muy importante.
         Hemos eliminado dinero de la economía porque…

Vocabulario/Gramática

C12-7 Asuntos locales

Step 1 Look at the budgets from the activity *Asuntos importantes (C12-6)*. Imagine now that you are working on a local committee in your community. You have been given $100 million to dedicate to addressing issues that face your community. Choose only three issues from the chart and allocate the money across those issues.

Modelo *Recomiendo que añadamos 25 millones de dólares contra la desigualdad.*

Step 2 Prepare to tell the class where your group has decided to put the money and why the issues are important. You also need to tell the class what you plan to do with the money.

Modelo *Hemos puesto 25 millones contra la desigualdad. Es importante que todos se sientan parte de nuestra comunidad. Hay personas que sufren discriminación todos los días. Con el dinero queremos tener actividades y clases para todos los miembros de nuestra comunidad.*

C12-8 Desastres naturales With a partner, read the following situations. Explain what you would do in each one.

Modelo Hay una inundación en tu ciudad.
Yo iría lejos del río. Buscaría un lugar alto. Llamaría a mis padres para ver si están bien.

1. Estás en tu habitación y hay un incendio.

2. Hay un huracán grande pasando por la ciudad donde vive un buen amigo tuyo.

3. Vives en un lugar que está pasando una sequía.

4. Estás en tu clase de español y hay un terremoto.

5. Hay un tornado que va a pasar por tu ciudad.

6. Hay un derrame de petróleo en tu comunidad.

Vocabulario/Gramática

C12-9 Un desastre natural

Step 1 The town of Tejedora has had a rough weekend. They had an earthquake and a hurricane. Look at the picture and with a partner state what condition things are in and what people have done to remedy them.

Modelo   *Los coches están dañados* (damaged).
           La niña ha encontrado dos gatos.

Palabras útiles: romper, dañar, destruir, escaparse, sobrevivir, salvar, ayudar

Step 2 It has been a year since the earthquake and hurricane. Tejedora has recovered nicely. Look at the current view of the town. With a partner, identify all the things the people have done and what condition things are in now in comparison to last year.

Modelo   *Antes los coches estaban dañados y ahora están en buenas condiciones.*
          Antes las ventanas estaban rotas y ahora María las ha arreglado.

Gramática

C12-10 Lo que he hecho

Step 1 Make a list of four things that you have done or that have happened to you and two things that you have not done or that have not happened to you. Take turns sharing your statements with a classmate. React to each statement to try and discover which are true and which are not.

Modelo   Student A: *Yo he vivido aquí toda mi vida.*
                  Student B: *No creo que hayas vivido aquí toda tu vida.*
                  Student A: *Es verdad que yo he vivido aquí toda mi vida.*
                  Student B: *¡Qué bien que hayas vivido aquí toda tu vida!*

Step 2 With your partner write down two or three things that you have both done or that have happened to you. Be prepared to share with the class.

Modelo   *Nosotros hemos viajado a México. Hemos votado en las elecciones.*

_____

_____

_____

C12-11 No hay nadie

Step 1 With a partner, write five sentences about things you think no one in the class has ever done. You or your partner should have done at least one of the five things.

Modelo   *No hay nadie en la clase que haya vivido en Canadá.*

_____

_____

_____

_____

_____

Gramática

Step 2 Form a group of four students. Your partner should be in a different group. Take turns sharing a sentence. See whether it is true that no one in your group has ever done it.

Modelo   Student A: *No hay nadie en la clase que haya vivido en Canadá.*
Student B: *Yo no he vivido en Canadá.*
Student C: *Yo tampoco he vivido en Canadá.*
Student D: *Yo he vivido en Canadá. Viví en Toronto.*

Step 3 Now, write some of your best sentences on the board. If someone in your group or the class has done it, write it in under the heading *Hay alguien que....* If nobody has done it, it goes under the heading *No hay nadie que....*

Modelos   *Hay alguien que: ha vivido en Canadá.*
No hay nadie que: haya vivido en la Antártida.

Step 4 Look at the list of things no one in the class has done. With a partner, come up with as many reasons as you can to explain why that is the case.

Modelo   *No hay nadie en la clase que haya vivido en la Antártida porque hace mucho frío y no hay ciudades ahí. Es difícil viajar a la Antártida.*

Vocabulario/Gramática

C12-12

¿Quién lo ha hecho?

Step 1 In groups of three, take turns asking and answering the following questions. Include additional information in your responses. Write down the responses.

Modelo   Student A: ¿Conoces a alguien que haya trabajado para el gobierno?
Student B: *Sí, mi madre ha trabajado para el gobierno como administradora en el centro de salud.*

1. ¿Conoces a alguien que haya trabajado en la política?
2. ¿Conoces a alguien que no haya participado en elecciones?
3. ¿Conoces a alguien que haya estado en una protesta o manifestación?
4. ¿Conoces a alguien que haya estado en un terremoto o un desastre natural?
5. ¿Conoces a alguien que haya vivido en otro país?

Step 2 Look at the responses you and your group gave and prepare statements to share with the class for each of the questions.

Modelo   *La madre de Ana ha sido la alcaldesa de su pueblo y unos amigos de Juan y Felipe han trabajado en la política.*

Step 3 Share the information you prepared with the class and then your instructor will ask whether you have done the same things.

Step 4 Look at the numbers on the board. Choose one set of numbers and write three or four questions you would like to ask the corresponding person or group of people.

Modelo   Una persona ha vivido en otro país.
¿En que país has vivido? ¿Qué comida has comido ahí?

Vocabulario/Gramática

C12-13 Mi especialización y el mundo

 Step 1 Find classmates who have the same or similar majors to yours. Work with a partner, or in a group of three, to make connections between your college major(s) and as many of the following issues as possible.

Modelo   *Las ciencias políticas tienen muchas conexiones con las elecciones. Analizamos los resultados y los datos demográficos. Trabajamos para los candidatos.*

noticias

desastres naturales

guerra

terrorismo

elecciones

salud pública

educación

medio ambiente

tecnología

crimen

desigualdad

(...)

Step 2 Now focus on two or three of the issues. Without disclosing your major(s), prepare several statements relating the issues to your major(s). Then have the class guess what your major(s) is (are) based on your statements.

Vocabulario/Gramática

C12-14 Antes de ser estudiante de la universidad

Step 1 Write down four or five things you had not done before becoming a university student.

Modelo   *Yo nunca había tomado una clase de español.*

Step 2 In groups of three, take turns sharing things you had not done before becoming a university student. After you share your statement, ask your group members whether their experiences have been the same as yours. Mark which ones you have in common and write down statements you hear and like.

Modelo   Student A: *Yo nunca había tomado una clase de español. ¿Y ustedes?*
Student B: *Yo tampoco había tomado una clase de español.*
Student C: *Yo había tomado una clase de español en la escuela secundaria.*

Step 3 Choose several of the situations that the majority of the group members have in common. Prepare statements for each of those situations and include the current situation.

Modelo   *Nosotros nunca habíamos estudiado español antes. Ahora estudiamos español todos los días.*
Nosotros siempre habíamos vivido con nuestra familia. Ahora vivimos con amigos y compañeros de cuarto.

Lectura

C12-15 Read the following journalistic piece about a record-breaking wave.

Una gigantesca ola de 19 metros de altura establece un nuevo récord mundial

National Geographic

Zacarias Pereira da Mata/Shutterstock.com

Una ola gigante de 19 metros de altura, la más alta conocida, **ha sido registrada por una boya automática situada en el Atlántico Norte,** entre Islandia y el Reino Unido, según reveló ayer la Organización Meteorológica Mundial (OMM) en un comunicado. La inmensa ola **fue registrada en la madrugada del 4 de febrero de 2013** y el récord mundial de altura que ha establecido ha sido ratificado recientemente por un comité de expertos de la OMM. El fenómeno **se produjo tras el paso de un frente muy frío,** que desató vientos de hasta 81 kilómetros por hora. El récord anterior, de 18.275 metros de altura, se había registrado el 8 de diciembre de 2007, también en el Atlántico Norte.

El récord de 19 metros de altura ha sido descrito como **"la mayor altura […] de una ola jamás medida por una boya",** según el Comité de [expertos] […] de la OMM, formado por científicos de Gran Bretaña, Canadá, los Estados Unidos y España. Wenjian Zhang, el subsecretario general de la OMM, destaca "la importancia de las observaciones y de las predicciones meteorológicas y oceánicas para garantizar la seguridad de la industria marítima mundial y **para proteger la vida de los tripulantes y pasajeros de las rutas marítimas de mucho tránsito".**

Las olas más altas **ocurren con más frecuencia al norte del océano Atlántico** que en el océano Austral o Antártico. En febrero del año 2000 se produjo un récord aparte: la mayor altura significativa de una ola jamás medida desde un buque, en la depresión de Rockall, entre el Reino Unido e Islandia. La altura de una ola se define como la distancia desde la cresta de una ola hasta el seno de la siguiente. Por otro lado, el comité de expertos de la OMM ha ratificado dos nuevos récords: **la mayor distancia y la mayor duración jamás registrada en un relámpago único,** en Oklahoma y en el sur de Francia, respectivamente.

C12-16 ## Después de leer

In small groups, write an 80-word summary of the article about the giant wave. Use your own words. When you are finished writing, share your piece. Pay attention to the other groups. What ideas and information did they use? How do the pieces compare?

El mundo de hoy: *What I learned while living abroad*

La semana que viene yo voy a regresar a mi casa, a mi familia, a mis amigos y a mi vida en los Estados Unidos. He aprendido muchas cosas aquí; cosas sobre el mundo y los seres humanos, cosas sobre mí misma, y claro que he aprendido mucho español. Estoy muy orgullosa de todo lo que he aprendido. Ahora puedo conversar en español, hacer preguntas, entender preguntas (jajaja) y puedo hablar sin sentirme nerviosa.

Aquí les comparto algunas cosas adicionales que he aprendido:

- Echo de menos a mi familia y a mis amigos; es bueno tener FaceTime y Skype, pero quiero verlos en persona. La familia es muy importante para mí.

- Estudiar español no es fácil pero me gusta aprenderlo y saber hablarlo bien.

- Me gusta la comida aquí y ahora quiero probar comida de muchos países.

- Puedo comunicar y expresar mis opiniones y las personas pueden entenderme.

- Soy una mujer fuerte e inteligente. Yo tengo control de mi futuro.

- Todos los seres humanos necesitamos las mismas cosas básicas: comida, casa y contacto con otras personas.

- Prefiero vivir en una casa con jardín y no en un apartamento pequeño; me gusta tener espacio.

- El medio ambiente es un problema global y TODOS tenemos que poner de nuestra parte para cuidar nuestro mundo.

El blog de Bella

Después de vivir en el extranjero y estudiar español por mucho tiempo, sé que no soy la misma persona de antes. Tengo planes diferentes para la vida. Tengo amigos internacionales y quiero mantener el contacto con ellos. Tengo una visión del mundo diferente. Sé cosas que no sabía antes y sé que hay mucho más para aprender.

C12-17 Blog: Estamos aprendiendo español

In small groups, discuss the following questions based on Bella's blog entry and what you wrote in your own final blog entries.

1. ¿Qué puede hacer Bella en español?

2. ¿Qué pueden hacer ustedes en español?

3. ¿Qué piensan ustedes que va a hacer Bella en el futuro?

4. ¿Qué van a hacer ustedes para mantener y mejorar su español en el futuro?

5. ¿Por qué es importante poder hablar y entender español?

6. ¿Qué sugerencias pueden darle a una persona que quiere aprender español?

Síntesis: Vocabulario

Nuestro mundo   *Our world*

los asuntos   *issues*

la contaminación del agua   *water pollution*

la contaminación del aire   *air pollution*

el crimen   *crime*

la democracia   *democracy*

los derechos humanos   *human rights*

la desigualdad   *inequality*

la discriminación   *discrimination*

la economía   *economy*

la educación   *education*

las elecciones   *elections*

las fuerzas armadas   *armed forces*

la guerra   *war*

la huelga   *strike*

la manifestación   *manifestation, demonstration, protest*

el medio ambiente   *environment*

la paz mundial   *world peace*

la protesta   *protest*

el terrorismo   *terrorism*

participar en   *to participate in*

suceder / ocurrir / pasar   *to happen / occur / pass*

votar   *to vote*

La prensa e Internet
The media and the Internet

el artículo   *article*

el asunto   *issue (matter)*

la entrevista   *interview*

las noticias   *news*

la página web   *web page*

el periódico   *newspaper*

la prensa   *the press*

la revista   *magazine*

el sitio web   *website*

entrevistar   *to interview*

estar al día   *to be up-to-date*

Los desastres naturales   *Natural disasters*

la causa   *cause*

el derrame de petróleo   *oil spill*

el derrumbe   *landslide*

el huracán   *hurricane*

el incendio   *fire*

la inundación   *flood*

de repente   *suddenly*

la sequía   *drought*

el terremoto   *earthquake*

la tormenta   *storm*

el tornado   *tornado*

el volcán   *volcano*

ayudar   *to help*

destruir   *to destroy*

escaparse   *to escape*

rescatar   *to rescue*

salvar   *to save (rescue)*

sobrevivir   *to survive*

Síntesis: Gramática

Relative clauses in Spanish

A relative clause is part of a complex sentence that has a main clause and a dependent clause. The dependent clause indicates when, where, or how the action in the main clause happens. The dependent clause is introduced by a relative pronoun, so the dependent clause is called a relative clause. The relative clause has a noun to which it refers, called the antecedent.

> **La casa** (antecedent) **que** (relative pronoun) **tengo** (verb) **está en la playa.**

English and Spanish have several relative pronouns: which one should be used depends on whether a pronoun refers to a person or an object and also whether it indicates possession.

English	Spanish
that	que
which	que, cual, cuales
who	quien, quienes
whom	(a, para) quien
whose	cuyo, cuya, cuyos, cuyas

The most common relative pronoun in Spanish is **que.** When the relative pronoun follows a preposition (*with whom, from which,* etc.) other relatives can also be used.

> El amigo **que** vi ayer fue mi compañero de cuarto.
> La profesora con **quien** hablé es muy simpática.
> El asunto del **cual** escribí es muy controvertido.

Relative clauses are useful for circumlocution, when you don't know a word for something.

> Esto es algo **que** sirve para comer la sopa.
> ¿Una cuchara?

Indicative or subjunctive with relative clauses

Relative clauses sometimes require the indicative and sometimes the subjunctive. If the combination of the antecedent + relative clause refers to something that, in the mind of the speaker, exists or has been identified, then the verb in the relative clause is in the indicative.

> Tengo **un amigo que sabe chino y árabe.**

When the antecedent is unknown to the speaker, the speaker does not know whether it exists, or it is not a concrete, specified entity, then the verb in the relative clause is in the subjunctive.

> Busco **a alguien que sepa chino y árabe.**

Past participles

A past participle is a verb form that is used to form perfect tenses (**He vivido:** *I have lived*) or to form adjectives (**dormido:** *asleep*). Some forms like *lived* in English are regular. They are formed by adding *-ed* to the verb; some others, like *slept,* are irregular.

Síntesis: Gramática

In Spanish, the regular past participle is formed by adding the ending **-ado** to **-ar** verbs and **-ido** to **-er** and **-ir** verbs after the verb stem.

estudiar	estudi**ado**
comer	com**ido**
vivir	viv**ido**

Here are some common verbs with irregular past participles:

abrir	**abierto**
decir	**dicho**
escribir	**escrito**
hacer	**hecho**
morir	**muerto**
poner	**puesto**
romper	**roto**
ver	**visto**
volver	**vuelto**

Past participles, when used as adjectives, must agree in number and gender with the nouns they modify.

> la ventana abiert**a**
> el libro escrit**o**
> los hues**os** rot**os**

The present perfect

The present perfect refers to past actions that started in a time that is still not finished, so the action is in the past, but the time frame is present or extends to the present.

> **Nunca he estado en España.**
> *I have never been to Spain.*

> **He comido en trece restaurantes esta semana.**
> *I have eaten in thirteen restaurants this week.*

Spanish uses the auxiliary verb **haber** to form the present perfect, which changes based on the person. The past participle **(estado, comido)** stays in the masculine, singular form.

yo	he	
tú	has	
él / ella / usted	ha	
nosotros(as)	hemos	vivido
vosotros(as)	habéis	
ellos / ellas / ustedes	han	

The present perfect usually appears with adverbs such as **siempre, nunca, ya,** and **todavía,** and expressions such as **esta semana, este año,** and **este mes.**

Capítulos 11 y 12

For this project you'll be examining world issues that are of importance to you. You'll do research on a topic such as a social issue or a current event that interests you and then formulate an opinion about this topic. You'll use the grammar and vocabulary you've learned in Chapters 11 and 12 to do this.

Project components

Activity	Points
UP6-1 El tema	10 points (individual)
UP6-2 Opiniones	20 points (individual / group)
UP6-3 Step 1 Step 2 Step 3	10 points (individual) 10 points (individual) 10 points (individual)
UP6-4 Sesión de pósters	30 points (individual) (25 points for presentation, 5 points as audience)
UP6-5 Conclusión	10 points (individual)

Proyecto 6: Artículo de opinión

UP6-1 El tema

Step 1 Think about a topic that interests or concerns you. See below for a few sample topics. Write six complete sentences that express emotion, hopes, and/or wishes on this topic. Post your sentences.

> la política: las relaciones internacionales, los derechos humanos, globalización
>
> el medio ambiente: contaminación, calentamiento global, ecología
>
> la vida: la comida, la salud, los deportes, la educación

Step 2 Read through the sentences posted by your classmates. Try to find three sentences about the same topic as your own and that express the same interest in or opinion about it. Comment on those three sentences with one additional, similar sentence.

UP6-2 Opiniones

Step 1 Write or type the following information and bring it to class. Leave room for additional notes in class.

1. Tu nombre
2. El tema que te interesa (en pocas palabras)
3. Las seis oraciones que escribiste para la primera parte del proyecto
4. Tres preguntas para tus compañeros de clase; las preguntas tienen que estar relacionadas con el tema de tu proyecto

Step 2 You will have a short amount of time to pair up with as many of your classmates as you can to share your topic and listen to them share theirs. State your topic and choose one or two sentences to share. If there is time, you can ask questions. On your paper, write down the name of the person you are talking with and his/her topic. Rate the topic based on how interested or uninterested you are in the subject: *una estrella, dos estrellas, tres estrellas, cuatro estrellas, cinco estrellas.*

Step 3 Look at the topics and the ratings you wrote down in this activity. Choose the top two topics that interested you. Find one of those people and, working together, ask and answer questions about each other's topics. Why did they pick those topics? How much do they know about each topic and where do they get information concerning them? Do they have specific opinions on those topics? Write down your partner's responses on your paper. Next, complete the following:

1. Are your topics identical, similar, or different? What do your topics have in common? What is different?
2. The person you are with now is going to be your partner later on in the project. Together, finalize a topic that you both find interesting / important / etc. It can be one of the topics you already have, or it can be a completely different topic.
3. On your papers, write the topic and why you choose it. Turn in your papers when you are done.

Investigación

Step 1 Working individually, answer the following questions. This will require some research. You will need to document the sources for your information.

1. What is the topic you and your partner have chosen? Write three reasons the topic interests or concerns you. (Why is it important?)
2. Give a recent example of the topic in (a) complete sentence(s).

3. Name a few people (two or more) who are important figures related to the topic. Tell why you feel they are important to the topic. How are they involved? Do they have a positive influence on the topic?
4. Research information about your topic. Write four to five sentences talking about numbers, data, and/or statistics.

Step 2 Working individually, use the information you collected in **Step 1** to write an opinion article about your topic. Your article should be two to three paragraphs. Include an introduction, the body of the article, and a conclusion. Proofread your article before you post it.

Step 3 Once your partner has finished **Steps 1** and **2**, you should complete the peer review.

1. Read everything your partner wrote for **Steps 1** and **2**.
2. In red, mark anything you think is grammatically incorrect. How would you fix the mistake?
3. In green, mark any information that both of you included.
4. In blue, mark anything that your partner included, but you did not.
5. Did you and your partner use any of the same sources? What were they?

When you meet with your partner, go over the things you have in common, the ideas you want to include in your poster session, and any corrections that need to be made. Make those corrections.

UP6-4

Sesión de pósters With your partner, prepare a poster for presentation. The poster should include your names, your topic, the key points you want to make, and the supporting statistics. It should be visually appealing and written completely in Spanish. During your time, you will have classmates listening to your short presentation. They will also ask you questions. You and your partner need to speak an equal amount of time and both of you need to show that you have researched the topic and can clearly express your opinions and the facts.

For part of the poster session you will be the audience. You should walk around and interact with the presenters. Listen to what they have to share. Ask questions and make comments. Make note of the posters and topics you find the most interesting; you will need this information for the next part of the project.

UP6-5

Conclusión React to one of the posters you found most interesting. Express your opinion and explain why you feel that way in three to four sentences.

Spanish-English Glossary

A

a cuadros plaid; checkered (10)
a la derecha (de) to the right (of) (4)
a la izquierda (de) to the left (of) (4)
a menudo frequently (9)
a pie by foot (5)
a veces sometimes (9)
abajo below (6)
abierto(a) open (5)
abogado(a) *m. f.* lawyer (8)
abrigo *m.* coat (10)
abuela *f.* grandmother (1)
abuelo *m.* grandfather (1)
aburrir to bore (6)
acabar to finish; to end; to run out of (9)
acantilado cliff (11)
accesorios *m.* accessories (10)
aceite *m.* oil (3)
acordarse to remember (5)
acostarse to go to sleep (5)
actor *m.* actor (8) (9)
actriz *f.* actress (8) (9)
Adiós. Goodbye. (P)
adjetivo *m.* adjective (3)
administración de empresas *f.* business administration (8)
aduana *f.* customs (6)
aeropuerto *m.* airport (5) (6)
afuera outside (4)
agrio(a) sour (3)
ahí there (6)
ahora now (6)
aire acondicionado *m.* air conditioner (4) (6)
ajo *m.* garlic (3)
al lado (de) next to; beside (4)
albergue *m.* hostel; inn (6)
alergia *f.* allergy (11)
alfombra *f.* rug (4)
algodón *m.* cotton (10)
allá over there (6)
allí there (6)
almeja *f.* clam (3)
almohada *f.* pillow (4)
alrededor (de) around (4)
alta definición high definition (HD) (7)

altivez haughtiness (11)
alto(a) tall (1)
altoparlantes *m.* speakers (4)
amargo(a) bitter (3)
amarillo(a) yellow (1)
anaranjado(a) orange (1)
andar to walk (5) (8)
anillo *m.* ring (8)
anoche last night (9)
anteayer the day before yesterday (9)
antes before (3) (6)
antibiótico *m.* antibiotic (11)
anuncio *m.* comercial (9)
añadir to add (3)
año pasado *m.* last year (9)
apagar to turn off (2)
aparato del aire acondicionado *m.* air conditioner (4)
apartamento *m.* apartment (4)
apellido *m.* surname; last name (1)
aplaudir to applaud (9)
aquel, aquella that (over there) (6)
aquellos(as) those (over there) (6)
aquí here (6)
aretes *m.* earrings (10)
argumento *m.* plot (9)
armario *m.* closet (4)
armarios *m.* cabinets (3)
arquitecto(a) *m. f.* architect (8)
arreglar to tidy up (4)
arriba above (4)
arroba *f.* @ (P)
arroz *m.* rice (3)
arte *m.* art (9)
artículo *m.* article (12)
artista *m. f.* artist (8) (9)
ascensor *m.* elevator (6)
así thus; like this (6)
asiento *m.* seat (8)
asiento de pasillo *m.* aisle seat (6)
asiento de ventanilla *m.* window seat (6)
asistente *m. f.* assistant (8)
aspiradora *f.* vacuum cleaner (4)
aspirina *f.* aspirin (11)
asunto *m.* issue; matter (12)
ático *m.* attic (4)
auto *m.* car (5)

autobús *m.* bus (5)
autor(a) *m. f.* author (8)
avión *m.* airplane (5) (6)
ayer yesterday (6) (9)
ayudar to help (12)
azul blue (1)

B

bailar to dance (2)
bajar to download (7)
bajarse (del tren, etc.) to get off (the train, etc.) (5)
bajo(a) short (1)
baloncesto *m.* basketball (2)
banana *f.* banana (3)
banco *m.* bank (5)
bañadera *f.* bathtub (4)
bañarse to take a bath (5)
bañera *f.* bathtub (4)
baño *m.* bathroom (4)
barbero(a) *m. f.* barber (8)
barrer to sweep (4)
barrio *m.* neighborhood (5)
batidora *f.* mixer (3)
beber to drink (3)
bebida *f.* drink (3)
béisbol *m.* baseball (2)
biblioteca *f.* library (5)
bibliotecario(a) *m. f.* librarian (8)
bicicleta *f.* bicycle (5)
bicicleta de montaña *f.* mountain biking (2)
bien well (6)
Bien, gracias. Fine, thanks. (P)
billete *m.* ticket (6)
biología *f.* biology (8)
bisabuela *f.* great-grandmother (1)
bisabuelo *m.* great-grandfather (1)
bizcocho *m.* cake (3)
blanco(a) white (1)
bloqueador solar *m.* sunscreen (11)
blusa *f.* blouse (10)
bluyines *m.* jeans (10)
boca *f.* mouth (11)
bol *m.* bowl (3)
boleto *m.* ticket (6)
bolsa *f.* bag (10)

bombero(a) *m. f.* firefighter (8)
borrador *m.* eraser (P)
botas *f.* boots (10)
botella de vino *f.* bottle of wine (3)
brazalete *m.* bracelet (10)
brazo *m.* arm (11)
broma *f.* joke (10)
Buenas noches. Good night. (P)
Buenas tardes. Good afternoon. (P)
bueno(a) good (1)
Buenos días. Good morning. (P)
bufanda *f.* scarf (10)
buscar to look for (2)
buzón *m.* inbox; mailbox (7)

C

cabeza *f.* head (11)
cable *m.* cable (7) (9)
cacerola *f.* pan (3)
cada uno(a) each (3) (6)
cadena *f.* chain (8)
caer to fall down; to drop (9)
caer bien (mal) (not) to like someone (6)
café brown (1); *m.* coffee (3); café (5)
cafetería *f.* cafeteria (5)
calabaza *f.* pumpkin (3)
calcetines *m.* socks (10)
calefactor *m.* heater (4)
caliente hot (3)
cama *f.* bed (4)
camarero(a) *m. f.* waiter / waitress (8)
cambiar el canal to change the channel (9)
caminar to walk (2) (5)
camisa *f.* shirt (10)
camiseta *f.* t-shirt (10)
campus *m.* campus (5)
canción *f.* song (9)
cangrejo *m.* crab (3)
cantante *m. f.* singer (9)
cantar to sing (2) (9)
cara *f.* face (11)
carne *f.* beef; meat (3)
carnicería *f.* butcher shop (5)
carnicero *m. f.* butcher (3)
carro *m.* car (5)

cartera *f.* wallet (10)
casa *f.* house (4)
casarse to get married (5)
casi almost (4)
catorce fourteen (P)
cátsup *m.* ketchup (3)
causa *f.* cause (12)
cebolla *f.* onion (3)
cejas *f.* eyebrows (11)
cenar to eat dinner
centro *m.* city center (downtown) (5)
centro comercial *m.* shopping center (5)
centro de información *m.* information center (6)
centro estudiantil *m.* student center (5)
cepillarse el pelo to brush one's hair (5)
cerca near (6)
cerca (de) close to; near; nearby (4)
cereales *m.* cereal (3)
cerebro *m.* brain (11)
cereza *f.* cherry (3)
cero zero (P)
cerrar to close (4)
cerveza *f.* beer (3)
césped *m.* lawn (4)
chatear to chat (7)
Chau. Bye. (P)
chica *f.* girl, young woman (P)
chico *m.* boy, young man (P)
chile *m.* pepper (3)
chimenea *f.* fireplace (4)
chocar to crash into (11)
chocolate caliente *m.* hot chocolate (3)
ciclismo *m.* cycling (2)
cien hundred (P)
ciencias de la computación *f.* computer science (8)
ciencias físicas *f.* physical science (8)
ciencias políticas *f.* political science (8)
ciencias sociales *f.* social sciences (8)
científico(a) *m. f.* scientist (8)
cierra closes (5)
cinco five (P)
cincuenta fifty (P)
cincuenta y uno fifty-one (P)
cine *m.* cinema (5); theater (9)
ciudad *f.* city (5)
ciudad universitaria *f.* campus (5)
clase turista *f.* coach (6)
clóset *m.* closet (4)
coche *m.* car (5)
cocina *f.* kitchen (3) (4)
cocinar to cook (2) (3)
codo *m.* elbow (11)

colgar to post (7)
colibrí *m.* hummingbird (5)
collar *m.* necklace (10)
comedia *f.* comedy (9)
comedor *m.* dining room (4)
comentar to comment (7)
comenzar to start; begin (4)
comer to eat (1) (3) (6)
comercial *m.* commercial (9)
comida *f.* food (3)
cómoda *f.* dresser (4)
¿Cómo está (usted)? (formal) How are you? (P)
¿Cómo están (ustedes)? (plural) How are you? (P)
¿Cómo estás (tú)? (informal) How are you? (P)
¿Cómo se dice…? Se dice… How do you say . . . ? You say . . . (P)
¿Cómo se escribe…? Se escribe… How do you spell . . . ? You spell . . . (P)
¿Cómo se llama? (formal) What's your name? (P)
¿Cómo te llamas? (informal) What's your name? (P)
compartir to share (10)
comprar to buy (2) (10)
compras *f.* shopping (10)
computadora *f.* computer (7)**; portátil** *m.* laptop (7)
comunicación *f.* communications (8)
comunicación interpersonal *f.* interpersonal communication (8)
comunidad *f.* community (5)
concierto *m.* concert (9)
condimento *m.* condiment
conducir to drive (3) (5) (8)
conectar to connect (7)
conexión *f.* connection (7)
congelador *m.* freezer (3)
congelar to freeze (3)
conocer (a) to be acquainted with (3); to know (6)
contador(a) *m. f.* accountant (8)
contaminación del agua *f.* water pollution (12)
contaminación del aire *f.* air pollution (12)
contar to count (4); to tell (4)
contrato *m.* contract (7)
conversar to talk (2)
corazón *m.* heart (11)
corbata *f.* tie (10)
correr to run (2) (5)
cortar to cut (3)

cortar el césped to mow the lawn (4)
cortarse to cut oneself (11)
cortinas *f.* curtains (4)
crear to create (9)
creativo(a) creative (8)
crema solar *f.* sunscreen (11)
crimen *m.* crime (12)
criminología *f.* criminal justice (8)
crítico(a) *m. f.* critic (9)
cruzar to cross (5)
cuadra *f.* block (5)
cuadro *m.* picture (4)
¿Cuál es tu número de teléfono? (informal), **¿Cuál es su número de teléfono?** (formal) What's your phone number? (P)
¿Cuál es tu correo electrónico? (informal), **¿Cuál es su correo electrónico?** (formal) What's your email address? (P)
cuarenta forty (P)
cuarenta y dos forty-two (P)
cuarenta y tres forty-three (P)
cuarenta y uno forty-one (P)
cuarto *m.* room (4)
cuarto de baño *m.* bathroom (4)
cubierta *f.* counter top (3)
cuchara *f.* spoon (3)
cuchillo *m.* knife (3)
cuello *m.* neck (11)
cuero *m.* leather (10)
cuerpo *m.* body (11)
cuñada *f.* sister-in-law (1)
cuñado *m.* brother-in-law (1)

D

dañados damaged (12)
dar to give (3) (7) (8)
dar de comer a (las mascotas) to feed (pets) (4)
¿De dónde eres? (informal) Where are you from? (P)
¿De dónde es (usted)? (formal) Where are you from? (P)
de confianza reliable (8)
de lunares polka-dotted (10)
¿De qué está(n) hecho(s)? What is it (are they) made of? (10)
de repente suddenly (12)
de solo un color solid-color (10)
debajo (de) under; below (4)
decir to tell (8)
dedal *m.* thimble (5)
dedo *m.* finger (11)

delante (de) in front of (4)
delgado(a) thin (1)
democracia *f.* democracy (12)
dentista *m. f.* dentist (8)
deportes *m.* sports (2)
derecho *m.* law (8)
derechos humanos *m.* human rights (12)
derrame de petróleo *m.* oil spill (12)
derrumbe *m.* landslide (12)
desafiante defiant (11)
desastres naturales *m.* natural disasters (12)
desayunar to eat breakfast (2)
descansar to rest (2)
descargar to download (7)
desear to wish (10)
desembarcar to get off the plane (6)
desgraciado(a) unfortunate (5)
desigualdad *f.* inequality (12)
desmayarse to faint (11)
desordenado(a) messy (3)
despacio slowly (6)
despensa *f.* pantry (3)
despertarse to wake up (5)
después de after (3); **después** after (6)
destino *m.* destination (6)
destruir to destroy (12)
detrás (de) behind (4)
dibujar to draw (9)
dibujo *m.* drawing (9)
dibujos animados *m.* cartoons (9)
diecinueve nineteen (P)
dieciocho eighteen (P)
dieciséis sixteen (P)
diecisiete seventeen (P)
dientes *m.* teeth (11)
diez ten (P)
difícilmente with difficultly (6)
digital digital (7)
director(a) *m. f.* director (9)
discoteca *f.* club (5)
discriminación *f.* discrimination (12)
diseñador(a) gráfico(a) *m. f.* graphic designer (8)
diseño *m.* design (9)
divertirse to have fun (5) (8)
doblado(a) dubbed (9)
doblar to turn (5)
doce twelve (P)
doctor(a) *m. f.* medical doctor (11)
documental *m.* documentary (9)
doler (cabeza, estómago, garganta, etc.) to hurt (head, stomach, throat, etc.) (11)
dormir to sleep (4) (8)

dormirse to fall asleep (5)
dormitorio *m.* bedroom (4)
dos two (P)
dos veces two times, twice (9)
drama *m.* drama (9)
ducha *f.* shower (4)
dudar to doubt (10)
dulce sweet (3)

E

economía *f.* economics (8); economy (12)
edificio administrativo *m.* administration building (5)
editar to edit (7)
educación *f.* education (8) (12)
efectos especiales *m.* special effects (9)
elecciones *f.* elections (12)
electrodomésticos *m.* appliances (4)
embarcar to board (6)
empezar to start; begin (4)
empleado *m.* employee (8)
en in; at; on (4)
en medio (de) in the middle of (4)
en vivo live (9)
enamorarse to fall in love (5)
Encantado(a). Delighted. (P)
encantar to love (something) (6)
encima / arriba (de) on; over; on top of (4)
encimera *f.* counter top (3)
encontrado found (4)
encontrar to find; encounter (4)
enfermedad *f.* illness; sickness (11)
enfermería *f.* nursing (11)
enfermero(a) *m. f.* nurse (8) (11)
enfermo(a) sick (5)
enfrente (de) facing (4)
entender to understand (4)
entre between (4)
entrevista *f.* interview (12)
entrevistar to interview (12)
enviar to send (7)
enviar un mensaje de texto to send a text message (7)
episodio *m.* episode (9)
época *f.* time period (4)
equipaje *m.* luggage (6)
es cierto it is certain (10)
es dudoso it is doubtful (10)
es evidente it is obvious (10)
es importante it is important (10)
es imposible it is impossible (10)
es mejor it is better (10)

es necesario it is necessary (10)
es verdad it is true (10)
ese(a) that (6)
escala *f.* layover (6)
escalera *f.* stairs (4)
escaparse to escape (12)
escena *f.* scene (9)
escoba *f.* broom (3)
escribir to write (1); writing (8)
escritorio *m.* desk (P) (4)
escuchar to listen (8)
escuchar música to listen to music (8)
escultura *f.* sculpture (9)
esos(as) those (6)
espacio *m.* space (P)
espalda *f.* back (11)
espectáculo *m.* show (9)
espejo *m.* mirror (4)
esperar to hope (10)
esponja *f.* sponge (3)
esposa *f.* wife (1)
esposo *m.* husband (1)
esquiar to ski (2)
esquina *f.* corner (5)
está(n) hecho(a)(os)(as) de… it (they) is (are) made of . . . (10)
Está lloviendo. It's raining. (6)
Está nevando. It's snowing. (6)
Está nublado. It's cloudy. (6)
estación de autobuses *f.* bus station (5)
estación de metro *f.* subway station (5)
estación de trenes *f.* train station (5)
estacionamiento *m.* parking lot (5)
estadio *m.* stadium (5)
estado civil *m.* marital status (10)
estampado(a) printed (10)
estampilla *f.* stamp (6)
estar to be (8)
estar al día to be up-to-date (12)
estar congestionado(a) to be congested (11)
estar mareado(a) to be dizzy (11)
estar resfriado(a) to have a cold (11)
estatua *f.* statue (9)
estatus *m.* status (7)
este(a) this (6)
estilo *m.* style (9)
estómago *m.* stomach (11)
estornudar to sneeze (11)
estos(as) these (6)
estudiante *m. f.* student (P)
estudiar to study (1)

estufa *f.* stove (3)
experiencia *f.* experience (8)
extenuado(a) exhausted (11)

F

fácilmente easily (6)
falda *f.* skirt (10)
faltar to lack (something) (6)
familia *f.* family (1)
farmacéutico(a) *m. f.* pharmacist (8)
fascinar to fascinate (6)
Fatal. Awful. (P)
filmar to film (9)
finanzas *f.* finance (8)
flores *f.* flowers (4)
fractura *f.* fracture (11)
frazada *f.* blanket (4)
fregadero *m.* sink (3)
fresa *f.* strawberry (3)
frigorífico *m.* refrigerator (3)
frío(a) cold (3)
fruta *f.* fruit (3)
frutero *m. f.* fruit vendor (3)
frutilla *f.* strawberry (3)
fuerzas armadas *f.* armed forces (12)
fútbol *m.* soccer (2)
fútbol americano *m.* football (2)

G

gafas de sol *f.* sunglasses (10)
garaje *m.* garage (4)
garganta *f.* throat (11)
gastar to spend (10)
gemelos(as) *m. f.* twins (1)
generalmente generally (9)
género *m.* type (9)
gerente *m. f.* manager (8)
gimnasio *m.* gym (2) (5)
golf *m.* golf (2)
gordo(a) fat (1)
gorra *f.* cap (10)
grabar to record, to save (7) (9)
grados centígrados degrees Celsius (6)
grados Fahrenheit degrees Fahrenheit (6)
grande big (1)
gripe *f.* flu (11)
gris grey (1)
guantes *m.* gloves (10)
guardar to save (7)
guardar cama to stay in bed (11)
guerra *f.* war (12)
guion *m.* dash (P)

guion *m.* script (9)
guion bajo *m.* underscore (P)
guitarra *f.* guitar (2)

H

habitación *f.* bedroom (4) (6)
habitación de fumadores *f.* smoking room (6)
habitación de no fumadores *f.* non-smoking room (6)
habitación doble *f.* double room (6)
hablar to talk (1); to speak (10)
hablar (bien) to speak (well) (8)
hablar por teléfono to speak on the phone (2) (7)
Hace buen tiempo. It's nice (good) weather. (6)
Hace calor. It's hot. (6)
Hace fresco. It's cool. (6)
Hace frío. It's cold. (6)
Hace mal tiempo. It's bad weather. (6)
Hace sol. It's sunny. (6)
Hace viento. It's windy. (6)
hacer to do; to make (3) (7)
hacer clic to click (7)
hacer cola to wait in line (9)
hacer compras to shop (10)
hacer doble clic to double click (7)
hacer ejercicio to exercise (2) (11)
hacer fila to wait in line (9)
hacer gimnasia to do gymnastics (2)
hacer un tour to take a tour (6)
hasta until (3); to (5)
Hasta luego. See you later. (P)
Hasta mañana. See you tomorrow. (P)
hecho(a) made (3)
heladera *f.* freezer (3)
helado *m.* ice cream (3)
herida *f.* wound, injury (11)
hermana *f.* sister (1)
hermanastra *f.* stepsister (1)
hermanastro *m.* stepbrother (1)
hermano *m.* brother (1)
hervir to boil (3) (4)
hielo *m.* ice (3)
hija *f.* daughter (1)
hijo *m.* son (1)
historia *f.* history (8)
Hola. Hello. (P)
hombre/mujer de negocios *m. f.* businessperson (8)
hombro *m.* shoulder (11)

honesto(a) honest (8)
hornillo *m.* stove (4)
horno *m.* oven (3) (4)
horno de microondas *m.* microwave oven (4)
horriblemente horribly (6)
hospital *m.* hospital (5)
hostal *m.* hostel (6)
hotel *m.* hotel (6)
hotel de cinco estrellas *m.* five-star hotel (6)
hoy today (6)
huelga *f.* strike (12)
hueso *m.* bone (11)
huésped *m. f.* guest (6)
huevo *m.* egg (3)
huracán *m.* hurricane (12)

I

idiomas *m.* languages (8)
Igualmente. Likewise. (P)
impermeable *m.* rain coat (10)
importar to be important (6)
improvisar to improvise (6)
inalámbrico(a) wireless (7)
incendio *m.* fire (12)
inexpugnable impregnable (11)
infección *f.* infection (11)
ingeniería *f.* engineering (8)
ingeniero(a) *m. f.* engineer (8)
iniciativo(a) initiative (8)
inodoro *m.* toilet (4)
insensatez *f.* foolishness (11)
instalar to install (7)
interesar to be interesting (6)
intrepidez *f.* fearlessness (11)
inundación *f.* flood (12)
invierno *m.* winter (5) (6)
inyección *f.* injection (11)
ir to go (8)
ir de compras to go shopping (10)
irse to leave (5)

J

jabón de manos *m.* hand soap (3)
jabón de platos *m.* dish soap (3)
jamón *m.* ham (3)
jarabe para la tos *m.* cough syrup (11)
jardín *m.* garden; yard (4)
jeans *m.* jeans (10)
jefe(a) *m. f.* supervisor (8)
jersey *m.* sweater (10)
jolgorios *m.* joys (11)
joven *m. f.* young (1) (4)
juez(a) *m. f.* judge (8)

jugar to play (4); (a sport) (2)
jugo *m.* juice (3)
jugo de manzana *m.* apple juice (3)
jugo de naranja *m.* orange juice (3)

L

labios *m.* lips (11)
lago *m.* lake (5)
lámpara *f.* lamp (4)
lana *f.* wool (10)
langosta *f.* lobster (3)
lastimarse to hurt oneself (11)
lavadora *f.* washer (4)
lavaplatos *m.* dishwasher (3)
lavar to wash (3)
lavar el coche to wash the car (4)
lavar la ropa to wash clothing (4)
lavar los platos to wash the dishes (4)
leche *f.* milk (3)
lechuga *f.* lettuce (3)
leer to read (1)
lejos (de) far from (4) (6)
lengua *f.* tongue (11)
lenguas *f.* languages (8)
lentamente slowly (6)
letra *f.* lyrics (9)
levantar pesas to lift weights (2)
levantarse to get up (5)
librería *f.* bookstore (5)
licuadora *f.* blender (3)
limón *m.* lemon (3)
limpiar to clean (3) (4)
limpio(a) clean (3)
línea aérea *f.* airline (6)
lino *m.* linen (10)
literatura *f.* literature (8)
llamar to call (2)
llegar (a) to arrive (at) (2)
llevar to wear, to carry (10)
llover to rain (6)
(lunes) pasado last (Monday) (9)

M

madre *f.* mother (mom) (1)
maestro(a) *m. f.* teacher (8)
mal poorly (6)
maleta *f.* suitcase (6)
malo(a) bad (4)
mamá *f.* mother (mom) (1)
manejar to drive (5)
mango *m.* mango (3)
manifestación *f.* manifestation; demonstration; protest (12)

mano *f.* hand (11)
manta *f.* blanket (4)
mantequilla *f.* butter (3)
manzana *f.* apple (3); block (in Spain) (5)
mañana tomorrow (6)
mapa *m.* map (P) (6)
marca *f.* brand (8)
marcador *m.* marker (P)
marisco *m.* shellfish (3)
marketing/mercadeo *m.* marketing (8)
marrón brown (1)
más more (6)
más que . . . more than (4)
más. . . que more . . . than (4)
mayonesa *f.* mayonnaise (3)
mayor *m. f.* the oldest (4)
mayor older (4)
me myself (5)
Me llamo… My name is . . . (P)
mecánico(a) *m. f.* mechanic (8)
medicina *f.* medicine (11)
médico(a) *m. f.* doctor (8) (11)
medio ambiente *m.* environment (12)
medios de comunicación *m.* media (7)
medios de transporte *m.* means of transport (5)
medir to measure (8)
mejor better (4); *m. f.* the best (4)
mejorarse to get better (11)
memoria *f.* USB flash drive (7)
menor younger (4); *m. f.* the youngest (4)
menos less (6)
menos que . . . less than (4)
menos. . . que less . . . than (4)
mensaje de voz *m.* voicemail (7)
mercado (de campesinos) *m.* (farmer's) market (5)
mes pasado *m.* last month (9)
mesa *f.* table (P) (3) (4)
mesita de noche *f.* night stand (4)
mezclar to mix (3)
Mi correo electrónico es… My email address is . . . (P)
Mi número de teléfono es el… My telephone number is . . . (P)
microondas *m.* microwave (3)
mirar to watch (1)
mirar televisión to watch television (2)
misterio *m.* mystery (9)
mojado(a) wet (3)
molestar to bother (6)
monitor *m.* monitor (7)
montar a caballo to ride a horse (5)

montar en bicicleta to ride a bike (5)
morado(a) purple (1)
morder to bite (4)
moreno(a) brunette (1)
morir to die (4) (8)
mostaza *f.* mustard (3)
mostrar to show (7)
motivado(a) motivated (8)
mover to move (4)
muchacha *f.* girl, young woman (P)
muchacho *m.* boy, young man (P)
mucho a lot, much (6)
Mucho gusto. A pleasure. (P)
Mucho gusto en conocerte. (informal) A pleasure to meet you. (P)
mujer de negocios *f.* businesswoman (8)
mundo *m.* world (12)
músculo *m.* muscle (11)
museo *m.* museum (5) (9)
música *f.* music (9)
música clásica *f.* classic music (9)
música country *f.* country music (9)
música pop *f.* pop music (9)
musical *m.* musical (9)
músico(a) *m. f.* musician (9)
(No) Muy bien. (Not) Very well. (P)

N

nadar to swim (2)
naranja *f.* orange (3)
nariz *f.* nose (11)
navegar por Internet to surf the Internet (2)
necesitar to need (2) (10)
negar to deny (10)
negocios *m.* business (8)
negro(a) black (1)
nevar to snow (6)
nevera *f.* refrigerator (3)
nieta *f.* granddaughter (1)
nieto *m.* grandson (1)
no creer not to believe (10)
no dudar not to doubt (10)
no es cierto it is not certain (10)
no es posible it is not possible (10)
no es seguro it is not certain (10)
no es verdad it is not true (10)
no estar seguro (de) not to be sure (that) (10)
no negar not to deny (10)
no pensar not to think (10)
nombre *m.* first name, given name (1)
normalmente normally (9)
nos ourselves (5)

Nos vemos. See you later. (P)
noticias *f.* news (9) (12)
noventa ninety (P)
nuera *f.* daughter-in-law (1)
nueve nine (P)

O

o or (2)
obra de teatro *f.* play (9)
ochenta eighty (P)
ocho eight (P)
ocurrir to occur (12)
oficina *f.* office (5)
oficina de correos *f.* post office (5)
ojo *m.* eye (11)
olla *f.* pot (3)
olvidar to forget (9)
olvidarse to forget (5)
once eleven (P)
ordenador *m.* computer (in Spain) (7)
oreja *f.* ear (11)
organizado(a) organized (8)
os yourselves (informal) (5)
otoño *m.* autumn; fall (6)

P

paciente *m.* patient (11)
padre *m.* father (dad) (1)
padres *m.* parents (1)
pagar to pay (8) (10)
página web *f.* web page (12)
palpitar to palpitate (11)
pan *m.* bread (3)
panadería *f.* bakery (5)
panadero *m. f.* baker (3)
pantalones *m.* pants (10)
pantalones cortos *m.* shorts (10)
pantalones de mezclilla (denim)
   m. jeans (10)
papa *f.* potato (3) *m.* pope (3)
papá *m.* father (dad) (1)
para for, to (7)
parada de autobús *f.* bus stop (5)
parecer to appear; seem to be (6)
pared *f.* wall (P)
parientes *m.* relatives (1)
parque *m.* park (5)
participar en to participate in (12)
pasaporte *m.* passport (6)
pasar to pass (5) (12)
pasar la aspiradora to vacuum (4)
pasear (al perro) to walk (the dog) (4)
pastel *m.* cake (3)

pastilla *f.* pill (11)
patata *f.* potato (3)
patinar sobre hielo to ice skate (2)
patio *m.* patio (4)
pavo *m.* turkey (3)
paz mundial *f.* world peace (12)
pecho *m.* chest (11)
pedir order (4); to ask for (3) (8) (10)
pegadizas catchy (9)
pegar to hit (11)
pegatina *f.* sticker (8)
peinarse to comb one's hair (5)
pelar to peel (3)
película *f.* movie (9)
película de acción *f.* action movie (9)
película de ciencia ficción *f.* science fiction
   movie (9)
película de horror / terror *f.* horror movie (9)
película romántica *f.* romantic movie (9)
pelirrojo(a) redhead (1)
pelota *f.* ball (11)
peluquero(a) *m. f.* hair stylist (8)
pensar to think (10)
pensar de to think of; to have
   an opinion (4)
pensar en to think about; to consider (4)
peor *m. f.* the worst (4)
peor worse (4)
pepino *m.* cucumber (3)
pequeño(a) small (1)
pera *f.* pear (3)
perder to lose (4) (9)
perfectamente perfectly (6)
periódico *m.* newspaper (12)
periodismo *m.* journalism (8)
periodista *m. f.* journalist (8)
pero but (2)
persignarse to make the sign of the
   cross (11)
persona *f.* person (P)
pescadero *m. f.* fishmonger (3)
pescado *m.* fish (3)
piano *m.* piano (2)
picaflor *m.* hummingbird; womanizer (5)
picante spicy (3)
pie *m.* foot (11)
piedra caliza *f.* limestone (4)
piel *f.* leather; skin; fur (10)
pierna *f.* leg (11)
píldora *f.* pill (11)
pimienta *f.* pepper (3)
pimiento *m.* pepper (3)
pintar to paint (2) (4) (9)

pintura *f.* painting (4) (9)
piña *f.* pineapple (3)
piscina *f.* pool (4) (5); swimming pool (6)
piso *m.* floor (P)
pizarra *f.* blackboard (P)
planchar to iron (4)
planchas de titanio *f.* titanium plates (4)
planta *f.* plant (4)
plátano *m.* banana (3)
plato *m.* plate (3)
plato hondo *m.* bowl (3)
playa *f.* beach (6)
plaza *f.* plaza (5)
poco a little (6)
poder to be able to (4)
policía *m. f.* police officer (8)
poliéster *m.* polyester (10)
pollo *m.* chicken (3)
poner to put (3)
poner to put on; to rub on (11)
poner to put; to place; to post (7) (8)
ponerse (ropa) to put on (clothes) (5)
por ejemplo for example (7)
por eso that's why (7)
por favor please (7)
por fin finally (7)
por lo menos at least (7)
por supuesto of course (7)
porche *m.* porch (4)
postre *m.* dessert (3)
preferir to prefer (4) (8) (10)
prendas de ropa *f.* articles of clothing (10)
prensa *f.* media, the press (12)
preocuparse to worry (5)
prepago prepaid (7)
preparación de la comida *f.* food
   preparation (3)
preparar to prepare (2)
presupuesto *m.* budget (9)
prima *f.* cousin (1)
primavera *f.* spring (6)
primera clase *f.* first class (6)
primero first (6)
primo *m.* cousin (1)
probar to test; to prove; to taste (4); to try on
   clothing (10)
productor(a) *m. f.* producer (9)
profesor(a) *m. f.* teacher (P); *m. f.* professor (8)
programa de realidad *m.* reality show (9)
programa de televisión *m.* television
   program (9)
programador(a) *m. f.* computer
   programmer (8)

protagonista *m. f.* protagonist (9)
protector solar *m.* sunscreen (11)
protesta *f.* protest (12)
psicología *f.* psychology (8)
publicar to publish; to post (7)
pueblo *m.* village, town (5)
puerta *f.* door (P) (4)
puerta de embarque *f.* departure gate (6)
pulmones *m.* lungs (11)
pulpo *m.* octopus (3) (11)
pulsera *f.* bracelet (10)
punto *m.* period; dot (P)

Q

¿Qué es…? Es… What is . . . ? It's . . . (P)
¿Qué tal? How are things going? (P)
quebrado(a) broken (11)
quedarse to stay (5); to remain; (in the case of
   clothing) to fit (10)
quehaceres *m.* chores (4)
querer to wish (4); to want (4) (10)
queso *m.* cheese (3)
Quiero presentarte a… I would like to
   introduce you (informal) to . . . (P)
Quiero presentarle a… I would like to
   introduce you (formal) to . . . (P)
Quiero presentarles a… I would like to
   introduce you (plural) to . . . (P)
quince fifteen (P)
quitarse to take off (clothes) (5)
quizás maybe (3)

R

radiografía *f.* x-ray (11)
rápidamente quickly (6)
rápido(a) quick, quickly (6)
ratón *m.* mouse (7)
rayado(a) striped (10)
recepción *f.* reception desk (6)
receta *f.* prescription (11)
recomendar to recommend (10)
recordar to remember (4)
redes sociales *f.* social networks (7)
refresco *m.* soft drink (3)
refrigerador *m.* refrigerator (3) (4)
regar las plantas to water the plants (4)
regresar (a) to return (to) (2)
Regular. Normal. (P)
reírse to laugh (5) (8)
relaciones públicas *f.* public
   relations (8)
relajarse to relax (5)
rellenar to fill out (7)

reloj *m.* clock (P)
repetir to repeat (4) (8)
reproductor de DVD *m.* DVD player (4)
rescatar to rescue (12)
reservación *f.* reservation (6)
residencia estudiantil *f.* student residence, dorms (4); dormitory (5)
respirar to breathe (11)
restaurante *m.* restaurant (5)
revista *f.* magazine (12)
rock *m.* rock and roll (9)
rodar to film (9)
rodilla *f.* knee (11)
rogar to beg (10)
rojo(a) red (1)
romper to break (9)
roto(a) broken (11)
rubio(a) blond(e) (1)

S

sábanas *f.* sheets (4)
saber to know (3) (8); to know (something) (6)
sacar fotos to take pictures (2) (9)
saco *m.* jacket or sports coat (Latin America) (10)
sacudir to dust (4)
sal *f.* salt (3)
sala *f.* living room (4)
sala de entrada *f.* lobby (6)
salchicha *f.* sausage (3)
salida *f.* departure (6)
salir to go out; to leave (3)
salir con amigos to go out with friends (2)
salmón *m.* salmon (3)
salón *m.* living room (4)
salón de clase *m.* classroom (P)
salsa de tomate *f.* ketchup (3)
salud *f.* health (11)
saludable healthy life (3)
salvar to save (rescue) (12)
sandalias *f.* sandals (10)
sangre *f.* blood (11)
se itself, himself, herself, yourself (formal) themselves, yourselves (formal) (5)
se trata de... it is about . . . (9)
secadora *f.* dryer (4)
secar la ropa to dry clothing (4)
seco(a) dry (3)
secundaria *f.* high school (5)
seda *f.* silk (10)
seguir to follow; continue (5)
según according (4); according to (6)

seis six (P)
sello *m.* stamp (6)
semana pasada *f.* last week (9)
sentarse to sit down (5)
sentir to feel (4)
sentir náuseas to feel nauseated (11)
sentirse bien to feel well (11)
sentirse mal to feel badly (11)
sequía *f.* drought (12)
ser un(a) líder to be a leader (8)
servilleta *f.* napkin (3)
servir to serve (3) (4) (8)
sesenta sixty (P)
setenta seventy (P)
siempre always (6) (9)
siete seven (P)
silla *f.* chair (P) (3) (4)
síntoma *m.* symptom (11)
sitio *m.* site (6)
sito web *m.* website (12)
sobrevivir to survive (12)
sobrina *f.* niece (1)
sobrino *m.* nephew (1)
sofá *m.* sofa (4)
solamente only (6)
solo alone (6)
sombrero *m.* hat (10)
sótano *m.* basement (4)
Soy de... I'm from . . . (P)
subir to upload (7)
subirse (al tren, etc.) to get on (the train, etc) (5)
subtítulos *m.* subtitles (9)
suceder to happen (12)
sucio(a) dirty (4)
sudadera *f.* sweatshirt; sweats (10)
suegra *f.* mother-in-law (1)
suegro *m.* father-in-law (1)
suelo *m.* floor (P)
suéter *m.* sweater (10)
sugerir to suggest (10)
supermercado *m.* supermarket (5)

T

tableta *f.* tablet (7)
también also; as well (2)
tampoco neither (2)
tan... como as . . . as (4)
tanto como . . . as much as (4)
tanto(a)... como as much . . . as (4)
tantos(as)... como as many . . . as (4)
tarde late (6)

tarifa *f.* rate (7)
tarjeta *f.* card (7)
tarjeta postal *f.* postcard (6)
tarta *f.* cake (3)
taza *f.* cup (3)
tazón *m.* bowl (3)
te yourself (informal) (5)
té *m.* tea (3)
teatro *m.* theater (5)
techo *m.* ceiling (4); roof (5)
teclado *m.* keyboard (7)
tecnología *f.* technology (7)
tejanos *m.* jeans (10)
teléfono celular *m.* cell phone (7)
teléfono móvil *m.* cell phone (in Spain) (7)
telenovela *f.* soap opera (9)
televisión *f.* television (7) (9)
televisor *m.* television set (4)
temporada *f.* TV season (9)
temprano early (6)
tenedor *m.* fork (3)
tener to have (7) (10)
tener catarro to have a cold (11)
tener fiebre to have a fever (11)
tener náuseas to feel nauseated (11)
tener tos to have a cough (11)
Tengo que irme. I have to go. (P)
tenis *m.* tennis (2)
terremoto *m.* earthquake (12)
terrorismo *m.* terrorism (12)
tiempo weather (6)
tienda (de música, ropa, videos, etc.) *f.* store (of music, clothing, videos, etc.) (5)
tina *f.* bathtub (4)
tirita *f.* band-aid (11)
toalla *f.* towel (4)
tobillo *m.* ankle (11)
tocador *m.* dresser (4)
tocar to play a musical instrument (9)
tocar un instrumento to play an instrument (9)
todas las semanas every week (9)
todos los años every year (9)
todos los días every day (9)
todos los meses every month (9)
tomar to drink (3); to take (5)
tomar fotos to take pictures (2) (9)
tomar la temperatura to take one's temperature (11)
tomar un refresco to have a soft drink (2)
tomate *m.* tomato (3)

torcido(a) twisted (11)
tormenta *f.* storm (12)
tornado *m.* tornado (12)
torta *f.* cake (3)
tostadora *f.* toaster (3)
trabajar to work (1) (6)
trabajar bien con otros to work well with others (8)
traer to bring (3)
tragar to swallow (11)
traje *m.* suit (10)
traje de baño *m.* swimsuit (10)
trama *f.* plot (9)
transmitir to broadcast (9)
trece thirteen (P)
treinta thirty (P)
treinta y cinco thirty-five (P)
treinta y cuatro thirty-four (P)
treinta y dos thirty-two (P)
treinta y nueve thirty-nine (P)
treinta y ocho thirty-eight (P)
treinta y seis thirty-six (P)
treinta y siete thirty-seven (P)
treinta y tres thirty-three (P)
treinta y uno thirty-one (P)
tren *m.* train (5)
tres three (P)
trompeta *f.* trumpet (2)
turista *m. f.* tourist (6)

U

ubicación *f.* location (6)
Un placer. A pleasure. (P)
una vez one time, once (9)
universidad *f.* (5)
uno one (P)
usar to use (1) (2)
uva *f.* grape (3)

V

vacaciones *f.* vacation (6)
vacuna *f.* vaccine (6) (11)
vaqueros *m.* jeans (10)
vaso *m.* glass cup (3)
vegetal *m.* vegetable (3)
veinte twenty (P)
veinticinco twenty-five (P)
veinticuatro twenty-four (P)
veintidós twenty-two (P)
veintinueve twenty-nine (P)
veintiocho twenty-eight (P)
veintiséis twenty-six (P)

veintisiete twenty-seven (P)
veintitrés twenty-three (P)
veintiuno twenty-one (P)
venir to come (8)
ventana f. window (4)
ver to see (7) (8); to watch (9)
verano m. summer (6)
verde green (1)
verdura f. vegetable (3)
vestido m. dress (10)
vestirse to get dressed (5); to dress oneself (8)
veterinario(a) m. f. veterinarian (8)

viajar to travel (6)
viaje m. trip (6)
vidrio m. glass (4)
viejo(a) old (1) (4)
violín m. violin (2)
vitamina f. vitamin (11)
vivir to live (1) (6) (10)
volcán m. volcano (12)
volver to return (4)
vomitar to vomit (11)
votar to vote (12)
vuelo m. flight (6)

W

wifi m. wifi (7)

Y

y and (2)
¿Y tú? (informal) And you? (P)
¿Y usted? (formal) And you? (P)
yerno m. son-in-law (1)
yeso m. cast (11)
yogur m. yogurt (3)

Z

zanahoria f. carrot (3)
zapatos m. shoes (10)
zapatos de tacón alto m. high-heeled shoes (10)
zapatos de tenis m. tennis shoes; athletic shoes (10)
zumo m. juice (3)